AREA CODE 212

AREA CODE 212

New York Days, New York Nights

Tama Janowitz

BLOOMSBURY

First published in Great Britain 2002

Copyright © 2002 by Tama Janowitz

Bloomsbury Publishing Plc, 38 Soho Square, London W1D 3HB

The moral right of the author has been asserted

A CIP catalogue record for this book
is available from the British Library

ISBN 0 7475 5828 0

10 9 8 7 6 5 4 3 2

Typeset by Hewer Text Ltd, Edinburgh
Printed by Clays Ltd, St Ives plc

For Paige Powell
Who has always made the journey
as fun as the destination

CONTENTS

ACKNOWLEDGMENTS

Some essays appeared originally in somewhat different form in the following publications: *Modern Ferret; AnimalFair, American Jam* (Japan); *Marie Claire* (UK); the *Evening Standard Night and Day Magazine; SmithBarneyMoneyStyle; London Review of Books;* the *Independent; Vogue* (US, Germany); *V Style* (Microsoft internet); *Ocean Drive; Frank; Allure; Hamptons Country; American Demographics;* the *Scotsman; Irish Tatler; Scholastic Awards; Marie Claire* (US); *Spin; 21 Years of Picador Books* (UK); *New York Press; Sotheby's* (catalog); *Bergen Kunst Museum catalog* (Norway); *Elle* (UK, US); *Hamptons; Edifice Rex* (internet); *Manhattan Spirit; Telegraph Magazine;* the *Daily Telegraph; The Express;* the *Independent on Sunday;* the *Guardian; Child Magazine* I would also like to thank some of the many fine editors with whom I have worked, among them: Gwyneth Cravens, Betsy Lerner, Mary Shefferman, Tom Allon, Nancy Novograd, Margot Guralnick, Kim Heron, Pat Towers, Barbara Fairchild, Pete Wells, Andrey Slivka, Crista Worthington, Dana Wagstaff, Richard Storey, Joanne Chen, Linda Wells, Karen Marta, Susan Boyd, Marian McElvoy, Kate Betts, Kim Brown, Lise Funderberg, Gael Love, Lucy Danziger, Ilene Rosensweig, Tom Austin, Glenn Albin, Stefanie Marsh, Catherine Sabino, Priscilla Eakeley, Luisa Nunez, Wendy Diamond, Lisa Grainger, Lisa Kerns, Linda Yablonksy, Kathy Henderson, Jill Kirschenbaum, Constance Gustke, Bob Guccione Jr. Glenda Bailey, Anna Wintour, Joanne Malabar, Christie Hickman, Louise France, Paul Davies, Lisa Grainger, Kazuko Matuoka, Dana Cowen, Constant Gustke, John Strausbaugh, Ellen Salpeter, Yasuaki Yamoda, Nic Illjine, Luc and Marianne Coorevits, Kristoff Tilken, Kathryn Holliday, Victoria Ward, Jessic Berens, Gunnar Kvaran, Jason Oliver Nixon, Jeff Slonem, Pamela Kaufman, Sadie van Gelder, Sue Ward Davies, Stephanie Marsh, Aymi Miyako, Priscilla Eakeley, Robert Mcgrew, Graham Boynton, Robert Longhecker, Alan Taylor, Matthew Hamilton, Rosemary Davidson, Jocasta Brownlee and many others whose names I have forgotten to include and who will no doubt now hate me for ever, only please don't, I beg forgiveness.

APOLOGIA PRO RATIOCINATION

This 'speech' we speak of – what can it be
if not translations, incoherencies,
ideograms, pebbles, shreds of silk.
It is a nest we build to entice others,
to make them want to hang around or else

it might be to 'communicate' a crust
of information such as, 'To get to Grand
Central Station take the crosstown bus.'
Perhaps we need to beat our kettle-drums
as counterpoint to chambered compositions,

lacking the brook-babble, buffalo-stomp
heard in earlier times, or moo of cows.
(Who can remember the redundancy of cows?)
Some think it might be one of those windy songs
connecting us to others of our school

or swarm. Of course it must be something innate,
something we really wish to do – although
how weighted and harsh with age my chords, my hands
often tremble, my famished face grows warm.
My instrument – it is not mine – and the words,

those tenuous twitches, gaffes, and glottal stops
do not fairly represent me – are not
what I mean to say. What a vast abyss
can separate flautist from cadenza played,
huffing maker from the vial made,
the lover and the kiss.

                                        by Phyllis Janowitz

Part One

Family Life

Performance Art

SOMETIMES, LIVING in New York, I got invited to movie premieres and screenings. There were all kinds. Usually a premiere was held in a cinema – tickets and the invitation for the party to follow came in the mail. There would be a big crowd gathered in front of the theater to watch the arrival of the celebrities, a velvet rope, security guards, Klieg lights on the streets lighting huge arcs in the sky.

Lining the velvet ropes on each side were masses of press photographers. Arriving was a humiliating moment for me. If the photographers knew who I was and took my picture, I felt embarrassed. I was just a writer, after all, and it seemed ridiculous that all those voices were suddenly shouting, 'Look here, Tama! Tama, over here!' I didn't enjoy having my picture taken the way the movie stars seemed to revel in it – even the ones who claimed not to.

On the other hand, if on that particular evening the photographers didn't recognize me, or a genuine star arrived and they ignored me, this was equally embarrassing. To make my entrance and be ignored, when only the week or month before I had been photographed, made me feel like a has-been. So either way a movie premiere was a shameful event.

After the movie there was usually a party of some sort. One I remember was held in the Plaza hotel, following a Western comedy: hamburgers and beans were served on paper plates. One was in the restaurant adjacent to the skating rink at Rockefeller Center. Another time the guests were taken in old-fashioned English double-decker buses from the movie theater to a restaurant.

I had lost the passes to get us on the bus, so I went around the line to ask the woman taking the tickets what I should do – if she would let us on the bus without them. Later, somebody wrote an angry article in a local free newspaper, about how I had thought I was so important I tried to cut to the front of the line. I kept wanting to say, That's not why I went to the front of the line! I went to the front of the line to find out whether or not I would even be let on to the bus without a ticket or should I find a taxi. But in this situation, my own personal equivalent to a movie star's getting a mean mention for behavior, there was nothing I could do.

Screenings were more fun; one got to see the movie in a little screening room, and some of these were incredibly fancy, with only twenty or thirty huge plush seats, high in a skyscraper, just a few of you at your own private movie in Manhattan. Sometimes after this the director might take a group out to dinner.

Of course the best premiere I ever went to was for the Merchant–Ivory film based on my book *Slaves of New York*. Bloomingdale's had opened a boutique with clothing based on the fashion worn in the movie. My Grandma Anne attended and each time the photographers tried to take my picture my tiny grandmother appeared out of nowhere and sprang into the picture alongside me, shouting, 'I'm the grandma!' She was so totally gleeful – at getting her picture taken – that I always felt good that I had given her that experience before her death. Then a red carpet was laid out across Third Avenue – the entire stretch, across the avenue – and traffic was stopped so that the attendees could leave Bloomingdale's and cross the street to the movie theater.

During the movie not one person laughed. Fortunately the next night my brother and mother attended (there was a second, different premiere) and even though on this night the theater was still totally quiet, my mother and brother were sitting directly in front of me, howling, screaming with laughter. So at least at that time, for the movie, there was an audience of two.

Another time I was invited to a movie premiere which was to be followed by a dinner at the Museum of Modern Art. Tim, my husband, was out of town so I invited a friend of his – who had become my friend, too – to be my date. I was very pleased to go to a premiere and to have a friend to go with, and it seemed particularly nice in the last days of summer, first days of early fall, to be having dinner in the museum.

I didn't feel so good, bloated and a little queasy, but I dressed carefully and put on black tights and a long flowing black skirt, with a T-shirt and a sort of long frock coat over it. I think it was an old design of Nicole Miller's, whom I knew and who had given it to me. I liked being covered up. My idea of a bathing suit would have been one of those Victorian things down to my ankles, but even at night it seemed best to keep every inch of skin covered. That way nobody could look at me and judge me; and since I am my own harshest judge, I knew what they were thinking.

The film wasn't particularly good but it wasn't unbearable and later it won all kinds of prizes. Afterwards everyone walked the block or so to the museum and we showed special passes to get in.

It wasn't the most glamorous evening, though it might have been if you had never done one of these things before, but it was entertaining in a peculiar New York sort of way, to be at a party in a museum that was closed to the general public, at night time. But neither of us really knew any of the other guests. That made things a bit awkward; it was like attending a cocktail party for a business in which you didn't work.

Then my friend bumped into someone he knew and introduced me and the three of us stood chatting near the top of the escalator going down.

Suddenly I realized my black tights were wet. They were completely soaked. Next it occurred to me my shoes were sodden, like two sponges. It seemed very peculiar. I looked and saw the shoes were full not of water but of blood. For a moment I didn't move. Drops of blood began to dot the floor. The floor was shiny and the dots of blood were very red.

'Excuse me,' I said and I went down the escalator toward the women's lavatory.

By the time I got to the bottom of the escalator my shoes were almost overflowing and in the toilet I started to bleed more. There was blood everywhere. I couldn't control it. Finally I mopped myself up a bit with toilet paper, and the floor and toilet. I went out and bought a sanitary napkin from the machine with my only dime, dripping blood everywhere.

Back in the toilet stall I bled through the sanitary napkin. There was blood on the walls, and all over the floor, it looked as if someone had been murdered. In a way it was sort of cool, I thought, even though I couldn't figure out how this had happened. I was getting a lot weaker.

Women were going in and out and it seemed a bit peculiar that no one called, 'Are you all right in there? Do you need help?'

Suddenly there was a commotion at the door; I peered out the crack in the toilet stall and saw that three men had entered with buckets and mops as well as two women, all five were in janitor uniforms. 'Somebody cut themselves?' one of the men was saying.

'There's blood all over the floor,' a woman said. She sounded furious.

'Going up on the first floor, too,' another man said.

They began to mop and scrub. 'Who did it?' said a woman. 'The blood led down here.'

They must have known it was I, I thought, since I saw there was a pool of blood leading directly to my toilet stall. Surely one of them might ask if I was OK. It was true I had made a

mess and was very ashamed, but after all, what if I was trying
to commit suicide and was bleeding to death in here, that
would be a lot more work for them. It occurred to me it might
be amusing to put on a couple of different voices, in a high
voice I could scream, 'Stop! Stop!' and in a deeper voice I
would say, 'I'm going to kill you!' Then I could bounce back
and forth between the walls as if I was being throttled. This
was a long time before the O. J. Simpson case. How surprised
the cleaners would be when they finally burst open the door to
my stall and found only me, covered in blood: it would be like
a Sherlock Holmes case, the attacker mysteriously vanished.

They finished mopping and left. The women's lavatory was
quiet and empty. Once in a while a woman came in to use the
facilities but I guess nothing appeared amiss. I tried to wring
out my stockings and clean up my shoes. Each shoe was so full
I tipped out the contents into the toilet. I was still bleeding, but
not as heavily, and I went out and got a lot of paper towels
since I didn't have another dime to get anything out of the
machine. In the mirror my face was absolutely blanched. There
was blood all over my hands and some had gotten on my face.
I had never seen so much blood in my life.

'You were gone for forty minutes,' my friend said. 'I thought
maybe you left. Where were you?'

I don't know why I didn't say having a miscarriage. 'I was in
the lavatory,' I said. 'It's not that much fun, being female.' I
was maybe three-quarters embarrassed and about one-quarter
amused. I don't know why it amused me, that I could so easily
have been left for dead in the lavatory of the Museum of
Modern Art, but it did. We went to the bar to get another glass
of wine.

*After this whenever there was some dumb girl in the
newspapers who went into a bathroom and gave birth
and left and then was accused of murdering her infant, I
always had sympathy for the girl. I was a lot older than*

my teens but at that moment if a full-term baby had slipped out into the toilet and drowned, along with all the blood, I probably wouldn't have known what was happening. If I was in my teens and nobody said, 'Are you OK? Are you alive?' I don't think I would have felt it mattered whether or not a baby was alive, if I even thought to look. And it would have served the lavatory attendants right if the next day one of them had found a dead baby.

Looks Good on Paper

I'VE ALWAYS *hated articles about the joys of mother-hood. Come to think of it, I also despise pieces about dogs, children, travel and coming-of-age. That hasn't stopped me from using these topics, though, apart from 'coming of age' – but only because I still haven't arrived at it yet.*

Days 1–2

We are in Beijing, on route to adopt our baby. Our group consists of eight couples and two single women, along with our leader, a woman named Xian Wen, who will serve as tour-guide for two days in Beijing before we fly down to Heifei to collect the babies, where Xian Wen will be doing the necessary paperwork. Heifei, a two-and-a-half-hour flight, is located in Anhui Province, an inland south-central area with the large industrial city of Heifei on a parallel with Shanghai.

Even though I had been so anxious, even desperate, to get our baby when we were back in New York, for some reason I calmed down the minute we arrived in China. The other couples are all frantic to get the kids, most of whom are around nine months old and whom we have only seen in photos. But after more than eight months of excruciating paperwork, now that we have landed I suddenly wonder: what's the rush?

The forms we had to acquire for the adoption had been endless. It was like a scavenger hunt: the FBI, for example, needed fingerprints to prove we weren't on their Most Wanted list. Birth certificates with original signatures had to be acquired, then sent to city departments, taken to state departments, government departments, then the Chinese consulate. Medical exams were needed; tax statements; letters of recommendation; our minds had to be probed.

All that time it seemed we never would get our baby, who was getting older by the minute and in the only picture we had of her, taken when she was two months old, had a surly expression already – by my standards, a positive attribute.

I might have adopted years ago, even before I met my husband almost eight years earlier, although I had never been entirely certain whether I had maternal tendencies towards babies. I knew I had maternal tendencies towards dogs; and I always knew any child of mine would have doggish qualities, so I wasn't too concerned. I worked at home, as a writer, so I had plenty of time on my hands: I could never write for more than a few hours a day, and when I was finished all that was left for me was to stare at the ceiling, wondering why I had picked novel-writing as a career. Fourteen years ago I had come to Manhattan in search of other human beings and had found myself only a short time later on the cover of *New York* magazine, standing in a meat locker with a lot of frozen carcasses and a successful novel. (The photographer asked where I wanted my picture taken; since I lived in the meat market district, I said, 'In a meat locker.' At the time it made sense.) Now, I felt, I was on to even bigger adventures.

I knew Tim would make a wonderful father. I rarely picked up friends' children, since whenever I did they burst into tears. Not so with Tim. But I never could believe that anyone would let us adopt a baby – we lived in a one-bedroom apartment. Two adults, three dogs, and both of us collected books (Tim is a curator), so that there really was scarcely any room. But the adoption agency assured us that two rooms were an improvement over a crib in an orphanage, and that once we were driven out of our minds we would double our efforts to find another place to live.

Soon we would be a family, or whatever the equivalent was at the end of the twentieth century. That was why, once in Beijing, I was so happy when my anxiety and apprehensions disappeared. We were taken to see the Great Wall, and the Forbidden City. In Tiananmen Square a woman got run over by a taxi – not someone in our group, though.

I loved everything about the place – the historical sights, and the shopping (cashmere sweaters more expensive than I thought, at a hundred dollars for top quality, in the richest, lushest range of hues I have ever seen – celadon, cinnabar, pea-green and candy-pink; huge cashmere shawls for a hundred and fifty; dresses similar in style to those found in New York, of fantastically patterned silk with prints that for some reason remind me of Paris in the thirties and forties, for thirty), and the antiques market (beautiful old chests of Chinese elm lined with camphor wood, fifty dollars, brilliant vermilion lacquer-leather trunks, forty dollars) and the restaurants. We ate in our hotel, which was a modern skyscraper – our last night alone as a couple – and I couldn't get over the menu, which was the most fabulous menu I thought I had ever seen. Under the category 'Danty of Sea Food' were listed:

Fried Fish Maw with Stuff and green Cucumber
Sautéed Cuttle-fish with American Celery
Braised Shark's fin in Brown sauce with Three Shreds of
  Seafood
Sea Blubber with Cucumber Shreds

There were also, under the 'Vetable' heading:

Braised Hedgehog Hydnun
Fried Whole Scorpion.
Dry-Braised Dick Strip in Brawn Sauce

'Let's stay away from the dry-braised dick strip in brawn sauce,' Tim said.

'OK,' I said, 'but why don't we try the fried whole scorpion? It's only ten cents, and it can't possibly really be a scorpion – it's under the Vetable heading.'

The waitress seemed astonished that we wanted fried whole scorpion. 'Maybe scorpion's out of season?' I said.

'Only one?' She shook her head. 'Only one?' she repeated.

'OK,' said Tim, to placate her. 'Two.'

A few minutes later two fried, whole, black scorpions – claws outstretched, tails curled – arrived at our table, each positioned on a rice cracker.

'Do you think people usually order a whole platterful?' I said. Tim was looking at the scorpions appreciatively, as if he was a connoisseur of this treat

'Well, here goes,' I said, shutting my eyes and putting the scorpion in my mouth. Under normal circumstances I probably wouldn't have done this. It might have been my last attempt at extricating myself from a situation – getting our baby – which, as the time grew closer, I was beginning, far too late, to question.

The scorpion was crispy, but did not have a distinctive scorpion flavor or any instantaneous venomous effects. I really did want a baby, as long as it was quiet and gurgled to itself in a crib. Anybody I ever knew who had had a baby had always said – almost continuously – 'You should have a baby. It's the most fantastic thing that can happen to you.' I could never figure out why they kept saying this, when the look in their eyes was that of a survivor of an airplane crash, but I figured it was something I would understand later.

Day 3

Everyone is relentlessly impatient on the flight to Heifei. The group keeps laughing – someone says he feels like we are Elvis fans, waiting for a glimpse of Him.

I am beginning to get to know our group a little bit. They are in their mid-thirties to mid-forties – among them, a physiologist, a pediatrician, a photographer, an editor, an insurance agent, an education researcher, a marine engineer. Eight couples and two single women, so we will be collecting ten babies. One or two of our group have grown children by a previous marriage. Two couples already have four-year-olds waiting for a new sister. It's the girls who are abandoned in China. The Chinese are only allowed one child per couple, and girls just don't have much status. In addition, the boys stay home and look after the parents in their old age. In the future, China will be like New York City, only reversed: the men will outnumber the women a hundred to one; when a single Chinese woman walks into a party, she will be as desirable as a movie-star-handsome billionaire bisexual bachelor in Manhattan.

Though perhaps under normal circumstances the people in our group would have nothing in common, the fact that we are all joined together in this adventure makes me feel like a timid opera buff who has signed up for a packaged Perillo tour to La Scala.

At the hotel in Heifei – another modern skyscraper – we all disappear to our rooms, still laughing, smiling: the next time we see one another we will all be with our smiling, adorable, happy little babies. We have swapped photographs – the babies are beautiful. I only wish I had brought other clothing. All the women seem to be dressed as Mothers, in long, floral print dresses or crisp linen outfits. A glimpse in the mirror as we get off the elevator on to our floor reveals a sophisticated crowd of parents-to-be and one hippie type with hair like black scrambled eggs, wearing a T-shirt Tim found for me that reads: 'CadvihKlein', with smaller letters beneath that explain it is 'uhderweqr'. The Chinese love T-shirts printed with words in English, but don't seem to care that almost always they are misspelled or make very little sense.

Two o'clock, two-fifteen, two-thirty. Tim and I pace back and forth, as if our wife was in labor next door in the delivery room. I keep running to the bathroom to brush my teeth. If the baby detects even a whiff of stale breath, it could put a damper on our relationship that might last for years. Finally, around three-thirty, the call comes: *SHE* is on her way.

After months of arguing we have decided to name her Willow. I had wanted to call her Thomasina, or Letizia. Tim, on the other hand, was thinking more in terms of Hortense or Hattie. It no longer matters. Maybe it will be a safeguard: the information and photograph of her that we received several months ago said that – for her age – she was extremely short and fat. With a name like Willow, this will have to change. The doorbell rings: Xian Wen, a baby-nurse from the orphanage, and Willow arrive.

Willow is *very* cute, dripping with sweat (the Chinese believe in keeping their babies bundled up in the heat), with giant ears. When the nurse hands her to me she smiles, even though she has been taken on a six-hour unairconditioned bus ride from the orphanage at dawn, along with the other babies, and then made to wait in a hotel room for many hours until our arrival.

'This is the first baby I've ever held who didn't burst into tears,' I say, smiling as I look into Willow's eyes.

'She doesn't cry,' says the nurse in Mandarin. Xian Wen translates. 'She likes to play.'

'She's just been fed,' Xian Wen adds. 'When you give her food, make sure it's boiling hot – that's what they're accustomed to. She should be fed at six a.m., nine, twelve, three, six and then she goes to sleep and gets fed again at eleven at night. Keep her warm – never let her stomach be uncovered.'

Then, handing us a box of rice cereal and a bag of formula that we are to combine in specific amounts at the next feeding, Xian Wen and Willow's nurse leave, while I continue to hold the smiling, happy baby in my arms.

As soon as they are out the door, Willow bursts into tears. It turned out the nurse was right – Willow doesn't cry, *as long as she is played with, every single second*. This is no cuddly baby. She wants to be bounced, rocked, swooped around the room, turned upside down, and stares grimly while adults flap their arms and hop around the room like parrots. Since she has been in cribs with the other babies for the past nine months after she was found in a park when two days old, she has no muscle tone – so all the swooping, jostling and jiggling has to be by the person holding her. The minute that person stops tossing her around, she screams.

Despite her physical weakness, she has an abnormal amount of energy. I am wondering, hyperactive? Part chimp? Her head has been shaved – another Chinese custom, to ensure a thicker, more luxuriant growth – but it looks to me like she must have had hair on her forehead that was shaved too. Anyway, she definitely has sideburns. It really may be that Baby Elvis, complete with all the troubles of his past life, has arrived in this new incarnation. I wonder if they selected her for us when they saw the picture of me and Tim that we had to send from the United States.

She cries non-stop, and since I have read somewhere that babies only cry for a reason, Tim and I decide to change her diaper. We put her on the floor and try to get her out of her clothes.

Though she is weak, she is able to fight like a wounded fox in a leg-hold trap, and even with the two of us working hard the task is next to impossible.

Unearthly howls fill the air. Through the opened hotel window, a chorus of screams joins in. Apparently throughout the hotel the other members of our group are occupied in a similar endeavor. My face is bright red; sweat pours off Tim, dripping on to the sweating baby. We look at each other. 'Is it too late for her to catch the bus back to the orphanage?' I say.

This diaper-changing takes around an hour. When she is back in her clothes with a diaper haphazardly strangling her midriff, her sobbing diminishes somewhat, which makes us realize it is time for her bottle. Trying to get the lumps out of the gruel with the lukewarm water provided to us in a thermos by the hotel takes almost another hour. By then, I can tell, she is *really* angry, and bored – obviously this was not what she expected.

The hotel has provided our room with a purple metal cage, a crib with bars spaced just the right distance to trap a baby's head. Willow doesn't like the crib. Being in the crib makes her very upset. If she was angry before, now she is furious. The toys we brought from the United States are lousy; any fool would have known. But finally after several hours of strenuous entertainment – silly faces, songs, the hora and other impromptu performances of folk dance, arm wrestling – and another feeding, we are able to convince her to sleep. We've got the crib in our room. By now it's quite late, though how so much time has passed it's hard to say. I was ready for bed hours ago.

Unfortunately, though she's already snoring, I can't sleep. What if we have unwittingly killed her and each snore is her last gasp? A kid that survives being left in a park, only to be murdered by two witless foreigners. If she lives, though, I don't know what we are going to do with a monster. It will be eighteen years before she's ready for college. I suppose we can send her to summer camp and boarding school in the meantime.

At least I know she's not dead when she decides – at three a.m. – she may take a second look at some of the toys. She discovers that by pounding a button, the electronic version of 'Gee, It's a Small World', a song I have always loathed, will play over and over.

Day 4

Dawn. First there is the feeding, the bathing, the changing, the attempt at cheering her up while the other adult member of our family unit tries to shower and put on some clothes and vice versa. At no time must she be ignored. The kid has no inner resources – can't read, write letters, put on nail polish – and seems to have nowhere to go.

It is now eight – it has only taken us three hours to get ready for breakfast.

In the lobby large groups are patrolling the halls and I see that – although they are speaking Norwegian and Swedish, or have Canadian accents – every single one of them is lugging a sobbing Chinese baby. No wonder the place was so noisy last night. What I thought was simply bad singing coming from the karaoke bar downstairs was a hellish chorus of babies.

I suppose things could be worse. What if I had checked into the hotel – a normal, non-baby-acquiring tourist – only to find I had arrived in some kind of babyland?

A woman approaches Willow in her stroller. Willow looks up at her and coos appreciatively, as if she is about to be rescued from what is obviously a mistaken placement. 'Oh, what a cute baby!' the woman says. 'I was supposed to get mine yesterday, but she's not going to be delivered until today. It's like torture, waiting for her.'

'You could take this one,' I offer.

Our group has already gathered in the dining hall for breakfast, tots in their strollers in a ring around the table. 'How's everything going?' I say weakly, expecting a response similar to the one I would have.

In unison the group shouts, 'Great!'

Day 5

The horror. The horror.

Day 6

By now the other adopting parents appear to have aged ten years and are so worn down they are at last willing to admit

everything is not perfect. Two babies cry constantly and if even
if they can be stopped will start again the moment anyone
looks at them. One baby is on a hunger strike. Two babies
have been given the wrong mixture of formula-to-rice cereal
and are severely constipated. I have definitely bonded with the
group, if not the baby. There is nothing like hearing techniques
for relieving constipation over breakfast to make one feel close
with another couple. There is nobody in the world like these
folks. At every meal we have the most fascinating conversations on topics as diverse as diaper rash, diarrhea and baby-
dandruff, as well as complimenting one another on the darling
baby-clothes the surly waifs are drooling on.

Day 7

How could I have been such an idiot? It was Tim who had his
doubts and apprehensions before we got her, and Tim who has
bonded immediately with her – no wonder, when she looks at
him so adoringly. He is a natural: strong enough to throw her
around, adept at changing diapers, laughs with honest delight
when she suddenly viciously inserts one sharp-clawed finger as
far up his right nostril as possible.

When she tries to pull out my hair by the roots, I can't help
but believe her intent is malicious. My arms are too weak to
toss her into the air. For this, it is obvious, she will never
forgive me. And I will never forgive myself for believing all
those girlfriends who kept telling me, 'You should have a baby.
It's so great!' I see now that it was their method of revenge. I
must remember to encourage others to do this marvelous thing
– adopting a hyperactive, sweating lunatic unable to change
her own diapers.

The Chinese paperwork is complete; our next stop is a week
in Guangzhou (formerly Canton) to complete the American
adoption process. After that, we fly back to the United States,
where, I suppose, the real nightmare begins, when she will

suddenly begin demanding Barbie dolls, Nintendo, pure-white Arabian mares, will take drugs, contract sexually transmitted diseases, insist on attending the fanciest, most expensive private schools, cry when she doesn't get into the college of her choice.

Postscript: Four Weeks Later

The above notations were found in my diary, obviously scribbled by someone other than myself. Perhaps some pages of my journal got mixed in with someone else's? We have been *extremely* lucky: our baby is so easy-going, laughing, laughing, laughing all the time. Sometimes she laughs so much, staring at her beautiful bud-like face in the mirror, that I, too, begin to cackle uncontrollably.

Honestly, no matter how many times anyone insists I wrote the above, I truly can never believe them. It must have been the jet-lag. Or something. She is so sweet! Just the other day our pediatrician told me not to worry – hopefully by college age she won't need a bottle and will be on to the harder stuff.

It's the most fantastic, wonderful thing a person can do. I'm really making the most of that brief time I have with her before she starts walking and having unprotected sex and experimenting with drugs and screaming on the floor in the supermarket because I won't buy her candy.

I have China to thank. China is so great about foreign adoption, making it simple for single people – both men and women – as well as couples of all ages. I don't see how or why anybody wouldn't do so. And the baby is so cute! So smart! It's easy to see how China is going to take over the world.

I'm thinking, maybe in the fall I'll looking into adopting one from India.

Yes, I can see her already: perhaps a bit older than Willow, one of those gypsy-street-urchin-waif types, with dark skin, a dirty face, gold bangles at her slim wrists and ankles, and thick, wild hair. I'll have to warn my friends to put away their valuables – jewelry, silver – before we come, but otherwise she'll be the perfect sister for Willow. I wonder just how long it will take to convince Tim.

A New York Marriage

P AIGE INTRODUCED me to one of her friends, an English guy in his early twenties. (This was many years ago, long before I met Tim.) Nigel came over one evening and told me that he was going to have to leave the country. His visa had expired, he didn't want to leave, they probably wouldn't let him back in. 'I want to find an American willing to marry me so I can get my green card and find work in the movies,' Nigel said.

I said I would try and think if I knew anybody.

It got late in the evening and we had quite a bit to drink and finally I said, 'I'll tell you what: I'll marry you.'

'Oh?' Nigel said. He slid over next to me on the couch and put his arm around me. 'That's awfully generous of you.' He leaned over to kiss me thank you, but his kiss missed my cheek and landed on my lips in a way that was slightly more than just friendly. 'Are you sure this is what you really want to do?'

'Sure,' I said. 'No problem.'

'Wow,' Nigel said. 'You won't be sorry? Later?'

'No,' I said. 'But we'll have to live together, you know. They expect you to prove it's a real marriage before they give you your green card.'

'Oh, I know,' Nigel said. His lips brushed the side of my neck.

'You can sleep on the couch in the living room,' I said. 'It's not a very comfortable couch, though, and it's kind of noisy in the front room.'

'Mmm-hmm,' Nigel said. He wasn't listening.

'The dogs need to be walked three times a day,' I said. 'You don't have to take them far, though. Make sure you keep Beep-beep away from other dogs – he attacks. And also you might have to carry Lulu, she's not really the type of dog who walks.'

'I like dogs,' Nigel murmured.

'I'm not particularly neat or clean, but I don't think it will take you that long to straighten up around here. The vacuum cleaner is actually pretty decent. And there's so much filing and paperwork!'

Nigel sat up and moved away from me a bit.

'I don't ever want to be criticized for stuff like leaving the cap off the toothpaste,' I said. 'By the way, if you want to smoke, you're going to have to go outside. Also, since I work at home, you'll have to be out of the apartment from nine to five every day, I can't stand it when someone's around while I'm thinking. Please make up the couch before you go. It'll be great having you here, though; Paige said you're a good cook, I like spicy food the best and I hate making coffee every morning!'

Nigel stood. 'I'm very flattered,' he said weakly. 'Why don't I let you think about it, overnight?'

'Oh, I don't need to think about it.'

'But what if you met someone else and fell in love? You would have a stigma.'

'I wouldn't mind, not at all. Gosh, it'll be nice not to have to cook, and clean! It would be worth it.'

'I wouldn't want to ruin your life,' Nigel said before he went out the door.

The City Dweller's Daily Writing Routine

T HE AWFUL thing about writing is that you can think of a word, which is a good word, that you like, only then you think of a different word, which might be a better word, only it might not. Then you think of yet another word, it might be a better word, it might be a less good word, or it might not even be the word to say what you set out to say in the first place.

But maybe what you were setting out to say in the first place isn't as good as what you've ended up saying, or the thing you set out to say in the first place is better, only the words you've ended up using to say something that isn't as good are better words than the words you used to say something else that was better only using words that were worse.

And if you put different words in different places long enough, sometimes you go on caring, only you're making it worse, and sometimes you stop caring and you know it is worse, only you no longer care, but you have to care in case you can make it better.

Then there is the editor, the editor comes in and says, this is a good word, this is a bad word, but does he or she really care? Even if you no longer care, they can't possibly care as much as you care even when you no longer care, and then there is the reader, whom you never see, you never know, and if your book or article does not get published it is not even possible to have friends who don't bother to read your work, there is nobody to read your work but even if there was somebody to read your writing it would be impossible for them to know what you were trying to say, since you yourself have changed the words.

Commencement Speech at the Community College of Beaver County

*O*NE OF THE *most frightening things I was ever asked to do was to give the commencement speech at the Community College of Beaver County (about an hour outside of Pittsburgh, PA). I had never even attended a graduation – none of my own – and at my brother's college graduation I had to leave abruptly in the middle of the commencement speech due to a sudden attack of paranoia when I became certain that my father – seated in a different part of the audience – was about to take out a gun and shoot my mother, who was next to me. So I didn't have a clue what I was supposed to talk about at a graduation. To make matters worse, I had bought a suit at the Salvation Army, in order to look respectable for the event, which I hadn't actually bothered to try on, since the jacket fit, only it turned out that the skirt was around twelve sizes too large, and was going to fall off the second I let go. I had to hang on to it while I spoke, which was difficult because I was wearing a cap – barely balanced on top of my hair – and gown. Still, as I recollect, it was a lovely melon color.*

The auditorium at the Beaver County Community College was also the sports arena and had been built in the style of a geodesic dome, only it was made out of some peculiar substance that resembled vast tufts of brown mold that I started to think were going to fall on me – and the audience –

while I spoke. And the sound system was defective, so that every time I said a word a shrill buzzing – some kind of feedback – blasted through the arena.

I remember looking out at a sea of blank faces, wondering whether everybody looked blank because they couldn't hear me, or because I wasn't making any sense. Afterward there was a reception. Everyone – the professors, the staff and secretaries, and a priest who seemed to be associated with the college – was very nice, but everyone also seemed completely perplexed. They knew somebody must have invited me to speak, but who? And why?

I haven't been invited to give a commencement speech elsewhere, but the following is my prepared essay.

I am delighted to be here this afternoon to celebrate this day with you, the graduating class of 1995. From what I have learned about your college, you represent a diverse body of students. You range greatly in age; though the majority of you are from Pennsylvania, many have come from other parts of the United States and elsewhere in the world. The highest numbers are graduating in the technologies and allied health fields, though others plan to go into business. Some of you will go on to a wide variety of jobs and careers; some will continue with further education; some will raise families; and some of you will sit around at home crying. I can tell you this by personal experience.

The smallest number of you graduating today have majored in the liberal arts.

This was my major at college, and in speaking to you now I cannot help but remember my own graduation, some seventy-odd years ago. In any event, I hadn't a clue what to do when I wasn't in school. I had to get a job – immediately, that much was certain – but then, as now, it was apparent to almost everyone I met that I was singularly unqualified to make it through life, let alone find anyone crazy enough to hire me for a job.

In high school I had wanted to be a stewardess; but my mother pointed out that my surly disposition, combined with the fact that flying on airplanes made me sick, should help me to figure out that I would make a poor stewardess.

While in college – taking classes in English, anthropology and creative writing – I met a woman who worked for a New York City advertising agency. After spending time with her, I decided I wanted to go into advertising more than anything. This woman was well paid; the company sent her on trips to other parts of the world; she always appeared to be having a lot of fun. I liked the idea of advertising: it wasn't hypocritical, it wasn't pretending to do something other than what it really did. If the ad agency was trying to sell you toilet paper, they were trying to sell you toilet paper – it was all very straightforward.

I wanted to be a copywriter. My friend in advertising told me that my first step in applying for a job was to put together a portfolio of imaginary sample ads. I had always drawn and sketched for fun – in college I helped out various theater groups by drawing posters, or doing the artwork for campus parties and events – so I decided to illustrate my own advertising copy instead of gluing down photographs.

I can't say my writing was exactly inspired. One ad, I remember, had a drawing of a hot dog – it was supposed to be knockwurst, actually – and the caption read 'The Wurst is the Best'. My drawings, too, were extremely bizarre, for I couldn't exactly draw representationally, and if I drew something that looked like a hot dog, for example, it always ended up wearing a suit, with a face full of three-day stubble needing a shave. I could draw rabbits that looked like men, or men that looked like rabbits. Anyway, you get the idea – nothing came out right.

Some months passed applying for jobs and during this time I spent my entire life savings. I was in trouble. Whenever I spoke to my father, he screamed at me to get a job, and didn't believe I was even trying, although since he was no longer supporting me I couldn't understand why he cared. I was a failure.

At last, out of money, no job, I had to move back home. My mother lived on an industrial ten-lane highway, outside of Boston. Most of the time I sat around and cried. Finally I mustered the last of my strength and applied to various ad agencies in the area.

A long time went by. Only one agency responded to my letter; but at least I was invited for an interview. My mother agreed to drive me into the city, since I had a driving phobia. It was obvious this was the last chance, the last hope, for a person such as myself.

A massive snowstorm hit town, and my mother insisted we depart for the city at dawn. In the morning I dressed carefully, selecting the following Job Interview Outfit: a very tight black skirt; black hairy sweater that smelled of mothballs; black fishnet stockings; an antique black velvet hat, possibly with a veil (I've done my best to repress this entire experience); pointy, black-leather spike-heeled boots; and, in a finishing touch, slung around my neck a moldy silver-fox fur piece with glass eyes, covered with bald patches, that I had found sometime before in an old junk store. The completed look: your basic Elvira or Morticia Addams.

My mother made no comment but went out to warm up the nearly frozen, ancient car she owned. She told me later that she thought my outfit somewhat odd to wear to a job interview, but she assumed that I had received some training or instruction while in college, addressing the issues of what to wear to a job interview and so forth.

In retrospect I think I must have had some reason for wearing this costume – maybe I really didn't want to have to get a job? When we reached the office building I grimly headed up the stairs, carrying my portfolio. For reasons that are now unclear to me, my mother followed at a discreet distance behind. It turned out that the job position I was being considered for (though in my letter I said I was applying to be a copywriter) was actually a position as a receptionist in the accounting department. There was one other woman waiting to be interviewed – and she was dressed appropriately.

However, no one paid the slightest bit of attention to her; instead, I was whisked into an office, a group of men looked over my portfolio carefully; and, amazingly enough, I was immediately offered a job. Not, however, as a copywriter, writing slogans for various products, but – because they preferred my illustrations – the position of Assistant Art Director. I was given what sounded to me like an incredible salary, as well as an office with many windows. And I knew that in the business world windows were the most important thing you could have.

The job began in a week. Now that I finally had a job, I figured I had better dress correctly. For my first day, I neatly tied my hair back in a braid, wore flat suede loafers with a little fringe – like golfing shoes – a plaid skirt and a blouse with a demure Peter Pan collar.

It took several hours to get into Boston by bus and trolley car. When I reached the office, the man who had hired me appeared completely astonished – and disappointed. I looked like somebody else. The confident entity he had hired was gone; in her place, apparently, was a timid, fourteen-year-old school girl. I was sent to my new, empty office, where I sat, waiting and looking out the window.

Finally I was given an assignment: to draw a storyboard – a series of pictures like a cartoon strip – 'a cowboy resembling John Wayne, going into a bar and ordering a can of Underwood Deviled Ham'.

There was only one problem: there was no way I could draw a picture of a cowboy resembling John Wayne, let alone a can of Underwood Deviled Ham. I could draw a man who looked like a rabbit, or a dachshund – but that's not what they wanted. Even if I had been able to draw a cowboy who resembled John Wayne, there was no way I could draw him in the next frame, at a different angle or in a different position.

But nobody had bothered, at the agency, to find out whether or not I was actually capable of doing this. That night I went home and cried. I went to the library, and attempted to trace pictures from children's books. Impossible. Nothing worked, though I did my best. Every few days my boss asked if the storyboard was ready. 'Not just yet,' I said. But at the end of the week I was called into the conference room and I knew I was going to have to produce something.

Eight men were seated around a huge conference table. 'Let's see what you've been doing, Tama,' my boss said. 'Let's see your work.' I held up my drawings. There was a lengthy silence. 'Ah,' said my boss at last. 'That's, uh, that's . . . OK. You go back into your office, and when we have something for you to do, we'll be in touch.'

For a long time I didn't see or speak to anyone. I just sat in that office. My boss did try to come up with other things for me to do. Once he asked me to take some pictures – photographs for a client – out of their frames, turn the mats around so that they were back-to-front, and put the rematted pictures back in the frames.

Two days later, when he came to collect them, he found me on the floor, struggling with photograph number one, and crying. Then he took the pictures, mats and frames away.

At other times I was asked to do 'mechanicals' – a term in the ad world which meant I pasted things down on my desk, sliced things up, glued, and so forth.

After a while nobody came into my office to ask me to do anything at all.

One day a new woman got a job as copywriter. She was a single mother, a good deal older than me, but I was happy at last there was another woman working there, with whom I might be friends.

We went to lunch. 'Tell me, Tama,' she said. 'What exactly is it that you do there in your office, all day?'

'Actually, Valerie, I just sit there,' I said. 'I sit there. And, um, I look out the window. And I get paid!'

'Ahh,' she said, a curious expression on her face. She said nothing further, but when we got back to the agency, she disappeared into the boss' office.

The next day, I was called in. 'Due to unexpected cutbacks in the Underwood Deviled Ham account,' my boss said, 'I'm afraid we're going to have to let you go.'

Well, after that I knew I wasn't meant for this working world: I got a scholarship to go back to school, money that gave me barely enough to live on, but it was during that year that I wrote my first novel – out of sheer terror and desperation.

What I suppose I would like this story to impart to you today is: who knows where life will lead you?* The main thing, I think, is to use your imagination; to be willing to take risks; to be able to see life as some kind of demented adventure; and, finally, not to be afraid of failure. I cried and cried, after I was fired; I was a complete and utter failure, unworthy, and would never amount to anything in life. Now I see it was all for the best, even though I still spend a lot of time crying.

But luckily for all of us, this is America, and you can invent whoever or whatever you want to be. If it's Morticia Addams, OK. I'm not suggesting any of you go out there for those job interviews dressed in a fox-fur piece and black spike-heeled boots – particularly the men – for in retrospect that I got the job was pretty much a fluke. As it turns out, however, determination, confidence and will-power can get you an awfully long way.

* Actually I'm not sure that this was the message of my speech at all. But I knew there was supposed to be some point to a commencement speech. And it wasn't until many years later that I learned a commencement speech was supposed to be elevated and full of noble sentiment.

What I am suggesting is that you view life, in some ways, as an extension of your college here – no matter how well or how poorly you do, you've still learned something. At least maybe you've figured out what subjects do or don't interest you. And usually if you bother your professor long enough, he or she gives up and changes your grade out of sheer desperation.

But the difference between life and college is that, in fact, there are no grades in life. On your deathbed there isn't going to be a professor telling you: That was an A+ life, or a C– existence. And all of you here, whatever choices you may make, whatever risks you decide to take, are successful today, by having followed and pursued your dream of graduation. And I wish all of you the hope that you may have fun, adventures, love and the pursuit of your dreams along the way.

I Was an Elderly Teenage
Extra in a Video for MTV

A FEW YEARS after I moved to New York a woman stopped
me on the street and said, 'Would you like to be an extra
in a party scene in a ZZ Top video?' I tried to pretend this kind
of thing happened to me often; in other words, that I was a
person who could barely step out of the house without being
discovered. That was why I forgot to ask her if I would get
paid.

'What would I have to do?' I said.

'Oh, it'll be fun,' she said. 'You go out on this yacht for half
the day.'

I liked the idea of going out on a yacht. Anyway, for half the
day, what did I have to lose? 'Sure,' I said. 'Why not.'

A few days later I got a call from a woman named Ellie,
telling me to be on a yacht named the *Selisa* at nine o'clock in
the morning. I should wear 'Jeans, sneakers – you know, party
clothing.' So I wore what I always wore to parties: tight black
pants, sneakers, and a dirty black sweatshirt.

I got to the yacht at nine in the morning. Maybe I was still
half asleep, but it seemed to me that, if a person wanted to,
they could call the *Selisa* a yacht, but as far as I was concerned
it was a boat. There were some men moving equipment at the
front end, but none of them spoke to me. I pointed to a ramp.
'Is this how I'm supposed to get on?'

'Don't fall off,' one of the men said, without turning around.

I crossed over and went to the back of the conveyance. There were three or four people siting in a room on leatherette couches and chairs. None of them spoke to me. So I went into the other room. There was a bartender behind a counter covered with coffee cups and Danish. 'I'll have a cup of coffee,' I said.

'Last week,' the man said, 'I was a bartender at a party for Pat Benatar.'

I looked around at the other extras. As usual, I was dressed inappropriately. The other ingenues were ten years younger and wearing slut boots, vinyl belts and hot-pink nylon shirts. It wasn't that I didn't have an outfit like that – I had worn mine to Le Cirque the night before. But I distinctly remembered being told to wear jeans and sneakers. The makeup artist blinked at me sadly and told me to sit in the chair.

'Go upstairs when your makeup is done,' said Ellie when she saw me.

Just then the members of ZZ Top came on board.

Two of them had the most luxurious of beards. Probably it had taken them years and years to grow the beards, which were long and sparse and flowed below their waists. They were clean beards, without foodstuffs. How fortunate it was, I thought, that these two men with their long beards had found one another. I could tell that each admired the other and his accomplishment.

Then one of them spoke. 'I need a scissors,' he said. Everyone jumped.

'Who has a scissors?' Ellie said. She turned to the makeup artist. 'Do you have a scissors?'

'What kind of scissors?' the makeup artist said.

'Just a scissors,' Ellie said.

'What for?' the makeup woman said again.

'For his beard,' Ellie said. I looked up with sudden interest.

'No,' the man with the beard shouted. 'No, no, no! Not the beard! I have a loose thread on my collar.' Then the costume girl came and took them downstairs to change.

The yacht was under way, headed down the Hudson river toward the World Trade Center and great adventures on the high seas.

The three other girls came upstairs, followed by two college-aged guys dressed in shorts and Hawaiian print shirts. Maybe the three girls and the two boys went together, but whoever had stopped me on the street had made a mistake. Even without a mirror nearby, I could tell we belonged in different videos. I had a sense of humiliation. But then, I always did. We all stood near a table covered with trays containing barbecued chicken and a vat of green potato salad.

'Move over here,' a woman said, pushing the back of my legs into a low metal tub filled with ice and bottles of beer. She grabbed a chicken wing and thrust it into my hand. Then a man appeared.

'In this scene,' he said, picking up a large video camera, 'In this scene, you're all dancing – partying – and having a good time. I want you to go really wild.'

An assistant turned on a tape cassette of ZZ Top. 'Dance!' the director said.

We rehearsed the dancing. I tried to look enthusiastic, even though under no circumstances could I ever imagine myself dancing enthusiastically to a tape of ZZ Top music on the roof of a boat with five strangers at ten-thirty in the morning.

'Put some streamers around their necks,' the woman told the assistant. So he threw red and pink streamers over us.

'OK,' the man said. 'This time, when you dance, go really crazy. You,' – he pointed at a girl with a blond frou-frou hairdo – 'you shake up the bottle of beer while you dance and spray it on everyone.'

This time the camera was on. The boat began to rock from side to side. The sky grew overcast. We danced wildly to the tape, a boy picked up a handful of greenish potato salad and stuffed it into his mouth, the other boy pretended to play the barbecue tongs as if it was a guitar, the girl shook up the bottle and sprayed it all over us.

The crêpe-paper streamers, wet with beer, began to bleed streaks of blood red down everyone's clothes. The girls jiggled back and forth, laughing ferociously, clapping their hands. The boat was rocking harder now, my legs smashed into the metal tub of beer. Near the Statue of Liberty I began to think I might possibly throw up. Yet I noticed the camera focusing on my face. I smiled wanly as I danced, shaking my head from side to side to demonstrate joy and goodwill.

'Now,' the man said. 'In this next scene, pick up the tray of chicken and toss it overboard, tray and all.'

'I feel sick,' a boy said. I had noticed him eating the green potato salad. 'That potato salad – there was something wrong.'

'It was old,' the woman said. 'It was just there for looks.'

'Now, you have to get it right,' the man said. 'Look like you're having a good time, count to three and toss.'

We crowded around the chicken, counted to three and tossed the chicken and the container over the railing. We watched as it tumbled into the water. The camera panned to follow. It was pretty much a non-event, I thought, as we all looked at each other. 'Clap!' the cameraman shouted abruptly. 'Applaud! You're having fun! Laugh! Hahahahaha!'

It wouldn't have occurred to me that throwing some moldy chicken off a boat into the Hudson could be construed as entertainment. We began to applaud politely and then stopped. 'Was that OK?' the blonde said.

'It was OK when you threw the chicken,' the man said. 'But then you all just stood around like dumbos.'

'OK, OK,' the woman said. 'You have one last try.' From under a plastic tarp she took out a large platter of spare ribs. They reeked.

'This time, after it hits the water, jump up and down and applaud,' the man said.

The spare ribs went high in the sky, splattering the deck with yellowish goo. We laughed and cheered. 'OK, that's it,' the man said. 'You're done. Please stay up here. You're in the way downstairs.'

The boat was going no place, circling endlessly in order to keep the Statue of Liberty in the same spot. The faster we circled, the more the boat rocked. The other girls went downstairs. I thought maybe the fresh air would do me some good, but then I thought,' If I don't go below deck, I'm going to die.' Something was terribly wrong. I had the sensation of having swallowed a quart of gasoline and too much sushi.

'What's this a video for, anyway?' I asked Ellie.

'It's a promo,' she said. 'MTV is having a contest. There's one winner from each state. The winners get to go out on a yacht like this.'

What kind of contest is that? I thought. The prize to me seemed the same as a punishment. I found a chair and slumped into it, shutting my eyes.

'Taking a nap?' someone said. I opened my eyes. It was one of the members of ZZ Top – the taller bearded one – dressed in a yachting costume of white pants, a blue blazer and a captain's hat.

'Dying,' I mumbled.

In my youth I had two aspirations: to be a fashion model and/or a groupie. Sadly, I was never able to explore either of these career choices. In the first I was prevented by my appearance, and in the second I was prevented by my lack of knowledge not only as to who the various rock groups were but how to obtain access to them and what I was supposed to do to in the event I recognized and met one. Actually, over the years I did meet one or two but they showed no inclination to have sex. That left writing, which, to this day, I continue to find a very poor third.

Style

F OR MOST of my life I have unintentionally worn the wrong
thing. Secretly I blame my mother, who always encour-
aged me to be a free spirit. I remember in first grade I
discovered in her closet a marvelous pair of shoes of very soft
suede. Most magical of all, the right shoe was mustard brown
and the left lemon gold. Whether this was how they were
meant to be, or whether my mother had bought them on sale, I
never found out. Immediately I insisted, demanded, that I be
allowed to wear them to school.

I hardly had to insist – my mother didn't mind at all,
although she did point out they were quite a few sizes too
big. While I don't remember exactly what happened, I must
have grown used to the attention I received, positive or
negative, and have continued to crave it ever since.

We shopped at the Salvation Army, where I could (and still
do) choose whatever I liked, or Marshall's discount department store. Everything in Marshall's was there for a reason: no
one else wanted it.

But as a child I didn't know that. In the early seventies, to
celebrate going to a new school, my mother and I selected an
item for me that was not on sale – a huge, floppy, red velour
hat, which I proudly wore that first day. At lunchtime a tiny
gray man crept over to me and said, 'Take off that hat and put
it in your locker at once.'

I gave him a gentle smile. Astonishingly, he plucked the hat
from my head. The poor man, I thought, and wondered why

my wearing a hat would upset him so. He turned out to be the principal and rushed back to his office to immediately issue an announcement over the public loudspeaker: as of this moment, it was forbidden to wear a hat of any kind in school.

To have no money, yet to have the courage (well, at least the chutzpah) and creativity (OK, at least insanity) to wear unusual things, is a gift and a curse for which, as I say, I blame my mother. Of course, this predilection may also be genetic – from my father's side: his mother, my Grandma Anne, wore clothes as if she were a gypsy; when one necklace would do she was happy to wear twenty. She sent me boxes of clothing, often with the price tags still on, though it was impossible to determine where she had ever found such schmattes:* a terry-cloth jumpsuit in bunny pink, a bead-encrusted cashmere sweater she had decided to wash in the machine, a brassiere sized 38DDD, and a jaunty pillbox hat made of genuine leopard skin. 'I hope you were able to use some of the things I sent,' she would say.

When I was five she sent me a plaid dress that was missing one shoulder (deliberately), which shocked me terribly. I burst into tears and fled the room, screaming that I would never wear it (I must have thought it had been intended for some deformed little girl), while my mother shouted after me that it was a very cute dress. But as I got older I began to acquire a taste for Grandma Anne's finds, and, curiously, I did somehow manage to put to use much of the clothing she passed along, even though some of it was stained even before I put it on. 'That way you won't feel so bad if you spill something on it,' she told me.

A few years later my mother and I discovered the Ladies' Auxiliary thrift store in Flushing, Queens, near where *her* mother lived. Thus, during college, I was able to wear many Chanel-style suits in startling shades of coral, orange and green

* Yiddish for rags.

long before the revival of that look; a remarkable floor-length dress, circa 1940, of pink taffeta covered with blue lace with a sweetheart neckline and puffed sleeves; a man's white silk shantung suit jacket; a black Balenciaga ball gown (which cost $2.50). All these fashions would eventually be revived – but at the time they were truly peculiar things to wear.

Right after I graduated from college, my cousin took me to a very fancy party for the Campari family, for which I decided the only appropriate outfit would be the Balenciaga. Of course, no one else was wearing anything remotely resembling a 1950s ball gown, black and huge and strapless. 'You know,' a man whispered to me, 'it takes a real woman to wear a dress like that.'

I cringed and nearly fainted. Quickly I dashed to the women's room. Perhaps the dress had slipped way down, exposing my socks – I had had to stuff the entire bodice, as it had obviously been made for a woman a great deal larger than I was.

I wondered how it was that other women always somehow knew exactly the right outfit to wear. It seemed that whatever I put on turned out to be (thrillingly) inappropriate for the occasion. Going out was both terrifying and curiously exciting.

Of course, in New York you can always just put on something black – what it is hardly matters. When I first moved here, wearing black was an indication that one belonged to the downtown SoHo art crowd. Slowly this color crept uptown, until for a while it predominated at every gathering.

What exactly did it mean? Black clothing had somehow, mysteriously, come to signify sophistication, elegance, power. Yet in Greece or the Ukraine – and in this country, too – women donned black for a year of mourning. As Grandma Anne might have said, 'Are we all in mourning here?'

A couple of years ago, attending an event out of town, I realized that even if I had a vague idea of what to wear in New

York, it didn't help me much in the heartland of America. The famous Kentucky hostess Anita Madden had invited me to her annual benefit gala and the following day to the Kentucky Derby. All I was told was that every woman at the Derby wore a hat.

A hat! I had none. (Where was my red floppy hat now that I needed it?) I quickly set out to find one. In Bergdorf's I fell in love – Anne Moore, a master of hat design, had several tours de force for sale. A huge straw hat was covered with artificial ivy and several gigantic silk roses. Alas, the price tag was $400. But why couldn't I create my own imitation? I found a big straw hat at Woolworth's ($10) and in Manhattan's flower district I purchased variegated silk ivy and pink artificial roses.

I hadn't bothered in Bergdorf's to find out how the plant life was attached to the hat, and time was running out. I bought some clear nylon fishing line, and, armed with a big needle, I got on to the plane and began to sew. Unfortunately, I've never been much of a seamstress, and the hat, when finished, was festooned with – in addition to the roses and ivy – a great tangle of what I hoped was invisible fishing line.

The day of the Derby I somewhat uneasily put on my creation, only to discover in the grandstand that every single woman knew exactly what sort of hat to wear, and it was nothing like mine. The correct hat was one of felt, medium-size, fuchsia, yellow or royal blue, and covered with a veil or feathers. There were certainly no straw hats to be seen, let alone giant ones covered with trailing strands of growth and fishing line. As we all rose to sing 'My Old Kentucky Home', a man next to me hissed, 'Poison Ivy!' and jabbed his friend in the ribs. The singing stopped in a circle around me as they all, now silent, stared in contempt.

Humiliating, and yet somehow a secret joy: to be able to upset people simply by wearing the wrong clothes! It's always been as if I were two different people, the sadist and the masochist. The sadist makes the masochist put on ridiculous outfits, and then forces her to go out and wear them while she stays home. And it must be the sadist who does the shopping, too. How else to explain the bell-bottom pants bought in 1984 at Patricia Fields, the platform shoes from Peter Fox in 1985? Nobody was wearing such things. If one half of me wants attention, it's not the half that goes out to parties – she's the one who wants to hide in a corner and observe. But since the other one has dressed her, she has no choice but to stand there wearing something not only dramatic but stupid. Still, I can never help thinking that if a thing was beautiful once, why should it be less beautiful now? And certainly when I appear in a striking piece of clothing made by my designer friend Stephen Sprouse, I am more than a little disheartened to be told (in a rather patronizing, know-it-all tone) that the dress I am wearing is last year's model. In New York people follow fashion so closely, a thing is barely in the stores before it is out of date.

Recently, however, I've begun to think the masochist is wising up. After ten years in Manhattan, I've finally realized that everything comes back over a twenty-year cycle.* The bell-bottoms are in fashion, as are the platform shoes, while the little Chanel suits acquired from the thrift store in the late seventies have just gone *out* of fashion. All it takes is to hang on to everything long enough, and eventually a year will come along when each one of my impulse purchases will look just daring enough. Still, it's only a matter of time before the Grandma Anne/sadist/loud part of me figures out that all she has to do is send me to *another* part of the country and I'll be a misfit all over again.

---

* Or, more precisely, a thing comes back into style the moment I finally get rid of it.

White, Single and Female
in New York City

'WHEN YOU walk into a party, married women run to their husbands' sides, as if the men need protection, or as if you've only come to try to steal one. Single men quickly run, as if by speaking to them you'll somehow trap them into something – making a date, or tricking them into having sex. This is all, if you even get invited to a party in the first place, as a single woman.' This is the complaint of my single girlfriend 'Natasha'. She's fed up, not so much with being single as with the fact that being single, as a woman, in Manhattan, is the equivalent of having some dread social disease – to be treated as if 'there must be something wrong with you; you must be out looking'.

Things may have been bleak back in the days when, if a woman wasn't married by age twenty-two she was labeled as a spinster – but at least back then one could get on with one's role, one's position in society, of 'maiden aunt', 'aging spinster', whatever. The maiden aunt may have been the butt of many jokes and caricatures in literature, but she was always there, invited, included, a person toward whom a charitable act might be performed. Now, at least in New York, even if one is not particularly interested in meeting a mate, in a city that prides itself on accepting all varieties of possibility in family households, singlehood, at least for women, is still viewed as an incredible personal failing.

Far more socially acceptable is to have divorced and remarried, as many times as possible – in fact, a sign of success, although once, for women, the label of 'divorcee' would have been tantamount to being totally ostracized by respectable society.

One night I'm invited to a party and take Natasha along. 'If you're a single man, straight or gay, young or old, you're always welcome,' she states. 'Married women are always looking for extra men – if it's a single gay guy, it's a possible confidant, or at least someone to fix up with other gay guys. Gay guys are always getting fixed up. If it's a straight guy, you're a possibility – a married woman might want to have an affair, or trade in an old husband, or, charitably, has a lone single girlfriend dating back from a friendship in first grade, which she's working on as a project. But if you're a single woman, gay, forget it – what if you made a pass at another woman? how awful – and if you're straight, that means only one thing: you're a desperate failure. Because in New York, the only reason people go out is to do business – and it's a natural assumption, if you're a single woman, your business is to look for some guy.'

'Even if you're a married man, you still get invited,' I tell her. 'I mean, as soon as I'm out of town, my husband gets endless invitations. Gay men pursue him, hoping he'll be the one straight man they can seduce; married women, wanting to flirt; bored, single women suddenly and abruptly deciding to throw a party. Believe me, I'm not saying things aren't a lot nicer for me, being married, in more ways than one – but the shocking thing is, when I was single, I thought I was treated so nastily and patronizingly because I was single. When I got married, I was immediately treated nastily and patronizingly – only with a difference. Now, it was "Oh, and this is Tim's wife." As if it were somehow the 1950s, and this was your accomplishment – landing a man.'

The party we attend, for a magazine, at the Russian Tea Room, is not perhaps the best place to judge whether or not what Natasha says is true. The men do all appear gay, or married (this is easy to figure out because their wives hold them firmly by the arms and they look miserable). In any event no one here really appears to be having any fun; it's too noisy, nobody drinks, let alone eats some of the huge roast beefs and turkeys that are being sliced by hairy waiters dressed in tiny, pre-Revolutionary red suits. People go out in New York to do business: it might not even matter whether Natasha is a single woman or a talking orangutan; there's nothing she can *do* for anybody, therefore she's invisible. There's no use anyone making friendly chit-chat with her, and if she tries, they turn their back.

A few weeks later, on a remarkably similar occasion, Natasha brings a date – a handsome, highly eligible bachelor – and suddenly, I'm amazed, Natasha and her date are standing in the middle of a crowd. In addition, I'm constantly approached: 'Who's that guy Natasha's with?' 'Is that so-and-so, who used to be married to . . .' 'Are they an item?' The crowd descend like wolves. And, a few days later, Natasha calls me in tears – the man, whom she had been seeing, has been dragged off by more than one woman from the party that night, women who had only just met him that evening, through Natasha, but who never would have bothered to include her when they took their father's airplane for the weekend to Miami Beach . . .

On television I happen to catch Bo Derek, the *10* actress. She's now forty-three, and her husband John Derek has died some time ago. She appears shy, and kind, self-deprecating . . . She met John when she was very young, her first husband, her only husband . . . Now, though she's not looking to get remarried, apparently she's having trouble even coming up with dates. To me, it all seems perfectly clear: at forty-three, she's too old to be a trophy wife for a man looking for a young thing on his arm to show off to other men; she's going to be judged on a physical standard of beauty in a culture that seems, ultimately, to value only youth as beauty. In any event, where is she ever going to meet anyone? A long-term marriage often results in the shutting down of the outside world, you have each other, after all . . . and it's not as if she's involved in some job where she might meet people of interest on a daily basis. If she ever were to get invited to a party, she would have to stand in a room full of people who are basically inspecting her looks, how much they have deteriorated, how her acting career has gone nowhere, and so forth . . . One wonders, had Sharon Stone not married when she did, who would have been left out there for her to go out with? But for a male actor, of equal renown, physical appearance, success and age . . . at forty his possibilities would have been limitless.

Recently an article in the *New York Times* ('Style' section) discussed women who lied about their age. One woman had a twenty-ninth birthday party, to celebrate the last year of her twenties. 'But how could she still be in her twenties, when I'm thirty-one and we both started in kindergarten at age six?' said one of the guests. Meanwhile, a class at an exclusive, expensive women's private high school held a meeting and decided, unanimously, they had all graduated together in 1993, not, as was the reality, in 1987. There was a slightly joking, sardonic tone to the article, but what the writer did not point out was that as a woman one is immediately categorized by the outside world, based on one's age. No longer, perhaps, is one a spinster at an unmarried twenty-two, but at thirty a woman is 'desperate' and by simply announcing 'forty' as a woman one is truly past the point of sexual desirability. I'm not saying I really believe it, but in a world that continues to truly value women for their physical appearance and sexual desirability based on youth, the marriage some years back of Ted Turner to Jane Fonda came as a bit of a shock – one had perhaps expected him to obtain, as a new wife, someone a great deal younger, and had a man of his wealth and age not married someone a great deal younger, marrying a famous movie star was only a distant second best. Women continue to be devalued as they age, and marry and remarry; while men (look at Warren Beatty, for example) can not only get old, and have screwed their way through hundreds, if not thousands, but are never viewed as 'used goods' but only seem to become more desirable. And I'm not blaming men. I can't imagine what it must be like to have a constant procession of virile, rich, handsome and successful studs all vying to steal me from my husband. Yet it's entirely acceptable for a variety of nubile rich and desirable females to, nightly, fling themselves on him; and, I suppose, were he to run off with one of them tomorrow, no one would think him the less admirable. It seems to me that while some things have indeed improved for women, career choices, job possibilities, that we no longer give birth to child after child until we die from it, in other ways things have not only not improved, they have literally deteriorated. And until we, as women, unite in some collective consciousness to render the current treatment and behavior of women (by women and by men) unacceptable, we are doomed to make our lives on this planet one of self-hatred, low self-esteem and despair.

The New New York Couple

W HAT I have come to call the New New York couple has always existed but has, I think become more commonplace of late. There is a new openness – perhaps even a new interest – in gay men who want to get married. Once gay men came to New York because there was a certain community to be found, an acceptance in being gay, that could not be found elsewhere in the United States. In small towns gay men were 'permanent bachelors' – possibly spending their lives living at home, forced to be as unobtrusive as they could. Some gay men married but for quite different reasons than an openly gay man who marries today.

In small-town America there was and is still a great deal of stigma attached to being homosexual – witness the recent events in which a closeted gay man living with his parents was killed in a Southern town and a gay teenager in Wyoming (who was more open about being gay) was killed by two boys in a brutal and vicious fashion. A gay man who married often did so to disguise the fact that he was gay. A friend's father announced to her mother, after twenty years of marriage, that he was gay and was leaving. My friend's mother was devastated; she had not, apparently, had a clue that her husband was homosexual. Women were more sheltered; or at least gay men were less open.

Gay men flocked to New York – here there were career opportunities in the arts (a recent article in *New York* magazine was about gays on Wall Street, where they are still forced to be relatively low-key about their sexual orientation) – as well as bars, nightclubs and sex clubs that catered to gay men. While there are plenty of lesbian women who came to the city for the same reasons – and also lesbian bars, nightclubs and so forth – it's the gay men who began, I noticed over the past ten years or so, to proclaim their interest in getting married to a straight woman. As one friend, very decidedly gay, who had lost his boyfriend of twelve years, said to me, 'I'm thinking I should just look for a girlfriend now and get married – women just can't be any trickier than guys are.' And he wasn't my only gay friend who said he was sick of going out with men and wanted me to find him a girlfriend.

Part of this sentiment stems from a desire to have children. I know gay couples and single gay men with kids, and in middle-class families books such as *Heather Has Two Mommies* (or is it *Daddies?*) are read to tots in order that they grow up accepting diverse varieties of nuclear families. Nevertheless, in order to produce genetic offspring it is necessary to have one person of each sex, and our society is still definitely geared to male–female couples. At a recent birthday party, attended by approximately a hundred people, I noticed at least half a dozen couples in which the men had been gay or were still gay but were married to heterosexual women; all of the couples had children, either biologically or through adoption.

The party was held in a penthouse apartment, full of art works, all modern, the floor was cement, the walls plywood – though the place looked like the owners had run out of funds and never bothered to finish it, the cement and plywood are the height of current architectural trends and the renovation probably cost upward of half a million dollars. The man was in his family's business, the woman owned and ran a clothing store in midtown Manhattan and the birthday party was her fiftieth. Everywhere there were masses of flowers, bartenders served drinks and hors d'oeuvres, loud disco music from the 1970s played over the loudspeakers. Everyone knew everyone else, there was a sense of family, as if the *Titanic* hadn't sunk but had simply drifted for so long there was no one else to meet.

Do the men have sex with the women? As we used to say about our parents with more than a little disbelief, they had to have had sex at least once (or multiplied by however many kids there were). The first couple I personally knew who were gay/straight were perhaps the most tragic: R lived with his boyfriend and broke up with him to marry L. Together they started a successful fashion firm and had a child. Then R got AIDS and died; so did L; and finally the child died. Another couple I know, with two kids, both continue to have affairs outside their marriage – he with a man and she with a woman – unusual perhaps only in that the man and woman with whom they have their extramarital affairs are also a married couple. In this case it's a case of two gay/gay couples, but the ones who hang out together, the half-dozen couples at the birthday party, are all heterosexual women who do not appear to have affairs, all of whom are married to men who may or may not be active outside the marriage but all of whom, on first meeting, do not seem to be in the least bit shy about proclaiming their homosexuality. At least two couples I know (who did not happen to be at the birthday party) have been married thirty-plus years; obviously this is not a new phenomenon but what is new is the openness about it and the camaraderie; the art crowd in which I hang out is a sort of private club for this kind of couple, it's impossible for a week to go by in which one spouse or the other doesn't have a birthday, or an art opening, or give a lecture followed by dinner to which the whole gang is invited. The central core of half a dozen to a dozen gay/straight couples is surrounded primarily by single gay men, who seem to dip in and out like butterflies sipping nectar, providing flirtation, flower arrangements and public back massages. Have the women given up on having sex? Since no one is shy about pronouncing their proclivities (if they are, there is always one of the pals around who will announce it for them), I think by now I would know if any of them were lesbians or having affairs, but it's only the one couple who are both openly gay. In fact, a lot of my single girlfriends actually prefer gay men to straight. Gay men are – anyway, can be – more sensitive, more verbal, funnier, more artistic, less likely to park themselves in front of a television to watch football. One of my girlfriends consistently finds gay guys who think they want a girlfriend; they talk to her about marriage, having kids, even go as far as kissing her before they get scared and bolt. She's always left high and dry, but the truth is, as she's discovered, whether the men in New York are gay or straight, they tend to lose interest in sex (at least with the same woman) quite quickly, and why not at least live an existence with someone with a similar sensibility? 'Besides,' she says, 'sex is fun for a little while, but I don't think I'd want to go on taking off my clothes, putting on some idiotic negligee and perfume and having to take showers three times a day for my whole life. There's too much chlorine in New York City water, it dries out your skin.' At least without sex you don't have to worry about getting AIDS, which nowadays you're probably more likely to get from a heterosexual husband than a gay or asexual (at least one who's not having sex with *you*).

Previous generations didn't have the same expectations for marriage that we have today. Often marriage was an arranged situation; couples were put together for business reasons, and men and women hoped they would love each other but did not 'fall in love'. If they were lucky they would love each other, but mostly people were aware, at a much younger age than people today, that life was short and people had to work hard; marriage was there in order to join families, businesses, and procreate.

Mothers

I WAS GOING to do one of those round-up pieces, what various women were hoping to receive on Mother's Day, and I called up a whole bunch of mothers I knew, women with various careers and occupations and things they were involved in, women I really admired, but it was difficult for me because I have a telephone phobia, which means I don't like to make calls, I don't like to answer calls, I don't like to return calls, the telephone panics me. I thought this had gone away, though I remember when I was a kid my mother and brother and I all had this phobia, which meant that when the phone rang one of us would say, 'The phone is ringing. Answer it,' and then someone else would say, 'I'm not going to answer it. You get it,' and the third would say, 'Who would be calling us? We don't know anybody.'

I thought I had outgrown this but it's returned. Nevertheless, I made a list of women I admired and wasn't too frightened to call up; I didn't speak to a single one, they were all too busy to pick up the phone, I didn't think it was because they had phobias, but I left messages and hoped they would call me back. Liliane de Castelbac is the designer for Morgane Le Faye, those beautiful dresses that I have always admired, things of beautiful chiffon, pleated, very simple, with a fancy shop on Madison Avenue and another in SoHo, and she has a ten-year-old daughter (the children's clothing is also incredibly beautiful, things for little girls of plush red velvet and huge skirts with tons of petticoats). 'I'd like a poem from my

daughter,' she said. 'Carolina is ten.' With so many beautiful
dresses that she had designed and could wear right at her
disposal (probably it was like having the largest closet in the
world) I would have chosen a dress rather than a poem, but,
whatever. I had called a shoe-designer friend, who makes
beautiful shoes and has two daughters, but I had to leave a
voice-mail message and a day or so later someone called and
when I picked up the phone she said, 'Is this TanJan?'

'Well . . .' I said.

'TanJan,' she said, 'I'm calling on behalf of' – she mentioned
my shoe-designer friend – 'who is in Toronto, but she'll be
back tomorrow, and shall I take down your number?'

'Actually,' I said, 'my name is Tama Janowitz, and I'm an
old friend of hers, if you could relay the message.'

'Could you spell your name? I'll let her know. She may have
time to give you a call next week.'

'I need an answer sooner than that,' I said.

'I doubt she'll be able to,' the secretary said sniffily, 'but I'll
let her know.'

I didn't hear from this shoe-designer friend, but I did hear
from Cristina Zilkha, who was trying to finish her article for
the *Times Literary Supplement*, which wasn't going well
because she had too much to say and not enough space to
say it in. Her daughter Lulu is fifteen and what she would have
liked for Mother's Day, though not necessarily from Lulu, was
a Daumier lithograph – maybe because she was working on
the Daumier story. 'Or, I don't know, make it a Daumier
watercolor,' she said. 'Might as well go all out.' A doctor
friend didn't get back to me, but I guess this made sense
because she's not only a full-time pediatrician but has a
four-year-old daughter and divides her time between Manhattan and Princeton.

Sophie Matisse, my artist friend, has a daughter who's just
turned seven, Gaia; Sophie paints these remarkable paintings
which are, say, a section of a Vermeer that in the original is

invisible (the part you can't see, for example, because there's a person standing there) incredibly fastidious and evocative. Even though Sophie was just on her way to St Maartin's in the Caribbean, she decided for Mother's Day she would like the Brooklyn Botanical Gardens. It's true the Botanical Gardens are presently in bloom, the lilacs, magnolias, flowering cherries, but to me that whole place is a lot of upkeep and work and I'd rather have one of her paintings. I didn't hear back from a friend who has a very hot PR company, and my good friend who is the director of a non-profit art space apparently couldn't think of what she wanted, although I had reached her in Miami on her cell phone, but my friend Margot Guralnick who is an editor at *Travel and Leisure* and very kind, with two kids, Asa, six, and Nell, three, found the time to call and say she'd like to spend the day in bed. I didn't know about that, because it seemed to me if you're a travel editor you'd get offers for discounts on trips or even free trips, but maybe with two kids and her high-powered job, she'd rather have some time to not move . . .

For some reason this whole thing, Mother's Day, and a round-up of what all these high-powered New York women wanted, was starting to make me feel kind of depressed. I did speak to my mother, though, which I do almost daily – she's a poet and a professor up at Cornell. 'So, anyway, what would you like?' I said.

'Another life,' she said, which I wasn't going to be able to provide. As for me, if there was something I could wish for, for Mother's Day, practically speaking I'd like to get over this phone phobia – and also to have some friends who would be able to find the time to call me back.

My Baby

I HAD ALWAYS wanted to adopt a baby, even before I met my husband, but I lived in two very tiny rooms and I figured nobody would let a single person in two tiny rooms adopt a baby. I had no desire to perpetuate my genetic lineage. I knew if I gave birth it would be to an infant who would announce, 'Tama! Is it really you? It's your poor old Grandma Anne. When might you next be appearing on TV, or is no one interested in you any more?'

I used to see people wheeling the most adorable Asian babies that looked like dolls and I thought, That's the kind of baby I want. This was probably politically incorrect thinking, but the Caucasian babies, compared to the Asian babies, looked so big and white and puffy. I heard about an agency, Spence-Chapin, and we went to one of the monthly meetings there. The director, Flicka Van Praogh, said to the assembled (there were maybe a hundred people), 'It doesn't matter if you live in one room – we know that when you get desperate enough you'll move. And the baby will be better off than in an orphanage. And we don't mind if you're a gay couple, but it will be better if you don't announce it.'

It all seemed very simple. It was a non-profit agency, they just wanted to get the babies into loving homes. They worked with a few different countries – at the time, Russia, Moldavia, Korea, China and I think one or two South American states. The countries represented were always changing, based on government rules and political situations.

The next step, after the meeting, was to sign up for an appointment with a social worker at the agency; getting an appointment might take months. When my husband and I went in for our appointment, we were asked every personal question you could think of, but the social worker seemed quite affable, I didn't feel under attack. She wanted us to decide on the country we wanted to adopt from. If a couple wanted a Caucasian infant they were expected and required to do the work themselves. They had to place ads in local newspapers around the country, saying they wanted a baby, and take out a toll-free number, and speak to obstetricians. I had noticed, any time I traveled, that in every local paper under 'Personal' there were a half-dozen ads from handsome professional, caring loving couples, hoping to adopt a white baby. How could anybody care what color their baby was? But until recently if you were both white they didn't let you adopt a mixed-race child in this country. Only recently have they relaxed this law.

A few weeks later we were told we were accepted to the program. Our choice of country was China. I was thrilled we were accepted, at the same time felt a bit irritated: after all, nobody has to be grilled by a social worker before getting pregnant.

After this we were assigned to a different social worker. She was about twenty years old and very charming, yet it seemed odd that our lives would be altered by someone so much younger than we. We were given a list of about forty or fifty things: the things we had to obtain before we could get a baby. I'm not talking about diapers. It was stuff like 'getting finger-printed'. How do you go about getting fingerprints? That sounds simple enough, I guess, you go to the police station. But after calling the local station for three days and being unable to find out what to do, I was told the fingerprint man would be there the next day, from ten to two, and that they only took personal checks. Of course when I got there the fingerprint man wasn't there and so I had to go downtown, to another precinct, and at that precinct they only accepted money orders. Once you had a card with fingerprints, they had to be sent to the FBI on another form, and you had to wait for approval. But that one item, getting fingerprints, actually had twelve or thirteen steps to it – getting your FBI card, sending it to the FBI with a check, sending a second set to the immigration bureau, and so on.

I've managed to repress the various steps and items. When I try to recollect what one had to do, the only parallel I can come up with is: it would be as if a friend gave you four hundred shirts from four hundred different stores and said, 'I don't have the receipts but would you mind returning these shirts and getting refunds for me?'

It wasn't as difficult as it was laborious, irritating, frustrating and so forth. You had to obtain your birth certificate, but since I was born in California, how do you do it from New York? And the birth certificate had to be signed, notarized, duplicated, etc.

It went on and on. Our social worker had to come for a home study – in England I had heard of people who when going through the adoption process had social workers who basically came and spied on them every minute for two weeks. Here, she stayed for only a couple of hours but it seemed like a lifetime. I kept expecting a disaster at any minute. If it rained, mushrooms grew in the bathroom almost immediately. If the social worker decided to open a closet, or opened a door by mistake, I knew so many things would fall on her head she would be badly injured. But it all went OK.

The whole thing took about a year, from the time we went in for our first meeting to the time we got our baby, but was actually only nine months from the time we were accepted into the program. Finally we got a photograph of our baby. She had been left in a park when she was two days old; by now she was seven months, and it would be another two months until we got her. As soon as I saw the baby's picture, I couldn't believe it. 'That's my baby!' I thought. 'How did they know? She's the most fantastic thing in the world.' In the photo, taken when she was two months old, she looked mean, smart, angry, and as if she was trying, secretly, not to laugh. Also, she had an awful lot of hair. In fact, later, when I saw the photographs of all the other babies in our group (there were ten in total) I saw that, of all of them, Willow had the most hair. After all those lengthy essays, in which I had written that I was interested in gardening, and others had written about their interests, I realized that ultimately the babies were matched with couples (there were also two single women adopting in our group) based on hair types.

The members of our group (those who had completed their paperwork at approximately the same time) met up in Beijing. For two days we were taken to tourist sites – the Forbidden City, the Great Wall – while everyone grew more and more anxious, awaiting the next stage of the trip, a flight to Heifei, an industrial city in Anhui Province, where we would receive our babies. Though our paths might not have crossed otherwise (one of us was a paralegal, another a doctor specializing in perspiration, one an insurance agent, another a former airline pilot) we instantly all bonded with each other: it was like being, perhaps, part of a movie crew, or a bunch of victims of the same accident.

Together we traveled on Air China to Heifei. It was a peculiar flight – not as rough as, say, Aeroflot, and yet a bit odd when, while waiting on the runway, the plane suddenly filled with vast clouds of fog which poured in through the ventilating system. 'Is this customary?' I asked the former airline pilot. He smiled weakly. I never did learn what it was.

The hotel in Heifei was filled with foreigners from around the world – Swedes, Canadians, Norwegians, Americans – lugging or wheeling screaming Chinese infants. We didn't have much time to see anything, though – we were sent to our rooms. 'The babies have come by bus, a six-hour trip, from Ma Anshan,' said Xian Wen, our guide/translator/mother superior. 'Each is accompanied by a nurse, the nurses would be thrilled to get a little gift from the West, it is hard for them to give up the babies. You must wait in your rooms, the babies will be brought to you one at a time, I will come with each nurse to translate so please limit your questions about them to ten minutes – others are waiting.'

My husband and I paced back and forth for what seemed like hours. Apparently we were one of the last to be delivered. Our hotel room, a small suite, was vaguely Western in appearance, that 1950s Soviet style designed by someone who had once seen a fifty-year-old picture in a magazine of a Scandinavian airport hotel and had been put in charge of building accommodation for foreigners visiting Communist countries. It was hot, airless, but it had a lavatory and bath with running – though non-potable – water.

At last there was a knock on the door. A tiny young nurse held our baby, accompanied by Xian Wen. The baby was handed to me; in gratitude I flung any extraneous items from my luggage over to the nurse – magazines, lipsticks, nail polish, sweets, mostly things a nurse living in a remote village in China could never use, but which I thought might be of interest to her on a six-hour bus ride back home.

The baby beamed. Tim and I looked at each other. We didn't really know what questions to ask. 'Um, what does she like?' Tim said after a pause.

Xian Wen translated to the nurse, then back to us. 'She likes to play.'

'Ah,' said Tim.

The nurse reviewed Willow's feeding habits: stir a cup or two of nutritionally valueless rice powder into boiling water available from down the hall. Cut a giant hole in the top of a nipple, pour gruel into bottle, let her guzzle. The hole in the bottle we had brought, we were told, was much too small. Quickly I procured a rusty old manicure scissors and hacked open the top of the nipple. The nurse and Xian Wen looked slightly apprehensive. The nurse began to cry – whether with sorrow over parting from her charge, or despair at the sort of mother it was likely I would be, I don't know – then they left.

Tim and I looked at each other. The baby looked at us and began to howl. For a moment I thought of running down the hall after the nurse, before it was too late. She was awfully sweaty, and by the time we had taken off her clothes (the Chinese believe in bundling babies up whatever the weather) not only did Willow turn out to be half the size she had been when she was first handed over, but the clothes had so many strings in knots that the nurse and Xian Wen had long since made their escape. And, by breakfast the next day, I – and the rest of our group – appeared to have aged so vastly, there seemed little point in looking for the 'Return' department. But even though everyone was so old all of a sudden, everyone thought they had gotten the best baby of all. Only Tim and I knew the truth, though – everyone *had* gotten cute babies, but ours was the best.

Of course, a few days after our arrival in China, my thoughts regarding motherhood had changed considerably. I still thought she was the most beautiful, fantastic thing in the world, but I now saw, first hand, that she was obstreperous, demanding, hot, noisy, needed no sleep, and could easily break my nose without trying. And that she would spend the rest of my life torturing me and driving me crazy, in exactly the same fashion as if I had physically given birth to her.

And Baby Makes Four

W HEN OUR baby, Willow, was about a year old, I had a revelation: there was a good reason why, in so many English novels and biographies, babies were looked after by nannies. I had always read memoirs where the author, as an infant, was cleaned and hauled before his beautifully dressed mother for a few minutes before she went out to dinner. In the mornings, as well, this same mother – generally still in bed, clad in a clean peignoir and surrounded by heaps of thick white invitations – could be visited briefly as she sipped her breakfast tea. Then the child would be taken back to the nursery to eat tapioca.

It had always seemed a cruel practice until our baby became adept at unplugging my Powerbook while I was in mid-sentence. It was amazing how, the second I didn't give her my undivided attention, she could turn even the most harmless item into a lethal weapon.

It wasn't that I didn't love being with her – I did, for up to fifteen minutes at a time. It was probably just that I have a short attention span. And though every mother I spoke to told me that she could spend all day watching her child with fascination (and even went on to have a second or third child) I noticed that the ones who said this were the ones who had nannies, day-care, au pairs, baby-sitters and military academies at their disposal.

A nanny is the one job where the employer wants to buy love. Anyone who has a nanny hopes – even expects – that the nanny will love the child as much as the parents but will, at the same time, raise the kid exactly as they are told. If you've grown up with servants, or even office staff, perhaps it is easy to know what to expect of a nanny and how to ask for it, but I didn't even know what I wanted. I mean, I knew the basics: I wanted someone who would love Willow, would be nurturing, trustworthy, wouldn't neglect her, or sit around looking depressed. These were the essentials.

Then there were the things that would be nice: for Willow to learn a second language; embroidery; flower-arrangement; playing the stock market; and maybe to sing 'On the Good Ship Lollipop' in the style of Shirley Temple.

But how was I supposed to find a nanny? I didn't have a clue. I went to the park with the kid, thinking that might give me an idea. There were two kinds of women there. The first sat grimly staring into space in a dull fury while the children threw sand and kicked one another. These were the nannies. The second kind had a desperate, friendly expression and sat grinning anxiously while their offspring threw sand and kicked one another. These were the mothers. They were bored out of their minds, I could tell, because they were attempting to make new friends with anyone, something simply not done in New York City. 'How old's your baby?' one lady said.

Both options for Baby seemed equal – grim nanny or desperate mother. In the long run, did it really matter? Everyone grew up to blame their parents, no matter how they were raised. As a parent, there was no way not to feel guilty.

I knew two women who actually were nannies. Isabelle had had complete nanny training in the UK, which even included learning how to make all those old-fashioned puddings English children are always eating in books. But maybe American children didn't like tapioca, because as soon as my friend got to the States she quit her nannying job and, after finding a job as a receptionist, was promoted with amazing rapidity to account executive. In the UK, Isabelle said, nannies are viewed with respect (Princess Di, for example, got her start through a nannying position). But in this country, 'Anyone who has something to do with child-care is viewed with contempt.'

The other person I knew who was a nanny had taken on the job because – she claimed – she couldn't bear to be separated from her own baby. So, though she was highly educated in a completely different field, she took her baby with her to look after other people's children, and got them to look after her kid while she watched soap operas, the field in which, I think, she had originally written her thesis.

I had read someplace that the writer Mary Gordon, when her children were small, hired a baby-sitter, told the kids she was going off to work and locked herself in the bedroom for the day so she could write. The only problem was, if the children heard her and realized their mother was still at home, they would scream and break down the door. So she had to be very, very quiet and lie in bed until nightfall.

I thought this would probably suit me as well. I called a nanny agency in the paper. The woman who answered wanted to know what I planned to pay. When I mentioned a sum she said that for that amount of money I could have someone – perhaps – for a couple of days a week. In addition I would have to pay the agency at least fifteen hundred dollars. She muttered, half under her breath, something about sending 'Selma from New Jersey' to meet me. My grandmother is deceased, but I knew who was coming.

For some reason I balked. 'You see,' I said, 'I have a book right here. Maybe you've heard of it – *Pettie: Memoirs of a Victorian Nursery?* I kind of like how this Pettie person sounds. Let me just read you an excerpt: "I made six frocks, twelve petticoats, six silk slips and six white serge for the winter." That sounds nice, huh? One of the children was going to be a bridesmaid and needed a dress, which Pettie wanted to make. "I was allowed to do so: it was pale blue satin with pale cream chiffon over, two rows of pretty lace insertions round the skirt, a low neck, a yoke and pretty puff sleeves. It was

worn with a large black hat, black shoes and stockings."
Anybody around like that?'

'Selma's wonderful. I've got her here with me now. I'll send
her over now. She won't come, though, unless you pay her taxi
when she gets there, and back to New Jersey.' The woman must
have put her hand over the receiver but I could hear her anyway.
'Ma! I got one! Hurry up, would ya? You're going uptown!'

I was momentarily out of cash. Since every day I read in the
newspapers that people were found living twenty to a room,
working in sweatshops for a few dollars a day, I found it
impossible to believe I couldn't find someone who loved
children, who spoke a second language (so Willow could be
bilingual) and who wouldn't expect to get more money than I
myself was getting paid. This is a city of immigrants and if my
baby couldn't be brought up with a Cockney accent (as had
apparently been the case with so many of those upper-crust
English children raised by servants) at least maybe she could
learn to cook Chinese take-out.

But I wasn't part of any Chinese community. For a while I
spent time going around to the local Chinese laundries and
restaurants, hoping to lure a busboy or seamstress. Much to
my surprise, however, they all looked at me suspiciously.

At last I remembered that, when I was an undergraduate in
college, Barnard had an employment service for students. I
called up the local universities. Perhaps a foreign student
would be so happy to have a place to live for free she wouldn't
mind sharing the room with a baby. Students stayed up all
night anyway.

Much to my surprise the phone rang that afternoon. A student
was calling about the position, not for her but for her mother.

Mei-mei and Pyahlien came to meet me. Pyahlien, the
mother, didn't speak any English – well, scarcely any – and
I certainly didn't speak any Chinese. For a while Pyahlien and I
sat looking at each other. We were both equally terrified.
Finally Mei-mei spoke. 'What, exactly, would you expect?'

'Um, I'm not sure, exactly,' I said. 'I expect I'll do whatever your mother wants.'

So my first employee was hired.

It turned out Pyahlien had no child-care references – which didn't bother me. After all, neither had I. I figured it was enough that her daughter had a full scholarship to graduate school, and was still speaking to her. Though I didn't learn all this immediately, since she really didn't speak English – in China, Pyahlien had been a senior marketing director for a chemical company, and she went to five different factories to use an electric drill, which impressed me a great deal.

In some ways, the fact that we could scarcely speak to one another was a relief. I had dreaded the idea that, working at home, I would have to make pleasant chit-chat. And for her it was nice, because she didn't have to keep telling me what I was doing wrong.

But it was apparent from the start that, because we couldn't communicate, certain problems might arise. One day when the baby was taking a nap Pyahlien tried to tell me something. I didn't have the faintest idea what she was saying. She got out her massive Chinese–English dictionary and ruffled through page after page before finally pointing to the line that said 'a canopy of leaves'.

'Um,' I said thoughtfully. I too had a book, called *Communicating in Chinese*. 'Zigh Bay-jeeng chwun-tee-in shuun-muh shr-hoe kigh-shr?' I read, which was translated as 'When does spring being in Beijing?'

It turned out Pyahlien wanted an extra blanket for the baby.

And the other morning Pyahlien – who by now has more phrases at her disposal – told me, 'Tim saw bread.' She made a sawing motion in the air.

Tim is my husband and I have often seen him sawing bread; it didn't seem all that remarkable. She repeated, 'Tim saw bread.' Perhaps Chinese men didn't slice their own bread.

'Yes,' I said, 'Tim can saw his own bread. Butters it himself, too, sometimes.'

'No, no! Saw bread! Saw bread!'

'Oh,' I said thoughtfully. 'A saw blade. A saw blade.' It was starting to sound a little like Chinese.

'Yes, yes, saw bread.' It turned out Pyahlien wanted to borrow Tim's saw – for the weekend. I was too exhausted to ask why. And it did make sense, in a weird way – needing a saw for the weekend was probably a cultural difference.

After all, anyone who hires a nanny has to be prepared for cultural differences. Even if you are American and hire an American to baby-sit, the baby-sitter may very well come from a background that featured a steady diet of potato chips of a different flavor than the one you were brought up on. In my case, Pyahlien wanted to feed Willow white rice, but I wanted her to give Willow brown rice. For a long time, I feel, Pyahlien accepted this as part of the picture of the brutish American she had read about. In China, nobody in their right mind would want to feed a kid brown rice when there was white rice around. Obviously, to Pyahlien, it had to be that for some peculiar reason, though I threw money around so wantonly, buying bottled water, feeding the dogs chicken, in this one area alone – white rice versus brown – I was determined to be miserly.

And in China babies are kept warmly bundled. I would decide to change Willow and, after removing her sweater, find a long-sleeved shirt underneath, then a sweatshirt, a T-shirt, another sweater, an undershirt – and, at last, the tiny hot kid. But to Pyahlien, it was equally horrific to arrive in the morning and find a semi-nude, obviously neglected kid.

By now, though, we've adjusted to each other's quirks and eccentricities. I can't imagine survival without her. I figure it's my duty – as her English improves – to teach her the American sense of humor and impress her with my knowledge of Chinese politics. When I catch her looking in disbelief over something I've done – eating cheese, for example – I explain it's all part of being a

Capitalist Roader and a Cow Demon. But she doesn't seem to get it. Even after I point to the picture of the cow on the carton of milk and make sounds like those in the movie *The Exorcist*, while pointing to myself, all she does is shake her head sadly.

This summer I took Pyahlien (and the baby) home to my mother. One of the neighbors had a block party, which we attended. 'You see, everyone here lives on the same street,' I explained. 'And once a week they all meet – to read from Chairman Mao's *Little Red Book*. Later, they go home and criticize one another.'

Pyahlien appeared astonished. Even when I burst into laughter, she only shook her head sadly. On the other hand, she might be getting into the swing of things. When she found me washing a spot on the carpet she clapped her hands in glee. 'I used to think, American women can do nothing,' she said. 'But you – washing spot – very good.' She waited until I was through before taking the rug outside and cleaning it all over again.

But whether or not she's kidding me, I still can't say. She continues to tell Willow to be quiet because 'Mama sleeping', which is what she seems to think I do all day. And this morning I found her drilling Willow upstairs. It sounded like some very traditional Chinese kind of teaching. 'Mother ha! Daddy ha! Grandmother ha!'

'Mama ha!' Willow repeated.

'Um,' I said. 'What does "ha!" mean?'

'Good!' Pyahlien looked at me with a pleased expression. 'Mother good! Father good! Grandmother good!'

'Ha! Ha! Ha!' Willow and Pyahlien shouted in unison. Then Pyahlien burst into laughter.

I still haven't figured out why a senior marketing director in China would go to five factories with an electric drill. It might be that this was simply her way of teasing me. Or it might be one of those inscrutable mysteries of the East. It's nothing I can remember reading about in *Memoirs of a Victorian Nursery*, though.

The New York Child

TIM WENT out with Willow, who wasn't yet two and a half. He took the big stroller, which had a basket underneath. After some time Willow imperiously announced that she wanted to get in the basket; her stuffed toy baboon was to occupy the seat. It was only because Willow was so small that she was able to fit into the tiny bottom basket, meant for holding diapers or a few groceries.

Tim wheeled the stroller. All that was visible in it was the stuffed baboon. People gave him strange looks. From time to time from underneath Willow would yell, 'It's raining!' Although it was not raining, this was a command to Tim to quickly put the rainhood over the baboon. Then he would inquire if it was still raining, and if she said, 'No,' he had to fold the hood back.

After a while he bumped into a friend, John Waters, the movie director. John gave him a strange look. He had just watched Tim – for an entire city block – wheeling a stuffed baboon in a baby carriage and covering it with a rainhood, although it was a sunny day.

The New York Jungle

S O WE moved to Brooklyn. It was August, the city was scorching and violent in that way it can get when the rich people have gone to the beach or the mountains and the people who are left are nearly naked. They played loud music in their cars and at night, along the West Side Highway, they set up barbecue grills in the parking lots and had parties. But that was Manhattan. Here we finally had some space, indoors – there was no way our new apartment would have cost less than a million and a half dollars in Manhattan, though it hadn't been a third of that price out here. It was a strange old building, with hundreds of apartments, and the tenants were mostly very old. It was a pre-Depression building, the original owner – and builder – had jumped from the roof just after the place was completed, in 1929, and though there was plenty of light there were all sorts of other peculiarities we discovered after we moved in, such as 1) very little water (we had four bathrooms, but in mine I could only flush the toilet around once a day and there was only a trickle in which to take a bath); 2) peculiar noises (the elevator screamed, moaned and whined, the wind howled like *Wuthering Heights*); 3) an odd smell (apparently from the apartment below ours, occupied by a man whom I had never met but who for some reason burned bread each night at around twelve and got up at six to hammer on the walls).

I had never thought of myself – of us, my husband, Tim, and our little girl, Willow – as the kind of people who would live in

Brooklyn. First I had fought against it, but now I no longer cared. Manhattan was boring. Everyone looked the same – they were all white, in their twenties, the women were the same shade of blonde and the men either the same gay man, apparently cloned (brown hair, small nose, tidy) or recent graduates from an American university where they had spent four years calling each other 'dude' and drinking beer before heading to Wall Street.

Every block had the same things: a Banana Republic clothing store, with window displays of black, white and khaki clothing; a Gap, with blue jeans and skinny, headless mannequins; a Starbucks coffee shop and an upscale Italian restaurant.

The Italian restaurants might have been a chain, or a franchise; even though they were called different names – Pietro's, Nick and Francesca's, Pasta Dreams – they all served the same things. It wasn't the American-Italian food we used to have in this country (overcooked noodles with a lot of red sauce), it was things like penne al'arrabiatta, or spaghetti puttanesca, which I guess was more authentic.

In Brooklyn we were opposite the park, Prospect Park, but we weren't in one of the popular, fancier neighborhoods. Around the corner was a Jamaican restaurant, operated by kids who were so stoned it could take an hour for them to prepare food-to-go. There was a Chinese take-away, with pictures of food displayed so you could point to whatever you wanted, and then slide your money through a window in a bullet-proof glass wall that kept the cooks safe, but visible, in the kitchen.

The liquor store had an armed guard by the door, and in the Everything 99¢ Or Less there was a box to donate money to the mosque.

I hadn't even noticed how rough it appeared until a friend who had grown up in the slums of Glasgow stopped by for a visit on his way to the airport and said he had walked around the block first but was able to defend himself, due to his upbringing. I guess I was so intrigued by living in a place that was like a foreign country I had forgotten to be nervous. But everyone was extremely friendly – much more so than in Manhattan.

Pushing Willow in her stroller, we always noticed stray cats making love, or stunted flowers in front of the old, once-grand apartment buildings. There was a kiddy park across the street, utterly filthy, with newish but mean equipment – things like a colorful jungle gym, made of pink and purple and green iron bars, which in the summer heated up to temperatures in the hundreds of degrees, enough to burn a child's hand, and which probably in the winter were good at freezing fingers to the bar.

There was a sort of wading pool, constantly slopping over – the mouth of a cement sea lion spewed what appeared to be sewage. But Willow liked it, and I felt I was getting to know the area. 'Mom, can we go to the carouself?' she kept saying. 'When can we go to the carouself?' She wasn't yet three, but she liked to ride on merry-go-rounds, which she called 'carouselfs' and which she found terrifying. I knew there was one in the area – in Prospect Park – but I hadn't yet found the courage or energy to search for it.

Tim is English and, even though he couldn't understand why the Americans worked in August, living in Brooklyn was interesting enough for him that it was like taking a vacation. He didn't get home from work in the city until late, but at night the steel drums could be heard rehearsing for the big West Indian Day parade on Labor Day, a few weeks away, and the museum, which was nearby, was open late on Saturdays. Anyone could wander through the nearly empty halls, looking at the collections. A couple of times we went to Coney Island, the three of us, by subway, and ate hot dogs and French fries. I waited with Willow, in the sour gray sand beside the boardwalk, while Tim went on the roller-coaster.

One weekend he had to go to Cleveland, where they had a

really big roller-coaster, though that wasn't the purpose of his trip. I told Willow we'd go to the carousel, since it was too hot to stay in, plus twenty-four hours a day with a three-year-old, in a neighborhood where I didn't yet know anybody, was getting on my nerves. So I strapped her into the stroller and we set out. The elevator stopped on the floor below and a portly man got on; immediately I smelled that odd smell, of burned toast and something else that continually wafted up into our place, so I assumed he was the man who lived directly below, and I said, 'Hi.'

He scowled and did not respond. I could tell his eyes were not good; they were small and rheumy, deeply set; apart from this he did not appear infirm, being stocky and barrel-chested – nevertheless, he clutched on to one of those wheeled carts that old people sometimes use and which in my case I supposed I would start using as soon as Willow was old enough not to need a stroller.

His was filled with rubbish: plastic bags, newspapers, part of a plate was visible and red-and-black stuffed dice; the contents of a bag of birdseed trickled on to the floor, as if he was creating a trail to follow home. 'Look,' said Willow with great excitement, 'look.' She pointed to the falling millet.

'I think we're your new upstairs neighbors,' I said, too brightly. 'You seem to be . . . I think you're losing your birdseed.'

He grunted with what sounded like irritation. I had the idea he felt he was being harassed, trapped in the elevator with the two of us, like an animal in a Victorian zoo who will never be accustomed to being prodded with an umbrella. When the elevator door opened he bolted, spewing his moldy seed. 'I was just trying to be friendly,' I muttered, and sniffed.

At the corner of the park, where it met Grand Army Plaza in a kind of point, was a big map and it showed the carousel as being straight ahead. 'You see, Willow, that's the map. It tells us how to get where we're going,' I said. The map was enamel, on steel, beside a very grand stone structure – columns, steps, bronze swans. Probably this was once a very fancy area, now either in decline or on the rise.

'Are we going to the carouself?' Willow said. She was a little whiny.

'That's where we're going.' From what I had experienced, the average almost-three-year-old spent approximately 8 per cent of waking hours whining. As an adult, I spent 80 per cent of my waking hours wanting to strangle her. Maybe I would outgrow it.

It was blistering hot. The grass had all died and the trees had that burned, ashen look they get in urban environments. Where people had been walking – and sleeping, and playing, and urinating – there was nothing to hold down the dirt, which was so dry it blew around in great gusts of brown powder.

An Indian man was selling ice creams and drinks from a little cart; Willow had an Eskimo pie (vanilla ice cream held together by a chocolate cookie, which for some reason has managed to escape being given a new, politically correct name) and I got a little bottle of water for a dollar.

The water wasn't very cold, but I was glad I had bought it; pushing the stroller in the heat was a lot of work and Willow was completely covered with sticky melted ice cream, so at least I could use some of the water to attempt to wipe her off. The path was paved but all of a sudden it split in two directions, something that hadn't been on the map, and I didn't know which way we should go.

'That way,' Willow said, pointing to the path we had been on.

'I don't know,' I said. There was a man walking toward us, wearing a dirty white sharkskin zoot suit and I asked him if he knew where we could find the carousel. I almost said 'carouself'.

The man looked frightened. He had two big front teeth, almost like a rabbit. The zoot suit made him look as if he had gotten thrown from a time machine by accident. 'The carousel?' the man said. He thought for a long time. 'There's a carousel, but it a long, long way. You go, that way.' He pointed to the other path. 'You go. Maybe one, two miles.' He raced off, abruptly.

I didn't see how that could be; on the map it didn't look all that far, but then the map hadn't shown that there were two roads. 'Are we going to the carouself?' Willow said.

'That's right,' I said. 'I hope.'

The path slanted downward and to the left and then in order to continue along it we had to cross the road. 'When the traffic light says "walk" we can go,' I said. 'When the word is white.'

'Walk,' Willow commanded.

The path kept going down, into a sort of ravine. It was a bit peculiar. The trees got very big. They were old, and this area of the park hadn't been cleared of underbrush. It was almost as if we were in a forest, a North American hardwood forest, only with a tropical temperature. Under the canopy of trees the stale air was a good ten degrees warmer than it had been on the parched-meadow terrain. There was a series of wide steps going further down.

'Here we go,' I said with artificial jolliness, bumping the stroller along. The steps went on and on. At the bottom, abruptly, the path was no longer paved. This didn't seem right to me, but I didn't think I had the strength to turn around and push the carriage back up. In any event, the path had to lead somewhere. I could hear cars on a road at the top of the ravine, but I couldn't see them; they were too high up, and blocked by the massive trees.

The path was bumpy and for some reason here the mud hadn't dried to dust – it was still mud, thick and gooey. It got darker and in an odd way, though the traffic was still audible, it was quieter. Willow got very quiet, too. It occurred to me I was in the middle of a park where a series of rapes had recently taken place. It wasn't that people didn't get raped and mugged in Central Park, in Manhattan, but I knew my way around – I wouldn't go to an isolated spot at any time of the day, let alone at night.

To be in a park that was empty made me nervous and the stroller seemed heavier and heavier. Along the pathway – if it was a real pathway, I wasn't certain any more – we suddenly passed a bench, a regular green-wood and gray-cement bench. There was a man sitting on the bench. He wasn't wearing a shirt and he was dripping with sweat. He must have weighed about three hundred and fifty pounds and looked ominous, his folds of skin glistening like fur. He didn't say anything.

I pushed the stroller faster. I couldn't imagine what he was doing there, just sitting, half naked, on a bench in a dark forest. Would a man rape or attack a woman with a baby in a stroller? Probably.

'Mama,' Willow said.

'Yes?'

'Are we going to the carouself?'

'I think . . . we're a little bit lost.'

'We're lost,' Willow repeated.

'Mmm.'

'I want to go home now.'

'Yeah,' I said. 'Me too.'

I heard something in the bushes and out of the corner of my eye I saw a man, lithe and sinewy, darting through the bushes. All at once I realized the woods were crawling with them – men. I don't know why I hadn't seen them before. They were everywhere: leaning against trees, sitting on stumps, alone, in groups of two or three. There were all sorts of men, fat and short and tall, and all of them were skulking. I had never seen so many skulking men, all in the same area at the same time.

'Mom?' Willow said. 'Are we lost?'

I remembered once going with Tim and Willow to a safari park. It was feeding time and the lions paced restlessly, prowling the perimeters of their drive-through cage, waiting,

I suppose, for the keeper to throw them hunks of meat. There, it was different: we had been in a car. The atmosphere was the same, though, something hulking, angry and restless. I pushed onward. Even though the path still wasn't paved, the path took an upward turn and after a while the heavy aura of testosterone lightened. Cars were whizzing along the highway and, nearby, a sign with an arrow indicated the direction of the carousel and the nearby zoo.

It was a perfectly ordinary summer day in Prospect Park. Other mothers – in pairs, and threes – were wheeling strollers in our direction, apparently correctly headed to where we had originally wanted to go.

'It's too late now to go to the carousel,' I told Willow. 'But now that we know where it is, maybe Daddy can take you when he gets back.'

There was a sidewalk along the highway and the heat from the cars and the August dust made my throat feel thick. 'We were lost,' Willow said. I hoped our experience hadn't permanently affected her. Usually her attention span – or ability to reminisce – would not have lasted quite so long.

I don't know if the road meandered, or if it was uphill, but by the time we got home it was late afternoon. All we had done was walk through the park – well, part of it – and then come straight home, but I was as exhausted as if I had gone someplace like the Amazon, where I had once been before Willow was born. It hadn't seemed quite so dangerous there, however, but I tried to remind myself that this was always how one felt, after a move.

'I want my blue blanket,' Willow said.

'You said you didn't need it, we'll find it when we get in.'

'I want my blue blanket.' She kept repeating this, as if it would make it appear.

The dogs were glad to see us when I unlocked the door. They only barked if I was home and thought they heard someone outside. Otherwise, as watchdogs, they were useless. 'Hello,' I told them. 'Let me get you some cold water.'

Willow climbed out of the stroller. 'I want my blue blanket!' she screamed.

'I don't know where your blue blanket is. You must remember where you put it,' I said.

She lay on the floor, sobbing, while I looked. It took me a half-hour to find it. She had hidden it under the rug in the dog's crate. I was somewhat hysterical. 'Here,' I said. 'Here's your blue blanket. Next time . . . next time . . .' I didn't really know what to say.

I put Willow in a tepid bath filled with bubbles and, when she was done playing, dried her gently with a fluffy yellow towel, one of the ones I had purchased for our new home. It occurred to me that quite possibly I wasn't cut out for motherhood. How was I going to make it through the rest of my life, trapped like this with a child and a husband and an apartment and cheap towels in a color I didn't even like?

But then Willow fell asleep, clutching the foul rag, and I put her in her bed – in what had once been the maid's room, back when whoever lived in Brooklyn had been able to afford a maid – and I poured myself a drink, and I looked out over the skyline of Manhattan, where the lights of the bridge were just starting to come on, and I thought, Well, I made it through the day and I only have another forty or fifty years to go.

A half-hour or so later the intercom began buzzing. At first I thought it was something dying in the kitchen, but then I remembered that was the way the intercom system in this building sounded. It was the super, Heriberto, saying he was on his way up. He was a big guy, with a goatee and long black hair, who had told me his mother was Chinese and his father had been half Jewish and half Puerto Rican. Because of this he spoke Spanish and Chinese and Yiddish. In a kind of brutish, Stanley Kowalski way, he was somewhat scary, and I had been scared enough for one day and didn't particularly want to see him.

So I stood in the doorway. 'The man downstairs is saying he

got a leak,' Heriberto said. 'He want to know, you got a new dishwasher install, maybe leaking.'

'You can look,' I said, gruffly.

He came into the kitchen. 'Now I got to go tell him, nothing leaking.' He looked at me confidingly. 'I hate going in those people apartment. Those people, they live like animals. They got a real bad smell in there.'

After he left I locked the door. It was a nice old building with heavy metal doors. In the event of a fire, it would be sealed out, or in. Everyone had said, however, that this building would never catch fire – even though many tall buildings often did these days – because the floors were made of concrete, two feet thick. Nevertheless, at least now I knew where the bugs were coming from, if the people downstairs with the leak were messy.

I tried not to think, which was difficult, and from one of the boxes I found a book to read – something some guy had written about traveling in China on a filthy train. I was just getting involved when there was a knock on the door. I looked out the peephole, but I couldn't really see anything, just a sort of blur. I would have to try and remember to tell Tim, when he got back, that this was another thing that needed repairing. The blur didn't look very large, however, and I decided to open the door; after all, I doubted the doorman would let in a criminal, and the blur looked like a small person, probably someone who lived here.

Anyway, I opened it. A squat woman, very short and chunky, burst through. 'Your kitchen – something is leaking, my floor has four feet of water!'

'Oh, gee, I'm sorry.' I said. 'But I haven't used anything in my kitchen, I don't see what could leak.'

'Where is the kitchen?' she said. She shoved past me and stumbled down the hall. When she reached the kitchen she looked under the sink and around the back of the dishwasher. Then she grunted, a disappointed, disbelieving grunt, and started into Willow's bedroom.

'Hang on,' I said. 'The baby's asleep in there, please, I finally got her to sleep after her bath.'

'Huh.' She snorted, turned, and bolted back down the hall. Then I remembered where I had seen her – or at least a similar entity – before. It was on one of those nature programs, *National Geographic* or something, where a rhinoceros decided to charge a Land-Rover, which drove away. To save face, the rhino, too, trotted off in a different direction, as if that was where it really intended to go in the first place.

A few years later the police were on the lookout for a slasher in the part of the park where we had gotten lost.

Willow, Aged Four and a Half

SOMETIMES SHE holds up two objects, say, a fork and a clock. 'Which one is different?' she says.

'The fork?'

'No!' She's indignant. 'Try again.'

Yesterday I was sitting beside her in bed. She reached over and tickled me under the chin. 'You're the cutest little thing,' she said, patronizingly.

A Miracle

IT'S RUSH hour, I'm riding the subway with Willow, aged four and a half; someone is kind enough to squeeze over to give her enough room to sit, she's wriggling, a long school day, can't sit still, finally she pulls up her school uniform, inserts a toy stuffed turtle and pulls down her dress. 'Look, Mom! Look!'

'I see.' I'm tired, nervous, anxious, carrying her school backpack, twelve bags of groceries, the whole trek home is fraught with difficulties. 'Do you see? Look at my tummy. What do you see?' She writhes and slithers.

'I see that you're pregnant and about to give birth in public.'

'No, no! What do you see? Raise your hand if you know the answer.'

'You're having a baby. Please don't pull up your dress in public and try to sit still, this woman was kind enough to move over to give you room to sit.'

'I'm going to have a baby. Look, look!' She pulls the turtle out from under her dress. 'Here's my baby.'

'It's a miracle,' I mutter, wondering how I'm going to get through the rest of my life.

Eat Your Peas

WHEN I was a kid it was my father who was the disciplinarian and I was scared of him. Of course I adored him, but there was that element, too: if a kid knocked over a glass of milk, he yelled. That was how a father was meant to be. But when we had our own child my biggest apprehension was that my husband would turn into Angry Dad. 'I want you to promise that, whatever happens, you won't force our daughter to eat her peas,' I begged.

This was not one of his fears. In his home his mother had been the disciplinarian. And, curiously, after we became parents, though to a degree I took on his mother's role, he did not take on my father's. In fact, as it transpired, my husband was the soul of international diplomacy. He knew everything there was to know about the art of negotiation. 'Which shoes would you like to wear, the brown or the blue?' he would tactfully suggest to our daughter, aged four, lying on the kitchen floor when we were trying to get out of the house; meanwhile I became the one shouting, 'Get your shoes on, now, kid!' It seemed to me, particularly in her early years, that my husband's methods were spoiling her. Certainly I didn't remember anyone offering me kindly choices or suggesting that as soon as I got my shoes on we would be able to do something exciting, such as take an elevator ride downstairs.

Much to my horror I found myself yelling at her to eat her peas; while my husband was busy pretending that the little peas were her friends who needed a safe place to hide in her mouth.

Guess which method worked best? Slowly, over the years, my husband's gentle method of training has rubbed off on me and now I rarely find myself barking commands like 'Go and brush your teeth!' Instead, knowing this will be a challenge she'll be all too ready to disobey, I simply suggest that one of her toothbrushes is feeling lonely, useless and bored and would love its turn to scrub her tiny teeth . . .

It's funny, though, because scared as I was of my father – and though we never yell at her for knocking something over; after all, does anybody spill a glass of milk deliberately? I fail to see the point of calling a kid a careless, stupid slob for doing so – there are times when I still grow irritated, exasperated, and long for my father's methods to be put into action. 'It's bedtime' seems to me a particularly useful command, when obeyed. But with one parent a born leader in the Nelson Mandela/Mother Teresa style, the other parent cannot be a dictator in the manner of Pinochet or Noriega.

The other night, overtired, cranky, my daughter announced furiously, 'I don't like my home. I don't want to live here any more.'

I myself was too tired to wonder what my husband would or might have said. Instead, I simply snarled back, 'Fine! Go find somewhere else to live.'

'No,' she said, 'because I won't want to live there, either.' This had me momentarily stumped. I didn't know what to say. I have a girlfriend whose child, when in a rage, will announce, 'I hate you.' When this happens my friend tries, tactfully, to find out the cause and to tell the kid, politely, that she is her mother who loves her very much, and that this unkind remark may hurt someone's feelings.

My instinct goes the other way. I've suggested to her that, the next time her kid says this, she should wish her good luck and suggest she go find herself a new mother. 'Gosh, if my child said that to me, I'd offer to help pack her suitcase.'

I know I'm probably wrong, and that my husband, with all

his diplomacy, handles things much better than me. My method just brings me down to her level – that of a five-year-old. At least, though, I say to myself, I'm being honest and saying what I feel. Some of the time I actually *am*, mentally, five. I'm a person, too, I think – even though this blunt attitude has never done me much good in life.

It seems to me that each generation tries its best to be good parents – and that there is no adult on the planet who doesn't blame his or her parents in some basic way for how they were brought up. It's been going on since, well, at least ancient Greece, when Oedipus had his complex.

When I later relayed this saga – about my kid being dissatisfied with her home – to my mother, she exclaimed, 'Why, that's exactly like you. That's exactly what you would have said.'

'And what would you have replied?' I asked.

'I guess I would have told you to go find somewhere else to live, too . . . I remember I would tell your brother, when he misbehaved, that I wasn't going to be his friend any more. And he would kick me and say, "You will too be my friend." "Why would I be your friend, when you kick me?" I would say.'

All of a sudden, the art of negotiation, the methods of discipline, made me feel connected with my parents – and those of my husband. And for the first time the mantra recited to me by my mother, throughout my childhood, 'Someday you'll be a mother, and then you'll know what suffering is,' made perfect sense.

Whether you discipline or not, your child will still blame you; and you'll always worry, as a parent, what you did wrong. And then it'll be your kid's turn . . .

Part Two

Breakthroughs in
Science and Medicine

Exhibitionism

I LIVE IN a city where nearly stark-naked people often lie in dirt. The city is New York and the people I am referring to aren't the homeless, the derelicts or drug addicts. They are apparently respectable middle-class men and women, wearing the tiniest bikinis, who sit in absolutely filthy parks. Central Park, Riverside – located next to highways where the grass has shriveled and the brown ground is littered with dog droppings, empty heroin balloons, crack vials and heaps of rotting food.

When I grew up – in rural western Massachusetts – if I was taken into town on a Saturday I had to change from my shorts and put on a dress or trousers. You would never think of being seen in shorts in public, not even children. When my mother grew up – in Manhattan, and this wasn't all that long ago – women had to wear skirts or dresses, they couldn't even wear pants, even if it was freezing cold. Nor could they go out without stockings, even if it was a million degrees outside.

In some cities women actually go around topless – but that is in Sydney, Australia, and for some reason it doesn't seem so shocking there. For one thing, it's on the beach, maybe ten minutes from downtown. The beach is clean, spotless, and everyone looks so wholesome there's something kind of natural about it.

On the other hand, it is a bit peculiar, because Australia is positioned right under that hole in the ozone layer. Every single city block has a Cancer Shop where you can learn about what the big hole is doing to you and the various types of skin cancer, such as basal-cell and melanoma. You can also buy sun-screen and bathing costumes, which all the children wear. These consist of French Legionnaire-style kepis with fabric backs and sides to protect their shoulders and necks, as well as long-sleeved mesh-net shirts and trousers to go swimming in.

In New York, a favorite male pastime is harassing women. In Central Park, recently, I was sitting on a blanket, fully clothed in baggy jeans and an oversized turtleneck sweater. The baby was toddling nearby and the stroller was parked alongside me. A man – more of a boy, actually, but maybe eighteen or twenty – came over to me and said, in a voice that was attempting to be that of a late-night radio DJ, 'What's happening? Looking for company? How are you, baby?' He wasn't talking to the baby, either.

I couldn't understand it. What did he think he was going to accomplish? I'm sitting in the park – fully, 100 per cent clothed, frowzy, no makeup, with my kid, a heck of a lot older than him, obviously unavailable – was I going to invite him back to my apartment? I couldn't really take the time to ask him what he thought he was doing, though, because just then a bunch of kids started yelling, 'Ooo, look at that stinky mess in the grass!' and it was over in the direction the baby was headed.

You could say that maybe this boy just had a thing for frowzy-haired, makeup-less, messy women who were a lot older than he was and had a baby with them. After all, there're men out there who have every imaginable (and unimaginable) desire.

But it wasn't that. It's just that some men in this city feel free to say or do whatever they want. The other day I was walking down the street (again, fully, 100 per cent clothed, and when I say 100 per cent that means practically not an inch of exposed skin) and some man on a corner yelled, 'You having a bad hair day! Whoops, I mean you having a bad hair month! I guess you probably having a bad hair life!'

Even on fancy blocks, the Upper East Side, say, doormen or men walking by feel free to jeer. I don't enjoy it. It's hostile. Even an admiring remark is an embarrassment because it announces how superior men feel to women and that basically women are just objects to them.

That's why I don't understand the concept of wearing a teeny-weeny bikini in a Manhattan park. It's not just that it seems like bad manners to be in a state of undress in a place that's inappropriate. It's not just the surrounding filth that makes it unappealing, nor the expanding hole up above. It's that it's beyond my comprehension to go out of the way to attract harassment.

Some would argue that anyone has a right to wear a bikini because they want to and they're not doing it to get attention. Just like a woman dressed provocatively isn't asking to be raped. And I agree with that absolutely. Nevertheless, one also has to consider the world and society in which we live. If you live in a dangerous city you don't go into Central Park at night, let alone wearing a miniskirt and high heels. It's sad but true. So I guess what it comes down to is that you're either an exhibitionist, or not. But I have yet to figure out what the pleasure in being an exhibitionist might be.

Sex, Unable to

I HAVE NEVER been able to write a sex scene in any of my fiction, not a real one. I was once able to write a scene in which a hand was raped (under a table, during a meal), but there wasn't anything sexy about it. I don't mind reading about sex, but I can't say I find it arousing, and when I do try to write about scx and really think about what it feels like, any erotic qualities vanish at once and I am left with the words 'penis' and 'vagina'. OK, so there's a penis, and it goes into a vagina and then the two people – or whatever – rub up and down for a while and then one or the other or both or none of them have an 'orgasm' and then they stop.

There's something inherently unsexy in the sex act itself.

I have a lot of books about the sex lives of animals, which can be fascinating: for example, at a certain time of year the luminous penises of a certain type of squid detach themselves from the male squid and go swimming off across the sea, somewhere near Polynesia, in order to search for a female. And people go out in boats to collect the luminous penises, which they net and eat, though the book did not provide any recipes. And there's a kind of male spider who makes a beautiful present out of an insect, all wrapped in silk, which he presents to the female and, while she's opening it, quickly has sex with her – the present has distracted her attention from what she really intends to do, which is eat him.

Another chapter describes the sex life of the hermaphrodite Roman garden snail. Apparently Roman garden snails are more passionate than human beings. One end of each is male, the other female. When he/she meets another snail and falls in love, from each of their heads a sort of dagger appears and they get into an argument, stabbing each other viciously. Sometimes one or both die. If they live, however, or are not too badly wounded, they get into some kind of really involved sex, where the male half of one is screwing the female half of the other, and vice versa, sort of simultaneous four-way sex.

I can't say that thinking about the sex lives of snails is, at least for me, particularly arousing but it is interesting.

It may be that my early reading as a child somehow interfered with my ability to write about sex. When I was about ten I read *Candy* by Terry Southern. The nubile and voluptuous heroine, Candy, keeps feeling sorry for all the various men she meets who want to have sex – so she does. I haven't read the book in a long time but I don't remember anybody getting much pleasure out of it, only that I thought Candy was stupid for having sex with all these men just because she felt sorry for them. The most vivid scene, however, was the one in which the hunchback urinated on a piece of bread and then ate it for a snack. Who would want to grow up, I thought, if that was what lay ahead? Adults were too peculiar.

I now know that the book was intended to be humorous, although it is still beyond my comprehension.

About the same age I read *Awake, Monique (The Story of a Young Girl's Discovery of Love)* by Astrid van Royen, (originally published in 1957 in Holland as *Monika*). In this book Monique's parents are killed in a car crash when she is very young and she goes to live with her incredibly handsome single uncle, and she falls in love with him and they have sex when she is about fourteen. They have to be secretive about it because obviously this is really bad, but she's really happy because she's so madly in love with this handsome uncle.

That was sort of sexy, I think, though I have no desire to go back and read the book again. Even though I didn't want my parents to be killed in a car crash, it's one of those fantasies you have as a kid when you're little and angry at your parents; and if they were going to have to die, then I would want to go live with this uncle, except my real uncle wasn't like the guy in the book, he was married to my aunt and a perfectly good uncle, for whom I never had any romantic feelings. The uncle in the book – he was really young, he had a sports car and went to the most glamorous restaurants and had mistresses and other foreign things. Besides, everyone in the book was Belgian, or French, I don't remember, so what I mainly learned was that not only were adults weird, Europeans were even weirder.

My father had a collection of *Playboy* magazines on one of the bookshelves and sometimes I would leaf through these; maybe I was eight or nine or ten, there was no erotic charge involved, though I thought the naked women were perfectly beautiful, they also seemed so *large*. In the pictures they seemed to fill entire rooms, huge breasts topped with gigantic pink nipples, acres of thigh and buttock; and there were always those strange little captions, about what they liked to do, ride horseback, or go camping, or cheerlead, which never seemed to have anything to do with anything – besides, they were far too huge to be able to do any of those things.

There were also stories and articles in the magazines, and the one that was the most shocking was *The Fly*, a science fiction novella in which a scientist accidentally gets his head switched with a fly.

The problem was, I didn't know this story was science fiction and it just seemed like another horrid thing that could happen once you reached adult years and had to start having sex.

You might grow into a giantess, or feel so sorry for some man you would take off your underpants, or be offered a piece of bread to eat on which some man had urinated, or fall in love with your own uncle.

And when I finally did see a naked man, for the first time, at a pool where people were swimming nude, the whole thing was so shocking and sad I had to avert my eyes.

So maybe it makes sense that now, as an adult, as a fiction writer, I can't write about sex, not in a sexy way. In fact, the whole topic doesn't even interest me very much – not sex between people, that is. I mean, some like to be tied up and some like to tie people up and some like men and some like boys and some like girls and so on. The whole thing is very limited. But the sex lives of *animals* – now that's a different matter. Did you know, for example, that an octopus can get so depressed over losing its mate that it will kill itself by ripping off its own tentacles? And that the female flatworm spends her entire life *inside* the male, the two of them conjoined in a permanent state of copulation? And that . . . well, I could go on and on, once I get excited . . .

I was initially commissioned to write this article for an on-line sex magazine. The editor rejected it. It didn't have enough sex. Many people assume I write about sex because the first story in Slaves of New York *used the word 'penis'. That was my attempt to write about men as objects in the way men had always written about women. Mostly nobody got this, though, and thought it was about sex.*

My Peculiar Affliction

I N COLLEGE my underarm perspiration turned bright green. This startled me. I changed brands of deodorant but my perspiration was still green. All of my clothes had green rings under the armpits. I made the mistake of borrowing one of my roommate's shirts and when I gave it back to her she was seriously alarmed as to my well-being. In addition, the perspiration stains were permanent and no amount of washing could remove them. She gave me the shirt to keep. I remember it vividly: the shirt had originally been black, patterned with white abstract shapes, a bit like a painting by Penck, only now it was black and white and green. This might have looked OK if the green parts had been evenly distributed, but they were not – the only parts that were green were two big rings under the arms. Some days the perspiration was a blackish gray, or gray-green; on others it was a brilliant blue-green.

I decided to go to the women's health center. The room was crowded. I filled out a form with my name and other details. The space that asked 'Reason for visit?' I left blank. Then I handed it in to the receptionist. 'You didn't fill out this line,' she said.

I looked down, embarrassed. 'I'd rather wait and tell the doctor.'

'You have to fill it out or you can't see the doctor,' the receptionist said.

I was only seventeen, a freshman in college, and my condition was, to me, humiliating. In the space I wrote, 'I perspire green.'

The receptionist picked up my sheet and read it. Then she said in a loud, almost hysterical voice, 'You sweat green? You sweat green?'

'Um, yes,' I muttered, looking down.

'What?' she said. 'Is that what you wrote? That you sweat green?'

By now everyone in the room was staring at me. On their faces were expressions of horror and general fascination. These were the women I would be attending college with, possibly for the next four years. Some of them went in to see doctors, came out and left; then new women arrived in the waiting room. My paperwork was delivered to a nurse. 'She sweats green?' Shrieks from down the hall.

At last it was my turn to see a doctor. I was examined and asked a number of questions. Had this ever happened to me before, when had it begun, and so forth. At last the doctor said, 'I don't know. I've never heard of this.'

When I left the examining room, now dressed, all the nurses who worked in the health service had gathered in the hall to look at me, poking one another and giggling. As I made my way back out through the waiting room I could hear their voices, loudly, 'She sweats green? She sweats green?'

A few months later my condition disappeared and it has not returned since.

Psychological Testing

A LONG TIME ago I signed up for some tests as a paid volunteer. It was somebody's research project. The tester asked me a lot of questions like 'What is the meaning of "A rolling stone gathers no moss"?'

'It means if a stone rolls down a hill no moss is going to stick on it.'

'One swallow does not a summer make?'

'If you see one swallow, it doesn't mean it's summer – it could just be some kind of lost bird.'

'Still waters run deep.'

'If there's a lake – or a pond – without ripples, it could be that the water is deep. But I don't agree with that. After all, a puddle can be quite still on the surface, but that doesn't mean it's deep.'

She kept trying to get me to offer other explanations but I couldn't. I had never thought about any of these sayings before and they all seemed pointless to me. After all, who cares if a stone rolling down a hill won't get moss on it? Why would there be moss on a hill in the first place? Usually moss is at the bottom of a hill, by a stream or some other water.

The testing went on for the whole day. There were other components to it – I had to use an empty yoghurt container and some weights to weigh or measure something, which I couldn't do, and make things out of twigs, or blocks. I knew I didn't do too well with these parts.

After I was finished I wanted to find out how I had done. She said that normally in a case like mine she wouldn't tell me the results, but since I had a novel about to be published, she felt I could handle it: according to some scale, or Piaget, or something, I was mentally retarded. Nowadays I guess they'd call it mentally challenged.

I didn't pay this any attention, I just took my twenty-five bucks and left. But around five years later, it suddenly occurred to me: I've been evaluated as mentally retarded! That's how I knew it was probably true, because it took five years for me to figure this out.

My mother said I should never repeat this story, but I'm proud of it. It makes me feel good about myself, because when I feel blue I think, yes, but for somebody retarded I've accomplished a great deal.

And I still think of explanations for things like 'Still waters run deep.' For example, sometimes if there's a noisy brook, it's shallow, but of course that's not always the case.

A Visit to Bellevue Hospital

W HILE I was away in New Zealand, Tim went to Jamaica where, playing volleyball, he scratched his leg on a rock. The cut was imperceptible, but around a week later his calf swelled and his temperature rose to 104°. In Queenstown I got a fax: 'The good news is that my visa has been extended for a few weeks. The bad news is that I may have to go into hospital. I have cellulitis and lymphangitis. But don't worry.'

I couldn't change my plane ticket. There was a message waiting for me at the hotel (we stopped overnight in Hawaii) from an unfamiliar telephone number with a New York area code. Although it was four-thirty in the morning back in New York, I dialed. The phone rang many times before someone picked up and said, 'The patients' phones are turned off between seven at night and eight in the morning.'

'I'm calling from Hawaii,' I said. 'Can I leave a message?'

She connected me to a main switchboard. I said, to this next person, that I wanted to leave a message. The woman asked for the patient's name, and when I told her, she put me on hold. Some time passed, then she got back on the phone. 'Yes, he is a patient here,' she said.

'Can you tell me how he is?' I said.

She put me on hold. After a while she returned. 'His condition is stable,' she said.

'What's wrong with him?' I said.

Before I could stop her she put me on hold again. A few minutes passed. My mother looked at me across the hotel room in disbelief. 'He has a medical condition,' the woman said, getting back on at last.

'That's what you're telling me?'

'That's right,' the woman said.

'But what kind of medical condition?'

'That's all I can say. He has a medical condition.'

'Can I leave a message for him?' I said.

She said she would switch me to his floor. I assume it was a nurse who answered; I asked if I could leave a message for Tim, and she said she would go and see if he was awake and I could speak to him. I waited for a long time with growing impatience and excitement.

At last she returned and said I should call him directly, on his own line. By now fifteen or twenty minutes had passed, long-distance charges, from a hotel. 'But his phone is turned off, until morning,' I said.

'Oh, she said. 'In that case, let me go and see if he can make it to the phone here.'

Another five minutes passed, finally she brought him to the phone. 'Sorry for the delay,' Tim said. 'The nurse couldn't find a wheelchair.'

'A wheelchair! But what's happening? Where are you?'

'I'm in Bellevue.'

The situation did not sound good. With no insurance – Tim had only recently arrived in the United States – he figured Bellevue Hospital, which was public, wouldn't charge much. Besides, since they had to take everyone, the hospital had become known for its expertise in tropical disease. Apparently a lot of derelicts, after living on the New York City streets, had to be admitted with various disorders and skin diseases unknown to the general population. Tropical diseases must have thrived in the pavement cracks. But this cellulitis diagnosis – 'I don't know,' I told my mother. 'To me it just sounds like flab.'

When I got home I raced down to Bellevue. Some kind of renovation was taking place: scaffolding surrounded the front of the building. Maybe it was just falling apart. There was a patch of grass, fenced, and a row of stunned-looking daffodils poking their way through the rock-hard ground.

A tall, deranged man accosted visitors as they made their way in, asking for money. He staggered across the path in front of me, but I ignored him and pressed on. Two men stood inside the front door, somewhat ominous. 'Hey, baby,' one said to me, 'come on over here for a minute.'

'We got whatever you want,' said the other.

Nobody had ever tried to pick me up in a hospital lobby before. I looked at them again. They were drug dealers. Nearby was a woman in a uniform – either a security guard, or a police woman sent to protect the drug dealers – and I asked her where I was supposed to go. 'Straight back to the information desk.'

There were two people at the desk giving out visitors' passes. A small crowd, pushing and shoving, had collected to obtain their passes. On the other side of the room a security guard was shouting at a child. 'No children under twelve years old!' Just then one of the men waiting to visit toppled over. He fell to the floor, apparently unconscious.

The crowd stopped shoving, to look at him. Two security guards appeared and stood nearby for a minute. The third, the one admitting visitors, joined them. One kind of shrugged. Then the first two left.

'Hey!' the third yelled suddenly. 'Where'd that little girl go?' He ran toward the elevators. 'She waited till my back was turned and snuck in!'

Nobody on line spoke English, and the receptionist had to switch from Spanish when he talked to me. The man who had toppled unconscious was still lying on the floor. I got my pass and stepped around him.

There were two banks of elevators, but apparently none of them were working, because a large crowd of people had gathered, waiting to go up. A few minutes passed. Just as one of the elevators arrived the two security guards who had been examining the unconscious man on the floor came racing out a door, wheeling a stretcher. 'Get out of the way!' one shouted. At top speed the stretcher slammed directly through the middle of the crowd. 'Out of the way! Stretcher coming through!'

I crammed into the elevator with the others and made my way out at the fifteenth floor. A patient staggered from a room as I walked down the hall. 'Pssst,' she said, grabbing my wrist with a bony hand. 'You got any cigarettes?'

Tim was in the next room. He was lying on a bed, surrounded by huge displays of orchids, roses, every sort of flower imaginable and baskets of food and fruit. There was another bed in the room and just as I entered the man in this bed got up and left.

'He went to the hall to smoke,' Tim said.

'He's smoking?' I said. 'In a hospital?'

'Everyone here smokes,' Tim said. 'The nurses can't do anything about it. They've given up. My roommate's very nice. Poor guy. He's got something wrong with his neck. He can't speak, and he doesn't understand any English. They gave him a tracheotomy.'

'How can he smoke with a tracheotomy?'

'Oh, he holds the cigarette up to the hole in his throat.'

There was a pause while I contemplated this. 'Pretty flowers,' I said. It occurred to me that if I were in the hospital, I would never have so many flowers.

Tim looked chagrined. 'I forgot to tell people, no flowers. It's a little embarrassing.'

'Why?' I said.

'Apparently nobody has ever got flowers in Bellevue before. The nurses come up from other floors just to look at them.' He took a sip of water. 'And then, Fred sent me this basket of food, from E.A.T.' E.A.T. is a restaurant/delicatessen on Madison Avenue. I had once gone in there. Then I left when I saw that a bowl of soup cost eight dollars. 'The doctor said,

"I bet that's the first time anyone at Bellevue has gotten food from E.A.T." I've been giving food and flowers away, to the nurses.'

A nurse's aide, charming, Asian, came in to take his temperature. She had a digital read-out thermometer she stuck in his mouth. After a pause she took it out and looked at the numbers. 'Your temperature's down,' she said, pleased. 'It's 93.2.'

She was just leaving the room when Tim said, '93.2?'

'That doesn't sound right,' I said.

'Isn't that if a person is dead?' Tim said.

The nurse's aide stopped. 'Um,' she said. 'Were you drinking some liquid?'

'Ice water,' Tim said.

'Oh,' she said. 'I'll come back then, in a few minutes.'

Two more nurses entered the room. 'When can he leave?' I asked.

'Oh, we don't want him to leave,' one said. 'Then we couldn't see these beautiful flowers.' They glanced admiringly at the expensive arrangements of tulips and anemones. Then they glanced admiringly at Tim.

'And we like his accent,' the other said.

'We've never had an English person in here before.'

'And especially not one so good-looking.' Giggling, they went back into the hall. 'If you don't take a shower, we're not going to give you your medication!' one suddenly shrieked.

'She's talking to the woman next door,' Tim said. 'She likes her medication. She gets it every night, and if she doesn't get it exactly at eight o'clock, she goes into the hall and starts screaming.'

'How did you end up here?' I said.

'I came to the emergency ward. I was there for three hours, and after a while I asked to lie down. Then a doctor saw me and I think she fancied me, because she made some calls and told them to speed things up for my admittance. I think she liked the fact that I wasn't making a lot of noise. Because when I finally got a stretcher to lie on, there were other people on stretchers moaning, and a man lying on one of them told me that everyone made a noise so that they could get admitted faster.

'The stretchers were double-parked along the hallway, and about half the people were handcuffed by their wrists and ankles to their stretchers. I was in a room with a lot of convicts, or prisoners, or something. I never saw so many police officers in a hospital. Finally they wheeled me up to X-ray. You have to be X-rayed before you can be admitted. It was three in the morning before I was admitted.

'But somebody must have liked me, because after I'd been in the ward with the prisoners for a couple of days, they moved me up here.'

'I guess it's not so bad here?' I said as a troupe of nurses in tight white uniforms arrived and stood giggling in the doorway.

'We came to see the flowers,' one said. The others burst into laughter.

'The view is wonderful,' Tim said.

'And it's . . . fairly safe?' I said.

'The only thing is' – he lowered his voice to a whisper – 'the other patients, they come in to steal your cigarettes. You have to be careful, because the minute you leave the room, hundreds of them stagger in to search your things.'

Some years later I met a famous aids AIDS doctor who also worked with lepers. There were thirty lepers left in the New York City area, he told me, and they all came to him at Bellevue. I don't know why, but this fact has always amazed me. Sometimes I'll be on the subway and I'll think, There are thirty lepers in the New York City region. I wonder if I'm sitting next to one? Because I know that it's treatable, and these lepers are just walking around, among us. But the first stages of leprosy are slightly coarsened features and I figure, before you get treatment you wake up one day and you have slightly coarsened features. Maybe later your fingers drop off and then you get treatment. But first you wake up and there's the other business. And I can't help it, on the subway – or even, sometimes, at a dinner party – I look at the others and think, He has the slightly coarsened features. Could be the early stages!

Old People

I was asked to write something for the Scholastic Awards, an association that gives prizes to kids for scholastic achievement. I forgot the topic, but I remembered that when you talk to young people you're supposed to lecture them in a patronizing tone.

I remember when I was in first grade how incredibly ancient the teacher and teaching assistant appeared. Now I realize that they were probably in their twenties, which is younger than I am now, and people in their twenties look incredibly young to me, even though I am not that much older.

I felt sorry for those old people, when I was six; they seemed to inhabit a different planet than the one I lived on. I never believed for one second that I was going to move to the same place. I half thought it was their own fault, for getting that way. Especially really old people, like maybe forty, or sixty (anything older than twenty was all the same). Sometimes a grandparent would say to me, 'I don't understand how this happened. Inside, I still feel like I'm eighteen years old.'

That didn't even make any sense, since if they were eighteen years old they wouldn't have looked the way they did.

When I was six an eighteen-year-old wasn't an ancient blur, like those people over twenty, but they were about as old as somebody could get and still have fun. They were scary, the eighteen-year-olds, but very glamorous.

Then all of a sudden it happened to me, I never thought I

would be twenty, but I was, and probably pretty soon I'll be eighty years old, looking into the mirror and muttering, 'I don't understand how this happened, because inside I feel like I'm still eighteen.'

Now I have a baby who's almost two, but I really don't remember what it feels like to be her age, apart from the fact that probably everybody appears incredibly ancient to her. Even though you never believe when you're young that you're going to get any older, it happens.

So you just have to try and believe it and make the most out of every second you're around. That's why if you start to do something you really enjoy, when you're young, like drawing or painting or singing or writing, on the day when you wake up and you're, say, twenty or thirty or sixty years old you'll be able to do something you really like doing and feel satisfied about, and can have fun doing – and it won't matter whether you're any good at it or not. What will matter is that you're having fun, and that the eighteen-year-old trapped inside you has an escape route. If you don't start when you're young, though, for some reason it gets a lot harder later on.

Maybe I am, Maybe Not

A MAN CALLED up and told me his name and that he lived in Chicago and that by doing research he had discovered that I was born male and possibly still was. Initially I had attempted to publish my first book, *American Dad*, under a man's name – Tom A. Janowitz – and somewhere he had read an article about my mother in which she referred to her 'two boys'. If I did not tell this man the truth, that I was really male, he was going to call up the media and he would also be calling my parents to get the truth out of them. 'I'm not going to tell you,' I said.

This was during a period when many homosexuals were being 'outed', which I didn't approve of. If someone wanted to say they were gay they were entitled to do so and if they didn't want to then they were also entitled not to. Did this man also want me to wear a yellow star on my sleeve? If someone wanted to keep things private that was their business. But some people were arguing that if someone refused to admit they were gay it was damaging to all gay people. I thought it would be quite sad if you couldn't tell your parents you were homosexual, but that would be your choice and decision. And then what would be next? That you would have to tell your parents what specific kind of sex you liked or participated in? Why did everything have to be everyone's business? So I called my father. 'Daddy, a man is going to call you and ask if I am your daughter or your son. Please don't tell him,' I said.

'What?' my father said but he went along with my wishes.

And the man called up my father and was very aggressive and unpleasant, threatening my father if he did not describe my primary sexual characteristics. There are a lot of people born with all kinds of sexual attributes, a mixture of two sexes, a penis and vulva, an enlarged clitoris, a tiny penis, no genitals at all, whatever. Why would it be anybody's business whatever the appearance of my sexual organs, unless I agreed to pose for *Playboy* or *Playgirl*. If anybody was in the news – any woman, that is – for almost any reason, there was *Playboy* asking her to take off her clothes for money. It always seemed very weird to me, whether it was Rita Jenrette or Jessica Hahn or Fawn Hall or Faye Resnik, Monica Lewinsky, or someone on some *Survivor* program, very soon you would read that they were getting offers from *Playboy* to take off their clothes. And if you were a person who didn't have any money, how difficult it would be to not respond to such an offer. And after all, was it such a big deal, to take off your clothes for money for a picture? On the other hand, what was wrong with men, that they were so anxious to see what someone looked like without her clothes on? What were men always imagining was going to be under the clothes? There would be one, two or three breasts, and a vulva, though only the pudenda might be visible. Hadn't they figured that out by now? Only in my case, there was no money involved, just this guy calling up my parents, and then he started sending out a newsletter, an actual newsletter, about this exciting discovery on his part, and he sent it to the newspapers, and *People* magazine. *People* magazine called me up and asked me would I write about it? 'But you'll have to say whether or not you are now or ever were a man,' the editor said.

'I prefer not to,' I said. It felt kind of good, to take a strong position. Friends kept calling me up and saying, 'You have to tell the truth.' Some wouldn't even speak to me for a while, they found it so upsetting that I refused to just be open.

When I wrote my first novel, American Dad *(1981), I sent out chapters under my name and they were rejected. Then I sent out the same chapters under a man's name (the novel was written in the first person of a male) and almost immediately the* Paris Review *called to accept the chapters (the same that had been rejected under my name) and I got a rather nice letter from a woman editor at* Esquire *inviting me to lunch (I was too chicken to go, though) so we could discuss my work in greater detail . . . I wanted to publish that book under the name Tom A. Janowitz because I felt I would be making a point, that things hadn't changed all that much since the Brontës wrote under men's names, and George Eliot and George Sand and so forth . . . but my editor at the time said that for copyright reasons I had to publish under my legal name.*

Part Three

Food

Gluttony

Here's my fantasy: I get into bed with so many unread books I have to push them aside to make room. Then I order the following: a pizza, extra-large, extra-crispy, extra-cheese. The crust is thin and crunchy, each slice has a different topping, mushrooms, onions, pepperoni, the whole thing is oozing, at once crispy, crusty and wet. Tomato sauce, long strings of cheese. I eat it.

Baklava, myriad flakes of phyllo pastry dripping with honey, walnuts. Indian food, chewy naan, roti, parathas, fiery curry. Chinese food, not greasy but fried, things that are sweet and sour and hot all at the same time. I don't care about the mess in bed. Maybe when I fall asleep, somebody creeps in and tidies. I am surrounded by boxes of really good-quality chocolates and an entire chocolate cake, thick and black, bitter-sweet.

I breakfast on donuts, dense, heavy, a crusty lump of sugary dough. Steaks, thick and rare, sliced thin, with a bone to gnaw on. Fried potatoes, potato chips, pommes frites. Biscuits, sugared nuts, wedges of assorted cheese: Stilton, Cheddar, Swiss, Havarti. Bowls of the blackest, sweetest cherries. Southern barbecue, ribs, with coleslaw, or a pulled-pork sandwich, the tenderest meat shreds slammed between two sides of a soft roll. Did I mention chocolate mousse? And the ice cream, flavor depending on my current mood – ginger, green tea, mocha chip topped with hot fudge sauce. Pistachio, butter pecan, maple walnut.

My job is to lie in bed and eat and read – oh, once in a while perhaps a masseuse will arrive to soothe and comfort, a handsome delivery boy with a fresh pineapple he will chop right there at the foot of my bed and present to me in chunks on the ends of toothpicks.

In my fantasy I have blond hair piled on top of my head, my face is jolly, my cheeks rosy pink. I am huge, I occupy the whole bed, mounds of luscious creamy flesh. There are small dogs, too, for companionship, little fluffy Japanese spaniels, I believe, who snore gently in my ear and who beg for little tid-bits.

I can think of nothing so dreamy, so decadent. It's an evil existence by modern standards. If only I had been born in the time of Rubens, or Titian's sixteenth century, when obviously obesity, or at least plumpness and cellulite, was considered a desirable, sexy attribute in women. Or in one of those Arab cultures where the bigger the belly-dancer's belly, the better. Perhaps I could have been a sultana, or a maharani, or the Queen of Hawaii.

Instead I live in New York City, at the end of the twentieth century, where women compete to be the slimmest. I've been at lunches where each woman consumes only a lettuce leaf and sips Evian. If I order a glass of wine, a rich dessert, the others look at me with smug satisfaction – they're getting some peculiar, vicarious pleasure from the fact that I'm consuming calories and they're not. It's almost as if they're having their cake and not eating it, too.

It's not enough, either, to be slim – one is also expected to be fit, one is supposed to run, to swim, to spin (whatever that is). Women are expected to be taut, sinewy, perfect machines, not an ounce of extra flesh or skin.

Basically the modern New York woman is expected to have the same shape as that of a really tough villager who lives in a primitive place and spends the day hunting and gathering, grinding corn, lugging heavy pots of water on her head, giving birth to babies in the field, never getting quite enough to eat.

At the same time this body shape is considered desirable, everything on the city streets is designed to lure and tempt: the pastry shops with their displays of delicate cakes, the restaurants serving creamy risotto, chunks of lobster, veal chops in a reduced, rich velouté. At the parties there are bars serving endless quantities of champagne, wines, events whose sole purpose is to introduce some new, calorie-high cookie or drink.

I know that ultimately I would be uncomfortable weighing three hundred pounds and doing nothing but lying in bed eating. But why does gaining even a bit of weight have to be looked on as a vice? Why do I have to live as if famine has swept the village, when there's coffee cake for sale just down the block?

I suspect that society's anger toward the fat person comes from some puritanical American feeling that someone obese is taking more than their fair share; the fat person represents the rich landowner, the spoiled queen bee whose sole duty is to lay eggs while the rest of us workers go out and collect pollen. But it seems odd that in a time when weight is despised, considered a vice, the other trappings or symbols of wealth are coveted – the Range Rover, the Manolo Blahniks, the pearl necklaces, the house in the country, the Tom Bell sculpture, all luxury items that have antecedents dating back to the Renaissance.

Or maybe it's just because we know a fat person will take up too much room on the alien spacecraft, when it lands and the aliens select their guests. After all, as far as I know, nobody has ever reported seeing a fat alien. Not even a mesomorphic one.

The Food Chain

I WENT TO the A&P to do some shopping. There was a small lobby area just beyond the entrance where a cash machine was located. Two people were standing at the window alongside the gumball dispensers. They both looked at me while I inserted my cash card and punched in my PIN number.

'Excuse me, miss,' the man said. 'Do you speak English?'

'Yes,' I said.

'Could you please help me? My wife and I have run out of money and our next welfare check isn't due for three days. If you could buy us a chicken and two boxes of Rice-a-Roni I know how to cook it so it would last for three days. Please say you'll help us out, please!' The man burst into tears. It wasn't often I had seen a grown person burst into tears, but real tears ran down his face.

'Yes,' I muttered, 'sure.'

'Great!' the man said. He stopped crying and ran into the supermarket. A sign flashed on the cash machine saying it was unable to process my request at this time. I was still in shock over the request from the man. His wife stood by the window, looking at me. How terrible, to run out of food and money and have to ask strangers. Nobody should have to go without enough to eat.

Since the machine wouldn't give me my money, though, I only had about ten dollars. 'Where did your husband go?' I said.

'He went inside,' she said. She seemed very quiet, slightly embarrassed and timid. 'He went to get the chicken.'

I went in. I thought about picking up a few other groceries for the couple – such as apples, or some vegetables – but then I saw the man already standing in the checkout line, waving at me. I had sort of wanted to get something for myself, but he appeared to be in a hurry. So I went over to him.

He was holding a chicken, a very expensive chicken. This brand of chicken cost a dollar and eighty-nine cents a pound. The regular kind of chicken was ninety-nine cents. The boxes of Rice-a-Roni were expensive, too.

'Just a minute,' I said as the man gestured for the cashier to begin ringing up the stuff. 'Isn't there a smaller, less expensive chicken?'

'Oh please, Miss,' he said. Tears began to roll down his face. It was very impressive. 'Please say you'll buy this chicken. We don't have any more food stamps; the Red Cross says at the end of the month they'll buy us furniture – we just got a low-income apartment, we got to move out of the shelter, but—'

'I'm going to buy you a chicken.' I said. 'I just don't want to buy you an eight-dollar-and-seventy-three-cent chicken, that's all. Let's see if there's a cheaper chicken.'

'With this chicken I know how to cook it so it will last three days,' the man muttered, but he followed me over to the refrigerated chicken section.

I began to look at other chickens. To be honest, the man probably hadn't made such an extravagant selection. The store-brand chickens were a peculiar gray color, like the skin of a heavy smoker after twenty years, and this week, for some reason, they were priced at a dollar and sixty-nine cents a pound – not much of a saving. 'Please buy me this chicken,' the man said, rocking the chicken he had been cradling. 'Oh, Miss, I'll do anything! I'll give you my hat.'

I hadn't noticed his hat. It appeared to be a knit acrylic hat, rather old and pilleated, if there was such a word, and definitely filthy. 'I don't want your hat,' I said, and was surprised that I sounded irritated. 'Here's a chicken.' I picked up a five-dollar-and-thirty-cents chicken. It wasn't a very plump one.

The man shook his head. For a second I wondered if he was going to refuse this inferior bird. If he hadn't been in such a rush, I would have gotten the couple two or three apples, or something else to vary their diet. It must have been somewhat tedious, day after day, to rise in the morning knowing that all they would have to eat was stewed chicken and Rice-a-Roni. I thought of other ways he might economize. What if he just got some rice to go with the chicken, surely that would be less expensive? But then I thought of all the herbs and spices that went with the Rice-a-Roni mix, and how the rice in the box was blended with pasta, something the advertisements stated was an indigenous San Francisco treat.

While we waited in line at the cashier the man said again that one chicken could last him, and his wife and their two children three days. He kept muttering about food stamps, and Welfare, and also the Red Cross, and that they had just been moved into this apartment on 106th Street, but I couldn't understand him since he was mumbling.

Also, I didn't want to judge him – I was just buying him a chicken, not telling him how to lead his life. I wondered if I would have enough money to get something extra, something they would be surprised and pleased to receive. There was a rack of candy right next to the cash register. I knew candy wasn't nutritious, or even very filling, but I thought that if I were poverty-stricken, I would want either a drink (something alcoholic) or a big slab of chocolate.

So I selected an Alpine White Chocolate bar. 'By the way,' the man said, 'Would you consider buying me this *TV Guide* so I can watch the Superbowl?'

For a moment I was speechless. The *TV Guide* cost seventy-five cents and I hadn't realized that the man even had a TV set on which to watch the Superbowl. But surely it was just a question of turning on the TV set and finding the right channel? Did one need to have a more extensive guide to be able to follow it? 'No,' I said angrily.

The cashier rang up the chicken and the two boxes of Rice-a-Roni and the candy bar. The total came to just under ten dollars. It turned out I had more than I thought in my pocket, almost fifteen dollars in crushed bills and change. 'Here you go,' the man said, pushing the candy bar over to me as the cashier put the chicken and Rice-a-Roni into a bag. 'The candy bar is yours.'

'It's for your wife,' I muttered.

'Oh yeah?' the man said, and then added, loudly, 'You bought her a candy bar but you wouldn't buy a *TV Guide* for me? You women – you always stick together.' His tone was mildly flirtatious, even coy. It was as if now that he had gotten what he wanted from me – or very nearly – I had become not his property, but his buddy.

'Goodbye,' I said, and hastily rushed out of the store before the man. I went back in to try the cash machine again. I hoped it would work so I could buy what I had originally come in for. I saw the man, outside the window, handing the candy bar to his wife. There was something very touching about this. Then the two of them walked off together.

The machine still refused my request, although I had money in the account. When I left I saw the couple walking up the street. I couldn't help but follow them, because I was going to a different cash machine. When I crossed the street I saw the couple stop a man and chat with him for a minute. After they had walked on, I was half tempted to stop the man and ask him, 'What did that couple say to you?'

Maybe they were approaching him for different, additional groceries for their stew? But I lost my nerve and went on.

A few days later I was walking on the block and a man came up behind me. 'Excuse me,' he said. 'Excuse me, do you speak English?' I turned around. It was the man I had bought the chicken for. I looked at him. 'I'm wondering,' he said. 'Miss,

my wife and I are real hungry. Would you be willing to buy us
a chicken? I know how to cook it so it can last . . .' Suddenly
he recognized me and walked away.

I supposed I had been the victim of a new kind of con. But
what kind of con was it? If the couple were drug addicts, where
could they possibly take a chicken and two boxes of Rice-a-
Roni and sell them to buy money for drugs? I couldn't imagine
a fence who would buy a used chicken.

My closest friend, Paige Powell, once befriended a home-
less family in the park. At the end of the summer she was
having her apartment redone, and offered them her old
air-conditioner, which still worked, her futon, and other
things. She figured they could sell the stuff and make
some cash. When they came to pick it up, they said,
'Great! We can use some of this stuff at our other house,
the one in the country.'

The Supermarket, Part Two

THERE WERE two women ahead of me in line in the supermarket. The first was very elderly and was having a great deal of trouble counting out her change. At first I was impatient, but then I remembered that someday – soon – I was going to be old, and I sighed and gazed off into space. The woman directly ahead of me was younger – perhaps in her early fifties – and dressed in a little pale-blue suit. She began to help the elderly woman, and, when the woman's groceries were finally paid for and she had left, the woman turned to me and said, demurely, as if by way of explanation, 'I really sympathize. That woman can't see very well. The same thing happened not long ago to my mother, and it's incredibly difficult to survive here if you're old.'

'Yes, yes,' I murmured, taking my things from the cart. We were having a dinner party later, and I had a can of Coco Goya Coconut Cream with which we planned to make a tropical punch.

'Oh, how lovely,' the woman said, spying the can. 'You know, I teach school in the area – elementary school – and the children come from all parts of the world. The other day we had an International Day, and one of the mothers brought in all sorts of Caribbean food, which I love. Just looking at that can of coconut milk, it looks so good it makes me feel like I'm going to come.'

I leaped back. Was I hearing things? Did I have some sort of a brain tumor that made me hear sexual expressions in innocuous statements? But no, the cashier was giggling.

Had the woman meant something other than what she seemed to be saying? Maybe it was an expression she had picked up from one of the children that she didn't fully understand. Worst of all was the thought that she, in fact, knew exactly what she was saying, and I was the one so far out of touch with the times I might have landed right out of the Victorian era.

I loved this A&P across the street from where we used to live. There were always tons of really elderly people who lived in a housing complex nearby. These poor old people, people were always getting mad at them, some of them had nurses, they would take hours to count out their money, some of them couldn't see, they would ask me for help, make me find various products, compare prices, get things off the shelves, generally boss me around for ages.

You always had to wait in line for interminable periods, with everyone getting more and more irritated; for some reason something was always going wrong. Half the time I'd get home and realize the food – cheese, or milk, or tofu – was so old it was rotten.

My favorite was the time I was waiting in line and somebody behind me let out a weird yelp. I turned around and there was a very large, sleek, healthy rat, about a foot long, so close that if I had stepped back I would have stepped on it.

To my surprise I found myself letting out the same weird yelp. 'A rat, a rat,' I started to yell, involuntarily. The rat glared at me before strolling to a hole underneath the frozen food section nearby.

The Dinner Party

THERE WERE a couple of friends in town and Tim said, 'Should I see if they are free?'

I said in a surly tone, 'That's fine but if they are free we're just going to call in for food, maybe Thai.' There was a Thai restaurant over in Park Slope that would deliver this far. I normally leave the house to collect Willow at four-thirty (it takes me an hour, her school goes until five-thirty) and then it takes us between an hour and an hour and a half to get home, she has homework, sometimes two hours' worth, her dinner, a bath. There was no way I was going to cook.

Then because he had to get home early to meet with a carpenter Tim said he would pick up Willow from school. So I now had more than two extra hours free. I went to the supermarket. It's a fairly marginal supermarket, though lately it's been going, or trying to be, more upscale, which means there's a small shelf containing some organic oatmeal and boxes of tabbouleh and couscous. I thought, you know, I'll just get two chickens, and some potatoes to roast. Then I saw a box of those tiny jewel tomatoes that are actually quite good, $1.79 so I grabbed those along with some Scotch bonnet peppers, very hot, usually used in Jamaican cooking, which our supermarket carries because this neighborhood is primarily West Indian.

Ninety-nine cents for eight ounces of mushrooms that looked OK – the loose ones were $3.79 a pound, which made no sense to me since they were pretty much the same. And some asparagus (lately, unexpectedly, there has always been decent asparagus here). That would be a simple meal but perhaps a bit nicer than ordering in things.

There had been several back-and-forth conversations, from the time Tim first called, and somehow, by now, there were going to be anywhere from four to eight people coming over to dinner, that is how these things go, although the exact number was, as yet, indefinite.

When I got to the back where the meat was kept I saw a large half leg of lamb. It was on sale, $2.29 a pound, the lower half of a leg of lamb, about six pounds, fifteen dollars' worth. I decided to buy the leg of lamb. Two big chickens would have cost the same. A chicken, here, was often risky. For one thing, I was anti-Perdu. Despite the packaging and ad campaigns those birds had never tasted very good to me. But usually that was the only brand available, though sometimes there was a store brand that I had never had much luck with either. The whole birds almost always cooked up tough, or greasy, or tasteless. I thought I would decide what to do with the lamb when I got home; in the dairy section I found a packet of flour tortillas (the store didn't carry naan and I didn't care for pitta) and a big container of yoghurt. I had to get a few other items as well, not for the dinner; the bill came to $63, which was quite shocking.

I thought I would combine a couple of different recipes, one from the second volume of the Silver Palate cookbook and another from Ismail Merchant's first cookbook. I sliced up the potatoes and a bunch of onions and salted them with some sea-salt and I threw these into the bottom of a roasting pan. Then I washed and threw in the tiny jewel tomatoes and then I decided, what the hell, and I sliced and put the mushrooms in, too.

I have a food processor so I took some cloves of garlic and a big piece of peeled fresh ginger and I put them in the food processor along with a few cloves, some whole peppercorns, half the juice from a fresh lemon and three of the Scotch bonnet peppers (which I was too lazy to de-seed). The mess was so spicy that when I opened the top of the food processor I started to sneeze. So I put plastic baggies over my hands and smeared the mix on the leg of lamb, which I had washed, and put the leg on a rack which I then put on top of all the sliced potatoes and onions.

The leg of lamb still looked a little bare to me, but I had one of those pretty containers containing 'herbs de Provence' so I grabbed a big handful of that and sprinkled the bald areas on the lamb. A fair amount fell over the potatoes and onions below.

The oven was preheated to 450°. I put the roasting pan with the vegetables and the lamb on the rack in the oven. Then I decided to make some lentils, again a sort of imitation of the dhal made by Ismail Merchant and Cyrus Jhabvala. I knew probably it wasn't what they would have done, but I didn't care. I threw a little piece of chopped ginger and some garlic in a pot with olive oil and then added a chopped onion and some whole cardamon seeds – about five, green ones – and then while it was frying I added about eight whole peppercorns and five whole cloves and in my hand I dumped about a teaspoon, of garam masala, turmeric, red pepper flakes and by accident about six teaspoons of cumin.

I put this in the pot and stirred so that the spices had a chance to brown along with the onions. If I had had bay leaves I would have added a few of these, or a couple of sticks of cinnamon and sometimes I like to chop up a couple of chipotle peppers from a can and add them with a little bit of the juice.

None of this was right, exactly, and also the order was all wrong. I knew that if Jhab had been in my kitchen he would have been telling me this wasn't the way to make dhal. However, it always came out OK, not authentic, but American-Eastern-European-Indian dhal, according to me.

While this was all frying I opened and washed a bag of Goya

yellow lentils and then I added these to the pot and stirred it so that the browning spices and garlic coated the lentils and weren't getting burned.

I added a can of chicken broth (though I could have used vegetable broth, if any genuine vegetarian friends had been coming). Then the contents of a giant can of whole stewed tomatoes, one of those 32 oz. cans. It still didn't look like enough liquid to me, so I poured in a glass of water. Sometimes in Indian cooking, in a recipe book, there are requirements to use all different kinds of obscure things, which you use once and then the recipe doesn't come out right and for the next seventeen years a nearly full jar or packet of something peculiar sits in the back of the cabinet. What I like about mock-Indian cuisine is that A) I can use whatever is handy; B) I throw in quantities of things at random; C) I make sure never to invite Indian people to my faux Indian meals.

What is most amazing about the cooking of Ismail Merchant and Cyrus Jhabvala is that they can go into a kitchen, mess around for ten minutes, and leave. Two or three hours later, the announcement comes, 'The food is ready' and on giant platters the most amazing meal is delivered. I was not that kind of cook. On the other hand, this was the sort of meal I could fling together.

By now it was almost a half hour later so I turned down the oven to 400°. I let the lentils boil and turned them down to simmer and hacked off the bottoms of the asparagus, which I was just going to steam, or at least cook by throwing into an inch of boiling water and covering. I figured, let the asparagus be plain, everything else was going to be rich.

Then Willow and Tim got home and also the carpenter arrived and I had to sit with Willow while she did her homework and by the time I remembered to go in the kitchen the lentils were a little dry so I added another glass of water. They were still a tiny bit chewy, so I kept them cooking, low.

Some guests started to arrive and the lentils were done and

the lamb had been in the oven for one hour and forty minutes; in retrospect I would have cooked everything for two. I turned off the oven and then I remembered I had bought some tortillas so I wrapped them up in aluminum foil and put them in the oven, which I turned back on, only at a lower temperature, and I steamed the asparagus.

Then I tried to make everything look nice by dumping the potatoes and onions and tomatoes and mushrooms into a clear bowl and the other things in serving dishes and the lamb on a cutting board.

It was incredible-looking with a nice black crust of herbs and spices. The lentils were tender but not mushy, each had kept its form. And the roasted potatoes had gotten nicely browned and blended with the slices of soft onion and tiny tangy tomatoes.

I had done brilliantly. It was all vaguely Persian or at least mysterious; juicy and delicious with a rare garlicky, gingery scent. Tim was in charge of carving the roast – it didn't matter, because it had been cooked perfectly, but the leg of lamb wasn't really such a great cut of meat, the shank bottom end, or else it wasn't exactly the best leg of lamb because there was a lot of fat which Tim had to remove. Nevertheless, as I say, it didn't matter, the garlic and ginger cut the grease and the lambness of it.

Normally I can't taste my own cooking, it has no appeal to me, but this was wonderful, with the warm tortillas and the smooth, rich lentils and the crusty pink lamb, garlicky and spicy but not too spicy, and the potatoes and onions which, from being roasted under the lamb, had all the flavoring that the meat had. I hadn't added white wine or any liquid, I was glad of this, it hadn't needed it – I think it would have made the potatoes soggy, though the Silver Palate cookbook had suggested otherwise – and I had thought initially of mixing all the spices with yoghurt before rubbing it on the lamb, but I was glad I hadn't done this either because the dryness of the mix had made the surface of the lamb nicely charred. And there was mango chutney from a jar and some home-made cranberry sauce.

The only thing I would have done differently was use the yoghurt to make cucumber raita by chopping a lot of peeled cucumbers, adding salt, fresh black pepper and a spoonful of sugar, but there wasn't time. And for dessert I served tangerines, but it would have been nice to have some chocolates or really good cookies. One friend had brought some Francis Ford Coppola Claret, which made everyone feel like a movie star. I think, though, that I could either cook or be a hostess, but the combination of two roles in one evening is too much for me. If I could choose one of the two, I'd stay in the kitchen. But not for the clean-up.

Salad

A MAN INVITED us to dinner. We went to his apartment. We looked at his paintings for a long time. He had painted them. We looked at each painting and said different things about them. We said nothing negative about any painting. Then the man said it was time for dinner. He offered us herbal tea. We sat down at the table. It was just the three of us. The man set the table and brought out a salad. It was a fairly large green salad. He gave us each some salad and we ate it. Then he asked if we would like some more. After a while we decided to have some more salad. Then a long time passed and we said we would have a bit more salad. Then the man brought out the herbal tea.

After a while longer we realized the meal was over and we went home.

City Water

WHENEVER I take a bath or a shower I remember some-day there's not going to be any water, and what little there is will be incredibly expensive. We're just going to run out. Then I'll be one of those old people who can say, 'Back when I was young, all you had to do was turn on a spigot and there was as much water as you wanted. It wasn't considered a luxury.'

To me, it is a luxury, though. This is why the packaging for water is getting fancier and fancier. Pretty soon the packaging is going to be so fancy there'll just be a teaspoon of water in a crystal perfume-type bottle. In a little while, there'll be hardly anyone left who'll remember what it was like to have more than a sponge bath.

Like the passenger pigeons. Once there were so many passenger pigeons the sky would be blackened for an entire day as they passed over head. There were so many of them that when they landed entire forests would be destroyed, and fields of crops. Settlers used to go out and shoot them and trap them by the millions. No one ever thought they would run out of passenger pigeons. One day there were only a few passenger pigeons left. So they decided to put them in zoos and breed them. It turned out they would only breed when they were flying around in groups of millions. Five or ten passenger pigeons, put together, forget about it. They weren't going to breed. They were too lonely. Or maybe they were like people. What if you were the only woman on the planet, and there

were five or ten guys, and you looked at them and thought: I'm
not going to breed with them, these guys are all creeps.

My grandfather got to see the last passenger pigeon alive out
of all those billions, in the zoo in Cincinnati. Her name was
Martha. Sometimes I fill up the whole bathtub, and get in.
Then I think, I can't believe I'm having a whole bathtub of
water. A lot of people don't even know there was such a thing
as passenger pigeons. In some parts of India, and elsewhere in
the world, you're lucky if you live in a place where there is
running water, and it's turned on for an hour or two a day.
These people would never believe I'm sitting in an entire tub
full of water. Maybe some day, no one will believe it.

New York Wrestling Restaurant

A FRIEND INVITED me and Willow to dine at the New York Wrestling Restaurant, followed by live wrestling at Madison Square Garden. He was going to hold the event for friends with children. We wandered around Times Square for a while, trying to find the place. There was a hot dog stand and Willow said, 'I want a hot dog.' She had chosen her own outfit for the party–glittery red high-heeled shoes several sizes too large; a voluminous Chilean folk dress, given to her by her godmother; hot-pink tights with runs – and had done her own hair, in two pointy pigtails similar to horns, on top of her head.

'We'll be at the restaurant in a minute,' I said. 'You can get a hot dog there. It's dinner.' Actually I wasn't sure if they'd serve hot dogs, but they would have something she liked. At five-thirty there was a long line in front of the place, behind ropes off to one side, but I wasn't certain what they were waiting for. A man was unrolling a red carpet.

'Is this the restaurant?' I said. He pointed to the stairs. So we didn't get in the line. Maybe they were waiting in line for something else. We went down the steps and there was another long line, off to one side, waiting to go into the furthest door, but there was a whole row of doors and I opened one.

'Is this the restaurant?' I asked. There was a huge room, totally empty, though there was a gigantic floor-to-ceiling screen on which twenty-foot-tall nearly naked men were body-slamming each other around a ring.

My friend had apparently organized three large tables (I

knew they were his because each one had buckets of champagne, and party decorations) on a sort of balcony area but nobody was sitting down or had arrived. Then a girl, about nineteen years old, came with her younger brother, who was around ten. She – and the younger brother – seemed to be in a catatonic stupor. Whether they were always like this or it was the effect of the restaurant I couldn't tell.

The roar was deafening, but nobody else was in the place. Though the lines outside had been so huge no one else ever seemed to come in. Maybe the genuine wrestling fans were all being led into special cell blocks. Then the host arrived and told me not to drink the champagne from the bottle on the tale. As usual he had his own private stash of superior-quality champagne, kept elsewhere, that he always arranged for in advance, and he let me have a glass of it.

The waiter brought menus, heavy leather folders made heavier by metal insets on the front, as if because of them being made extra heavy you wouldn't want to steal them. 'I want a hot dog,' Willow said.

Nervously I perused. There were hamburgers and cheeseburgers and salads and chicken fingers. The choices went on for two pages of very tiny type, different kinds of pasta, pork chops, everything between ten and twenty dollars that a wrestling fan would probably want to eat, what you would call, I guess, American food. Finally under Children's Menu I found a hot dog and shoe-string fries. I thought for a while about getting a steak, there was a filet mignon and a strip steak, both twenty dollars, and I thought for a while about getting the vegetarian burrito, which I turned down because of the herb mayonnaise, and the chicken in a tortilla, which I also decided against, though I no longer remember why. I opted for the Buffalo-style chicken salad, a salad which was lovingly described, the bacon, the onions, the tomato, the crumbled blue cheese and blue-cheese dressing on the side, with chicken. 'Good choice,' the waiter said approvingly.

It was hard to imagine what you would really want to eat while watching big nearly naked men punch at each other.

Then some other people arrived – the host; a pop star with her son; some other couples and two little girls about nine years old; a man with his godson, who was about ten; a newspaper reporter with his son, who was nine.

The little boy who had come with his nineteen-year-old blonde sister was shouting, 'I want the lobster!' At the other table the host was saying that everyone could order whatever they wanted. 'I want caviar,' one of the little girls screamed.

While we were waiting the waiters kept bringing around platters of chicken pieces and dipping sauce. Some chicken pieces were fried and covered in orange sauce; others were boneless and fried. You could cover them with two different kinds of sauce, one yellow and one white. There were also shrimps stuck on skewers on a pineapple. When you tried to pull a skewer from the pineapple the whole pineapple came with it. 'Why are the shrimp stuck in a pineapple?' Willow yelled before jumping up to sit, uninvited, on various laps. The waiter brought over a plate of chicken wrapped in tortillas and cut up, though it might have been something else, and then a huge plate of raw meat he said was steak tartare, which really was the last thing I wanted to eat while on-screen men, oil-slicked, gnawed each other's legs. The huge torsos rutted like beached sea elephants in mating season.

I lured Willow back to the table just as her hot dog arrived. It was the saddest, baldest hot dog I had ever seen, on a plate with white French fries. The nineteen-year-old had ordered the cheeseburger, which was also quite bleak. Two tiny cheeseburgers, again with those white French fries, only the cheese on the two burgers had not been melted. It was just two slices of hard cheese. But for some reason the man opposite had one large cheeseburger and the white fries and his cheese was melted, though it did not look any more appetizing. 'Isn't the cheese on a cheeseburger supposed to be melted?' I asked the bored girl.

'I know,' she said.

My salad was a large platter of shredded iceberg lettuce, two triangles of pale tomato, some chunks of onion, a few crumbs of bacon, a tureen of what appeared to be white glue but was in fact the dressing, and a gigantic slab of breaded and fried chicken meat in orange.

The little boy who had wanted the lobster got, instead, a giant slab of ribs, or at least what appeared to be small brown ribs, hundreds of them, covered in brown sauce, served with white French fries.

Willow had almost finished her hot dog and was now harassing the pop star's son, who wore an earring and was not unfriendly. 'Willow, if you had some steamed broccoli I would let you get an ice cream sundae, or some cake,' I said.

'But I don't want an ice cream sundae or cake.'

'Have some steamed broccoli anyway,' I snarled politely. The poor waiter in the middle of this din and racket, the naked men flinging each other around and the screaming announcer on the taped video coming from some New Jersey match, and my daughter who kept leaping up to fling herself on men's laps, and tripping the waiter with his huge troughs of teeny greasy chicken tid-bits. It was as American as you could get; especially with the Moët and Chandon champagne. I couldn't help but enjoy myself. The only thing that would have made me happier would have been to bring a group of cloistered nuns to dine here, or at least a foreigner from a pure, remote region of laughing, singing shepherds.

They let other children in the restaurant up to the balcony to get the signature of the pop star, though it was obvious the kids didn't know who she was and had been sent by their parents. The pop star, now surrounded by pigtailed little girl wrestling fans, looked as if, momentarily, she was going to be devoured à la *Suddenly Last Summer*, that movie where the street kids ended up cannibalizing someone, I forget who.

Then a huge practically uncooked head of broccoli arrived –

everything was inedible, but speedy – and naturally Willow
didn't want it, or couldn't eat it – and a man on the other side
of the table reached for it and said, 'Thanks for the broccoli.'

In this restaurant a steamed vegetable did not seem out of
place, it merely seemed as if someone's mother was trying to
get a kid to eat – or at least look at – a vegetable. I thought for a
minute they probably had them back there in the kitchen for
use as scientific displays for people who came from certain
regions of New Jersey or Long Island, something special you
might see on a night out on the town in Manhattan.

The surprise lay in that it was undercooked, rather than
overcooked. 'If you eat it, you can have ice cream,' I told the
man. He looked slightly pleased, maybe at being ordered to eat
his vegetable in a wrestling-themed restaurant.

Then a giant wrestler arrived, part of the festivities, with a
woman who might have been a wrestler, only I couldn't tell if
she was a wrestler or one of those women who were in the ring,
sometimes, to aid with the increase in testosterone level.

'Where's the celebrities?' said the wrestler.

'Yeah, where's the VIPs?' said the woman. They stood for a
moment alongside the wall, surrounded by four or five men.
Suddenly the wrestler noticed Willow. He seemed to be on
another planet, maybe because he was so much taller and
bigger than other people, and he slowly bent over and, unexpectedly, picked her up from her chair. Then he held he close
to his face. 'Do you know how beautiful you are?' he said to
her in a booming yet seductive voice. 'Has anyone ever told
you how beautiful you are?'

Willow looked suspicious. I hoped she wasn't going to hurt
him. He was supposed to wrestle, later on. The week before
she had head-butted me, and though it was an accident the soft
cartilage of my nose had been shoved into my brain pan with
such force I was doubled over in pain for several hours. Then
there was that fellow in the elevator who got off on the wrong
floor after that blow to the groin.

The wrestler finally put her down, it seemed to me reluctantly. Willow was still staring at him like he was nuts.

A few minutes later the wrestler – and the woman, who turned out to be a woman wrestler – was called over to one corner of the balcony and the host announced that the children could go now to get their books signed (the kids at the party had all gotten gift bags containing a book of poetry in cartoon form about wrestling; a T-shirt; and a baseball hat) and have their picture taken. All the kids – around ten or twelve of them – ran over. 'Go with them, Willow,' I said. 'You can have your book autographed. It will be your first book signed by an author.'

I didn't think the two had written the book, but I wasn't sure it mattered. She was so tiny that she disappeared in the crush. The kids – and their parents – had their pictures taken with the man and the woman, and then the host yelled for me to come up and get my picture taken with Willow and the two wrestling celebrities. I squeezed through the tables. The man was holding up Willow. 'Do you know you're beautiful?' he was saying lovingly. Fortunately it was time to leave.

Limousines courtesy of the New York Wrestling Restaurant took us to Madison Square Garden. They were huge limousines. In ours the TV blared some game show and one nine-year-old was pretty quick with some difficult answers. The journey from 43rd to 33rd seemed to take many hours. The pop star put on her sunglasses and bolted from the car with her son, perhaps hoping to rescue him from my daughter. The rest of us trudged up many flights of stairs.

We didn't last long after we had found our seats, though, way at the top and to one end. My daughter wasn't really a wrestling fan, more at the age, or stage, when she would have appreciated Barbie on Ice. After some loud firecrackers were set off to announce the arrival of a bad guy – or a good guy – I decided we should go home, even though we were going to miss seeing the wrestler whom Willow had left unscathed. The host asked if he could have our ticket stubs back.

It wasn't until we were past the sign that said 'No Return Entrance' that Willow announced she had to go to the toilet. I asked the guard at the gate for the location. We couldn't go back in, he said, but if we made a right and went down one level, into Penn Station, we would find one. I was a little queasy from all the champagne and dipping sauces. We were bundled in our winter coats, I was carrying a bag with the gifts from the party and Willow's security blanket and stuffed toys and fake-fur scarf, along with her knapsack containing her homework and school books. I saw an elevator to the right. It was marked 'Handicapped' but two non-handicapped people were getting on, and so we followed.

'No,' said the elevator operator. 'You can't come in. Where are you going?'

'The security guard said to go down one level to find the toilet for her.'

'Where are your tickets?'

'Upstairs,' I said. 'We were leaving. I left my tickets.' It dawned on me that this elevator was not going to the main level of Penn Station but carried people to some backstage wrestling area, for wrestlers, or for Very Important Wrestling Fans. The woman passenger smirked at me as if I was a wrestling groupie, who traveled with a kid and pretended the child needed a toilet in order to crash backstage areas and in that fashion pick up wrestlers, only she knew what I was really up to.

'Where are your tickets?' he asked the other couple. The man showed the elevator operator two tickets.

'You have to leave,' the elevator operator told us.

'Nice try,' the woman cackled triumphantly as the elevator doors began to shut, leaving them in and us on the wrong side. 'Nice try. Ha!' Wearily into the night we began to trudge descending into the maw of the train station in search of a public toilet; still the hollow echo remained alongside. '*Nice, nice try!*'

An Evening at the Very Fine Pierre Hotel

I THOUGHT IT would be extremely interesting to attend the salute to Chita Rivera, a gala evening for the Drama League Guild which was to be a black-tie dinner event at the Pierre Hotel. I wasn't exactly sure what the Drama League Guild was but I imagined the members would include rather grand figures in the New York theater world, among them Jed Harris, Lucille Lortel, Bob Fosse, Laurette Taylor, the Lunts, Flo Ziegfeld and so forth.

I felt good about myself that night: I had on a flesh-colored dress with matching coat, from Shaw's of Roslyn, beautifully made with a knee-length chiffon flowing skirt, the top part of a heavier material perfectly draped with lead weights, and a matching belt with a diamond buckle that snapped open at inappropriate moments; the long coat of the same color had matching diamond buttons at the cuffs.

And I wore my hair up in a mushroom formation which I believed to be highly effective, although I wasn't certain what effect I was aiming for, exactly.

The Pierre is a serious place with mirrors and thick carpeting and vitrines displaying red kidskin slippers studded with beads and ladies' resort wear if you were going to go back to Atlanta, things like a beige jacket with no lapels to be worn with a large rhinestone pin in the shape of a butterfly.

It was fun to watch the men and women arrive, the women dressed in huge voluminous skirts and fitted tops, in shimmery taffeta, blond hair neatly coiffed – it was a bit like going to another city in the US, maybe a gala charity event in Lexington or Louisville, Kentucky, where people were still members of a country club although none of the people I mentioned was visible and to be honest none of them looked like theater people at all, but maybe doctors and doctors' wives who had all paid around ten grand for a table.

Then my husband arrived who looked very handsome in a tailor-made suit, made by his tailor David Mason with the pinstripes *going the wrong way*. It was very daring, and it was good that both of us were so daring otherwise neither of us would have dared to be with the other.

The drinks reception was held upstairs but for white wine there was only Chardonnay, with which I have a problem, in that I won't drink it, and so I opted for a Bloody Mary; after my recent anti-hors-d'oeuvres tirade I was somewhat relieved that no hors d'oeuvres were being served, only that on little tables around the sides of the conference or convention hall held bowls containing 1) mixed nuts, 2) large blanched salted almonds, and 3) potato chips.

I found this unusual, although I very much admired the daring of serving two varieties of nuts. Normally, even if there are no hors d'oeuvres served by waiters there is the customary large display of vegetables such as broccoli, carrots, and radishes, along with a rather liquidy unidentifiable dip.

For me the potato chip is one of the world's most perfect food products. One year, however, I cancelled my subscription to *Consumer Reports* after they did a report on potato chips and told the reader which was the best. I felt, truly, that Consumer Report had no business comparing and contrasting the varieties of potato chips. I think the result was something like Pringles being given the top vote, on the basis of freshness and cost, but to my mind Pringles is not a potato chip, it is a potato food-thing. Maybe that was not their choice, but to me the potato chip has always been a matter of personal taste and I would not be told which to buy.

If a person really likes a sour-cream and onion-flavored potato chip, or barbeque flavor, that is his or her problem, or they have inferior tastebuds, far be it for me to dictate.

The American potato chip is not the best in the world, though I have always been fond of Ruffles and Cape Cod has also been mentioned as being highly rated; but the American potato is not so flavorful, at least not the ones used in chips; the oil is not the most flavorful, many times one might simply be munching on highly caloric deep-fried construction paper covered with salt.

Each potato chip has ten calories. Basic rules of mathematics would suggest that ten potato chips will equal a hundred calories in a matter of approximately seven to nine seconds.

I like the idea of those potato chips made with indigestible Olestra (possible side effect: diarrhea) but in fact I don't think those are much less caloric and they don't taste right, really. I have found some of the world's best potato chips in England and even the flavors there seem interesting – salt and vinegar, lime chili – or those small packets of chips (crisps, to citizens of UK) containing, separately, a little parcel of salt; in addition, there one might also find chips that are thick-cut, or with the skins left on, and among them I would rate, internationally supreme, the premium Kettle Chips, which I believe is an American company out of the West coast and if I have found that brand here it doesn't taste the same as over there.

Finally, I would also rate the potato chips of India, again not simply for the quality of the potatoes, of which I'm uncertain, but rather for the interesting and pungent seasonings available, things that don't sound good (tomato ketchup potato chip, for example) but in fact do taste great.

At last it was time to shuffle into the other hall or ballroom for dinner.

For the second time in a week an event occurred which the other diners found upsetting. The first course was already on the table. A few days before it had been at a L'eggs Pantyhose luncheon, hosted by Vanessa Williams, who I much admire, in a corporate dining facility on the 35th floor of a Park Avenue building.

Here the first course was a salad inside a crisp tortilla-like object: roast vegetables and greens. Since the guests arrived at different times, everybody began eating randomly. And now, at the Pierre, the first course was a thin plate-shaped-and-sized piece of salmon; four toast points; and a rather pretty arrangement of teaspoon-sized dollops of capers, pink roe, egg yolk and a couple of other things which I couldn't see because a) it was too dark and b) it was time to get fresh contact lenses.

There was also a lovely lemon half in his or her own gauze bag, tied in a flounce at the top, which I initially thought was a beggar's purse or dumpling of some sort. There wasn't anybody else at our table, however, so nobody besides my husband would have noticed, had I eaten it, but I didn't. We weren't even really expecting anyone else to join us at our table, either. That is because for many years we would go to some benefit or charity dinner and though the room would be full there was never anyone else sitting at our table. We had dined out alone at tables for ten more times than we could count. Sometimes even others came, sat down at their assigned table (ours) and then left. But by now we were used to it.

In any event, having the first course on the table seemed to me to be a new trend *in this country* but it is commonplace in Russia and even in Russian restaurants here – if you have a reservation for, say, ten people at eight o'clock, when you get to the restaurant the first course of many appetizers and hors d'oeuvres will already be out on the table.

Sometimes this is frightening, as if the food has been sitting there all day, or as if the table was hoping to lure some guests. Sometimes it is all even covered in plastic. But that is simply the style and eventually one comes to understand they want you to feel welcome, and expected. So now this custom appears to be befalling the city.

Then some others came and joined us. They were all young people, in their twenties, who might have been from an F. Scott Fitzgerald novel if he was writing today, clean and glossy rich-appearing youth: a theater producer attempting to get a rock-opera off the ground, who 'already has 70 per cent of the backers'; a publicist for a jeweler; a woman on a magazine and a Princeton type who claimed to be a hypnotist (shortly, however, he was made to leave because he wasn't meant to be there – or here – and he was replaced by a newspaper reporter). Nobody seemed to have much connection to the theater, apart from the faintly suspicious young producer. But I liked him because I told him I was a dog-groomer and he didn't flinch but asked intelligent questions until I pointed out that I was a messy person who couldn't groom.

The next course was a large piece of meat, possibly filet mignon, in a brown sauce, accompanied by a tomato stuffed with something green and another thing, stuffed with other things, and three small puffy potatoes which were not stuffed with anything.

The problem was, it was good food for a gala dinner. Sometimes or usually at a gala dinner the food is either a) chicken in white sauce or b) salmon. But even though it was good food for a gala dinner, it was still not food I wanted to eat. How can anybody serve food simultaneously to several thousand people? Only by preparing all the food in advance and then keeping it warm, which to me always gives the food a kind of dead taste – as if it's been on a steam tray, or microwaved.

And the dessert was a pyramid of crispy pastry stuffed with flavored cream and accompanied by six pink halves of what might have been strawberries. Then came the homage or salute or tribute to Chita Rivera. We didn't stay for the whole thing, but the parts I saw were 1) Elaine Stritch singing with Russell Knight, and 2) a group of young men doing a strip act, which amused me. There were simply loads of in-jokes and remarks which I didn't get because they were all regarding the career of Chita Rivera, which remains a mystery to me.

I didn't really have a clue as to what was going on or why I was there, which I could pretty much say about my whole life.

But it did make me think about what I would serve if I was hosting a dinner for one thousand. Some dishes don't mind the abuse of being reheated. Lasagna never seems to mind, although it is not fashionable, although for a time at Barocco they served a kind of lasagna that was very flat, solid and square, more like a little firm lasagna cake than a big oozing ricotta-and-mozzarella-with-spaghetti-sauce explosion.

Indian food often does not mind being reheated. Or I suppose one might serve little individual chicken pot pies, with crusts made of phyllo dough and interiors filled not with a cream sauce but with a reduction of butter, flour, broth and sherry (I know there's a name for this, but I don't know what). But the rule is always, chicken or meat and/or fish *without any flavor in case someone is allergic to garlic.* (Or in case one person is allergic to peanuts, pepper, onion, shrimp paste, ginger – by the time the chef has ruled out the things one person in the thousand might be allergic to, he or she is left with nothing.)

So, I think, by trying not to offend anyone out of the one thousand people, here I am, offended by the fact that my night out becomes an airline-cuisine experience. But I still would like to try the real restaurant, in the hotel lobby, with the thick rugs and little sofas and ceiling painted like the sky, and only the two of us at our table on purpose, so I could pretend to see Vivien Leigh and Cole Porter cross the room on their way to meet Tennessee Williams. And Leonard Bernstein.

The Black Hole in the Donut

N EW YORK IS represented by the bagel, not the donut and for a time it seemed that the donut, that heavyweight fried cake, would disappear from the city altogether; it was, somehow, never destined for total extinction but rather had become a faintly Midwestern or rural farm product – a nostalgic American antique that made one think of, I dunno, country fairs or Rodgers and Hart tunes. It was not sophisticated or even quite kitsch.

In the city there were no longer many cheap diners with counters where one would consume a cup of bad coffee and munch a donut alongside a flatfooted policeman – it was all Starbucks, cappuccino and espresso. A sophisticated cup of coffee requires at best perhaps a muffin or biscotti. There were still, to be sure, the occasional Dunkin' Donuts but these in the city seemed anachronistic, out of place.

In any event, a donut had and has more than four hundred calories.

For the majority of women, at least women I know, at least for New York City women, this would be something around half of their daily caloric intake.

But they were never completely slaughtered and around four or five years ago, thanks to careful conservation and the reintroduction of new breeds, the restoration and renovation of frying vats, the donut began to return to its former city habitations.

Krispy Kreme (such a hateful name! Not just the 'k' used in

place of a 'c' but how can cream be crispy?*) had a great deal to do with donut preservation.† The advent of these stores brought new attention to the species. And on the way to my daughter's school a year and a half ago on Brand Street a sign went up announcing the arrival of 'The Donut Plant', a small store that eventually opened one year ago; shortly thereafter a second sign went up announcing 'as seen on Martha Stewart'. I admire Martha a great deal but this news made me uneasy.

I devoted some time and energy to collecting samples of donuts from the Donut Plant, Krispy Kreme, Gourmet Garage (many donut devotees rate these highly), Dunkin' Donuts and, in a rare bit of luck, the miniature donuts of Cuzin's Duzin, as well as the store-carried brands – Hostess and Entemann's.

The comparison taste-testing frightened me, however. For one thing, its seems to me that taste in food must by nature remain highly personal. I once met one of the vegetarian daughters of Linda McCartney who told me that her favorite food was mayonnaise sandwiches. One has only to think of the cookbook of Elvis Presley's favorite cuisine, with its recipe for Fool's Gold Loaf ('spread the butter generously over all sides of the loaf . . . meanwhile, fry the bacon . . . fill the loaf with peanut butter and jelly . . .') to know and understand that Elvis, like me, would not wish to eat eels.

I don't care how you prepare them, white baby eels in garlic and olive oil, large eels in Japanese broth with soba noodles, conger eels in the *style anglaise*, I don't really give a damn what you do to an eel, I don't like the taste, I don't like the texture,

---

* Then there is also the age-old scholarly debate on the spelling of the word 'donut' – or 'doughnut' – itself.

† According to *The Life and Cuisine of Elvis Presley*, by David Adler (Crown Publishers 1993), Krispy Kreme Donuts, a favorite of Elvis's, have 'a special ingredient that accounts for their crispiness: they're made from potato flour' and the Krispy Kreme corporation 'prides itself on how healthful its doughnuts are'. Apparently The Donut Plant is not alone in its need to advertise its product as healthful.

therefore, what sort of food critic could I ever be? On the other hand, let's say Joe Food Critic tells you that the eels prepared one way or a certain way or at a particular restaurant are really the best, but you, as an eel lover, taste those eels and disagree – neither you or Joe is right or wrong, it's just a difference in likes and dislikes.

I'll say right now, I would put ketchup on my scrambled eggs.

My husband would put ketchup on macaroni-and-cheese. How can I teach him he is wrong?

And in reading a review of a restaurant how does the reader know whether or not the reviewer likes Marmite? And if one did know, why would one ever ever trust his or her opinion?

I remember once I went out with a very famous restaurant reviewer at the *New York Times*; this job was fascinating, it was many years ago and the reviewer was obliged to dine out practically every night of the week and find friends to go with him. It was a massively difficult job – oh, not at first, perhaps but night after night, eating and eating and eating – every single night he had to have more food! – and he took me and several others to an Indian restaurant where the food was not terrible, just bad, and later he gave the restaurant a glowing review.

On the other hand while the restaurant didn't justify a glowing review the people seemed so nice there, how terrible to be in the position to put a restaurant out of business or discourage people from coming there and the owner's livelihood and staff's jobs at stake, while for the reviewer it was just another night out.

Anyway, I recruited a bunch of friends and acquaintances to write down comments regarding donuts. I didn't feel worthy of carrying the whole assessment alone. I spent the day rounding up the donuts. In the Fulton Mall in Brooklyn, in a food court in the basement, the Cuzin's Duzin (I had noticed the sign on the front of the mall earlier) proved to be a small stand selling cookies, pizza and fruit drinks, and a tiny greasy machine filled with deep deep wells of stale-looking dirty grease. How delightful.

This enabled me to have a Proustian flashback of the madeleine-and-lime-tea variety. Years ago as a student in England, on the old Victorian piers in Brighton, half collapsing into the gray sea (the piers, not me) with fortune-tellers and antique machines where one could bet a penny on a toy racing greyhound or buy a souvenir Brighton mug I came upon an ancient donut machine.

Here, for five pence deposited into a slot one could watch the first automaton of fast food – a terrible metal claw would slowly descend, clutch a handful of dough from a vat and deposit it in a huge trough of bubbling grease. Slowly, slowly, the ball of dough would chug along through various Rube Goldberg waterfalls of boiling fat, into blackened tunnels, turned by sluggish, filthy watermill blades, descend a chute and at last be thrown by another craven metal hand into a drainage tray where a shower of powdery sugar would snow atop it and at last the tray crankily raised itself and the donut – burning hot, sugary, delicious, crusty on the outside and fluffy within, would come spurting out through a trap door.

The hot sugary donut, the cold gray salt air, the tang of the real grease – it was a donut as a donut was meant to be, as good as a hot potato for a kid, roasted over an open fire when the kid is really hungry. It was a donut that for ever spoiled me for all others.

But the machine at Cuzin's wasn't working, or at least I was told it wouldn't be working for fifteen minutes. They only made tiny donuts, nine for one dollar, twenty for two. I spent a half-hour wandering around the mall. It was the grimmest, bleakest mall I have ever been in. I loved it more than any place. Everything plastic, cheap, artificial, not so cheap but awful. The music, the noise, it was all the aura of a biosphere on Mars inhabited by exiled Americans who had been there for generations, inbred. All the stuff junky, imitations of reproductions. The crowds milled aimlessly, no one seemingly over twenty, Indian, West Indian, African American, Muslim families with women and little girls with covered heads; gangs of adolescent boys in puffy down coats or black leather with insanely baggy jeans, sparks of testosterone and aggression flying as they roamed the circular halls.

The cacophony, the epileptically flickering lights; it was far worse than any brave new world of Huxley or futuristic vision by Orwell. It would have been a million times worse than their worst nightmares. And though when I returned the filthy donut machine was working and the tiny donuts slowly chugged along in their own personal hell, there was something about these donuts (shaken, in groups, in waxed paper bags with confectioner's sugar or cinnamon) that did not satisfy, not in the way my Brighton donut had. No, these were greasy and soggy without being . . . well, real. They were one step closer to a real donut – but just a step.

On the other hand it had a sort of hard skin on it which the donuts of the Donut Plant did not. And to my mind the donut should be slightly crusty on the outside and cakelike within. Nor should the donut care about whether or not it is made with pure spring water (as the Donut Plant proudly announces) and pure vegetable oil. Nor should the donut be ginger-flavored, or pistachio, again available at the Donut Plant. On the other hand the donut should not be covered with pink frosting (Dunkin' Donuts). But that was just my taste; maybe for somebody else they want a pink, ginger-flavored donut covered with peanuts and made from pure water and which comes in a box from the supermarket and who am I to judge?

I decided to abandon the whole project, because I don't even remember the donuts from the Gourmet Garage and Krispy Kreme, and all the guests looking in disbelief at the rows and trays of hideous donuts and being forced to write down comments and the whole thing was just a disaster and I never want to think about a donut again as long as I live.

I failed in the attempt to compare and contrast donut species of New York City.

One thing about a donut, you eat one, you've made a commitment. It stays in your stomach, like a rubber tire, for days, as it settles in the dump, disgorging upward from time to time decaying grease and sugar fumes, the sour reek of pudgy dough . . . lunchtime passes, then dinner, far into the evening donut reminds you of its weight, its substance, and girth – the indigestible ingredients that compose its DNA.

Donut does not believe in the big bang theory. Donut should have been a great auk, a moa, a ponderous dodo bird; but donut is not extinct. You cannot, you will not forget your donut; it is devoted, so devoted, to having a long-term relationship with you.

Hors d'Oeuvres

O N ONE OF the news programs on TV a reporter said that New Yorkers will attend an average of two parties over the holiday season, but I don't see how that's possible unless she meant two parties a night. Since well before Thanksgiving the mail has been stuffed with invites, mostly for things we will never attend, maybe a party to celebrate the publication of a photographer's book of pictures of fashion models (which commences at ten at night), or the one-year anniversary of a restaurant in an area of midtown Manhattan from 6 to 8, which I could not only not reach in time but, if I did, I wouldn't know anyone there and would stand in a corner wondering why I had come to a restaurant's one-year anniversary.

Nevertheless, excluding 99 per cent of the events during this holiday season still leaves many, many parties that I must, should or want to go to, and in addition keeps me in touch with the bizarre world of hors d'oeuvres. On the television show the reporter explained that for those attending the festive events, hors d'oeuvres contain many calories. The statistic that continues to haunt me is the pig-in-a-blanket, 475 calories. Fortunately this obviously once-popular treat is served but rarely, or perhaps never, at the Four Seasons where I attended a business cocktail event determined to make an authentic study of the hors d'oeuvres.

What is with these nasty little things? Try as I may, I have a mental block each time I try to spell it. You are holding a drink, talking to someone, and suddenly there is a waiter standing between you holding a tray of some repugnant artifact. Out of nervousness, or politeness, one reaches involuntarily for the bit of, say, raw fish on toast, which the waiter introduces to you as tuna tartare. Now you have a drink in one hand, a napkin in the other, and a mouthful of rank raw fish, and are still trying to communicate, feebly, cocktail-party-style, when a third party comes over to introduce him or herself. Transferring drink to the greasy fish hand, you reach out to shake hands and speak, all the while trying to swallow and breathing a foul fish whiff-cloud of the raw tuna, or, worse, the cold dollop of caviar, while the boggy ball of old boiled potato on which the deposit of caviar was initially laid to rest plummets down your gullet.

The next time the waiter comes around, you do your best to avoid him but no, accidentally, it happens again, your hand of its own accord has shot out and reached for, I don't know, something that's been announced as 'coconut shrimp' or 'chicken saté' and this time you're left with a mouthful of soupy peanut butter and a pointed wooden skewer you have to do your best to shove back into some old lemon half or pineapple before the waiter runs off leaving you with a dangerous and dripping weapon.

And the worst of all is that, after hundreds of these mean entities you have consumed thousands of calories and are still hungry and hoping for dinner – the endless mouthfuls (which even if initially warm are always, by your part of the room, ice-cold) have done nothing to quell or diminish the hunger pangs and have now gone to war, deranged, in your stomach, the Crab Egg-Roll and the Spinach-and-Feta Spanikopida battling the Foie-Gras-and-Crème-Fraiche in some kind of global cuisine nuclear stomach war.

Apart from an airport one would be hard pressed nowadays to think of a current construction project that permits as much space as the Four Seasons. The layout of the place is oddly reversed (one checks one's coat on entering, then goes *up* the free-floating staircase straight into the restaurant). Though the upstairs space is grand, one cannot make a grand entrance; one pops up into the room like one of those goby fish in a public aquarium. The massive room, several stories high, with the dangerously dagger-like glass chandelier above the bar, is familiar and comforting, as if one is a global citizen attending the World's Fair of 1964.

The design must be forty years old by now, but so worthy there is none of that nostalgia associated with it in the way that, say, an art-deco restaurant or even an inferior 'modern' piece of architecture might have.

In my mind it's always remained firmly a place to have lunch. The lunches I've eaten there have been exquisite and there's a sense that whoever is dining there is powerful, an important business venture is about to be launched. On occasion when I've had dinner, the room is oddly without energy and, for some reason, the food hasn't tasted quite as good – there's more of the idea, for me, of first-class tourists traveling on the SS *France* when the Beautiful People have long since taken to jet flight. At dinner the wheeler-dealers have fled, the air sags slightly with fatigue.

Yet on this night the air, the atmosphere, the restaurant, has pulled itself out of its nightly torpor, it's got the same fervor as at lunch, only more glittery; the chandelier, that stalactite nest of icycle crystal spikes, the bubbling fountain, the great sheets of glass windows – upstairs a little jazz combo belts raucous sacky strains – if only the crowd was not quite so dismal in black, it seems a little sad, as always, the men are sharp in charcoal suits but why do women have to be wearing sack-cloth or the equivalent of djellabahs? I suppose it's easier, knowing that whatever part of town you go to you'll fit in if you wear black, but in that case why bother with fashion at all? Why is there so much emphasis on it in this town, when at an event it's only pale faces above a sea of darkness?

I'm already uneasy as I approach a table where two men

stand behind trays of little neck clams and oysters on the half-shell, pink and white curls of huge shrimp, and a giant bowl of lobster meat. I just can't muster the interest in collecting a plate of seafood – even though it's possible to take the plate and sit at one of the empty banquettes. To indulge in an occasional raw oyster, for me, would be something best performed as a solitary act in the privacy of my own home. Who would want to put this ungainly object in one's mouth in public?

Yet there's something rather jolly about seeing them – oh, oysters, come and walk with us! – lined up on their half-shells, something Christmassy, and English, and American – they would have been found a hundred years ago, at Sherry's or Delmonico's, being wolfed down by 'Diamond' Jim Brady. And yet, really, it makes me wonder at what point Japanese and American cuisine took such different paths – like the moment of separation on some evolutionary tree of two separate species, with raw oysters in common.

At last I point to the heap of lobster meat. Really, I adore lobster, it's just that . . . I don't want to be sitting here nervously chewing away on the white and pink chunks. It's not that I'm not hungry, either; it's just that it's not possible to enjoy or participate in two activities at the same time. Am I alone in feeling eating is basically a solitary pleasure? Like an animal who's got a bone, I want to be able to gnaw alone in the private safety of a cave.

Meanwhile, the waiters and waitressess are circulating: wild mushrooms on toast (a quick mouthful and the overwhelming taste of soft, moldy forest floor); tuna tartare (canned catfood, maybe?); bruschetta (oily bread without taste, tiny cubes of tasteless vinegary tomato); tempura vegetables (cauliflower, broccoli, red peppers, zucchini – soft, bland vegetables in soggy batter); caviar in potato boat crusts; smoked salmon on pumpernickle toast points, and – oh no! – sautéed chicken on skewers with peanut sauce (maybe somewhere, somehow, someone's got this right. But I don't know when it turned into something American, like peanut butter and jelly, some kind of Elvis Presley dish, peanut butter and chicken – surely what it's become isn't right?).

The regatta of hors d'oeuvres sails past, modern, proud, fashionable (gone are their companions of yore, the stuffed celery, the deviled egg halves of the '60s, the chicken-liver-bacon-water-chestnut rumaki of the '70s, the cheese straws of the '80s long exiled to some distant shore).

It's not the food. I don't want to be mean, I adore the Four Seasons. It's me. It's the lack of thinking time between mouthfuls one cannot savor because one's too busy shaking hands, or worrying why one's not. I know it's my problem: if I could eat it at home, in bed, on a tray, the mouthfuls of sponge or spores from the ocean floor would be worth mulling over, I wouldn't feel I was getting hit in the face with some wet fish. I would be happy. Here? It's sensory overload, too much to deal with. If I'm going to have a plump raw oyster, please don't make me do it in public. I don't want to be the walrus or the carpenter. I want to eat hors d'oeuvres alone.

Bar and Grill

IN THE morning I woke next to a huge signed cookbook called *Alfred Portale's 12 Seasons*, a card saying 'Gotham Bar and Grill, Adrian Gjonbalaj, Manager' and a diagram of a vagina with arrows pointing to various parts with notations such as 'stainless steel labia majora', 'raised copper clit' and 'perforated steel labia minora'. Another note said, in scribbled handwriting, that the vagina tables were in a restaurant called NV, which had been designed by Paul Carroll.

Apparently I had been out to dinner the night before. When I went into the kitchen for a cup of coffee I saw that the refrigerator was stacked with seemingly dozens of take-out containers, filled with melted ice cream, tiny cookies, a large oozing piece of chocolate mousse cake, a steak, a salad, and so forth.

My downfall had commenced on my way to a cocktail event at the Sky Club, located on the fifty-sixth floor of a building on Forty-fifth Street at Park Avenue. It was one of those strange crispy gray spring days in Manhattan. On my way through Grand Central Station at rush hour everyone seemed so busy, a symphony of scuttling commuters going in a thousand different directions, none of whom crashed into each other. And on the street was the smell of upper East Side grilled food; people on their way home from work were popping into bars for a drink, as if they were escaped inhabitants of John Cheever's stories.

Everyone looked busy and grown-up, and in a hurry, as if they knew where they were going. I suddenly had a flashback to twenty years ago when I first moved to the city and didn't know anyone and I thought everyone knew people and they all lived in fancy apartments in high-rises and I was alone in this place of rich and sophisticated people. And everything frightened me.

Only now it was twenty years later and I was on my way to a cocktail party for the YMCA in the Sky Club; once this thought would have terrified me. I would have been shaking with excitement that I, TJ, alone, wrongly, badly dressed, pimpled, too scared to talk to anyone, was attending an event that was the epitome of glamor.

Of course, then I never got to do such things. Now that I did, I was not only not nervous, I didn't even care. And in a way I missed that trembling, idiotic, excited self.

Nevertheless, the Sky Club was very impressive, to be up on the fifty-sixth floor, with a lavish buffet of roast beef sliced to order and smoked salmon and grilled eggplant and steamed asparagus and shrimp and raw oysters, and a view of all of Manhattan spread like thick butter in a Gershwin rhapsody across the floor-to-ceiling windowpanes.

When I heard that my friend wouldn't be at this event and probably not at dinner, either, I thought I would just make a feast here and go home, even though it had taken all my strength to leave my kid – she had regressed, this week, and was once again sobbing that I was going to leave her with a baby-sitter, and even though I knew by the time the elevator arrived at my apartment she would have stopped crying and calmed down and started to have fun, my evening was totally wrecked at the trauma of abandoning the sobbing waif. So I was just as happy to quietly munch vast quantities of ratatouille and roast beef and head back to Brooklyn.

Then my friend did arrive, and since he had made the effort to get out of his bed (he had just had a minor operation) I couldn't really bail out and not go to the dinner at Gotham Bar and Grill.

There were two beautiful twins, identical, who were going to accompany us as well, and another tall girl, very beautiful; the twins' husbands were going to meet us at the restaurant, and another man, whose birthday it was, was meeting us outside the lobby in a car.

The twins were stunning: tall, slim, with shiny black hair. I had been quite friendly with one twin, years ago, and we had had many long and pleasant chats, then one night I saw her and I said hello enthusiastically and she responded by ignoring me. It wasn't until six months later I found out the girl with whom I had been friends had a twin, and that it was the twin who had ignored me; even so, it took me a long time to forgive the girl, I never quite trusted her after that, even though it wasn't her fault.

The Gotham Bar and Grill had been around for twelve years but I had never eaten there. I liked the look of the place. A long room, with high ceilings and big puffy light fixtures, it was bright enough to see and there was no loud music playing and the noise level was low, even though the place was packed; obviously if you could see and hear, that meant the restaurant wasn't super-fashionable but the sort of place I could eat at, a restaurant for grown-ups and it looked like the kind of place you could bring your parents, if they wanted to take you out and feel they were getting to see a part of the city.

Then the menus arrived and I realized there was no way I was going to eat. I had eaten already, what would I do with ricotta ravioli in braised oxtail broth, celery root and reggiano parmesan, $16, sweet prawn and baby artichoke risotto with prosciutto di parma, lemon and chervil butter, $21, warm asparagus soup with morel mushroom and white truffle custard, crème fraiche and chervil, $15.50.

And these were only a few of the appetizers. These were all appetizers for hungry people, if you weren't hungry they simply couldn't or wouldn't appeal.

Years ago on a weekly or twice weekly basis I used to go out

with Andy Warhol and Paige Powell and we would have
dinner (the 'Blind Date Club') and Andy and Paige didn't
eat, and I would start drinking out of nervousness and by the
time the food came at nine or ten o'clock or later I was totally
smashed, and then it turned out that Andy and Paige had eaten
before we went out.

But it would never have occurred to me to eat first, because
we were dining, after all, in some of New York's finest
restaurants. The point for them was, which I now understood,
if you were going to be around people in a restaurant having a
conversation it wasn't possible to eat, the two activities were
antithetical, like swimming and talking on the phone. Now the
champagne kept being poured and poured (my friend only
drank very good quality champagne) and even though I had
already eaten I was getting sloshed.

To be honest, looking at the menu now in the harsh glare of
daylight, I don't know what appetizer I would have chosen
had I been hungry. I don't think I would want asparagus salad
with baby beets, poached quail eggs and organic greens
because quail eggs are very very strong and remind me of
an unfortunate experience in Macau.

A wild striped bass carpaccio – I'm not going to go for a
dried fish prepared like a meat and the striped bass reminded
me of an unfortunate childhood dining experience in which my
father, who fished, attempted to force me to eat wild striped
bass he had caught, after he had removed its many parasites,
aka worms, which most wild fish harbor. If you want to catch
your own wild fish, you can see for yourself.

I wouldn't try the seafood salad with scallops, squid, Japanese octopus because I have never been able to eat a scallop
since college when a boyfriend decided to cook me dinner and
made a dish with scallops that called for flour but he accidentally used sugar instead.

It was grown-up food in here, food for the sort of people I
had once believed to occupy the city, who wore suits and lived

in clean apartments filled with modern furniture and doormen. Among the main courses were: grilled salmon, roast cod, seared yellow fin tuna, grilled saddle of rabbit, your organic free-range chicken, a squab, rack of lamb.

It was by this point, I believe, that I had consumed at least six glasses of very very good champagne and the conversation turned to the vagina tables, designed by the husband of one of the beautiful twins. 'How can a table be like a vagina?' I asked, which is how I ended up with a diagram next to my bed in the morning. What I really wanted to ask is, why would anybody want a table like a vagina? but in order not to seem rude I added, 'And how is a raven like a writing desk?' Nobody seemed to know what I was talking about, though, and instead they explained that the tables also squirted. My self of twenty years ago would have thought she was out of her league. And perhaps, twenty years ago, the idea of a vagina table would have had some shock factor.

I decided to order the steak and take it home. I am an eater of left-overs, and a steak eater, because I am not very far evolved on the evolutionary scale. If I was far evolved I would be a vegetarian and it makes me sad to be unevolved but it's a character flaw I've grown used to.

It used to be I would have a craving for steak once or twice a year, but now I feel steak is in jeopardy, shortly it will be unavailable altogether, too dangerous to eat, and I had better get as much as I can while it is still believed to be safe in this country.

I would feel even worse about myself, that I am not only not spiritual but will probably get a terrible disease from eating meat, except that recently I read Richard Rhodes's book *Deadly Feast*, which describes all the diseases people and animals can get when they turn or are forced to turn cannibal: kuros, scrapie, mad cow, all various spongiform brain viruses, but then he explained that in the future, when hundreds of people every day will be going to euthanasia centers as they

lose their minds, vegetarians will not be excluded as they have
been eating vegetables fertilized with animal products such as
bonemeal, blood and manure, which also are going to harbor
the various brain-destroying viruses.

I'm reducing his factual information, of course, into my own
language.

Anyway, I took the steak home. It was great, sliced, in a
sandwich. It wasn't too dry or lacking in marbling, which is
what sometimes happens in a really fancy restaurant, and it
wasn't greasy or tough or chewy. At least I had my night out,
in a grown-up restaurant, the kind of place where I had,
twenty years ago, imagined myself eating, though at that time
I hadn't foreseen that I wouldn't be hungry, and that, at my
age, I would drink too much champagne and see twins.

Part Four

City Life

A Heck of a Town

MOST PEOPLE think of New York City as Manhattan, but in fact there are five boroughs which constitute New York City – Manhattan, the Bronx, Staten Island, Queens and Brooklyn, where I live. In most of these areas below the buildings is a very hard rock called Manhattan schist, which is so hard that, unlike in London, they could never build the subways very deep and even, in some places, had to run the tracks above ground. Though I have lived in New York for many years, until a year and a half ago I had rarely, scarcely ventured into Brooklyn – I had no idea how fascinating and diverse an area it was. But by a Manhattanite the other boroughs are generally looked on with disdain. During my childhood I would often visit my grandparents – we lived in Massachusetts and they lived in Flushing, Queens, an area perhaps best known for being the site of the home of Archie Bunker, the star of a popular sitcom, *All in the Family*, which was based on a similar program in England in which the equivalent to the right-wing, racist reactionary was a Cockney named, I believe, Alf.

But the Queens of my grandparents was nothing like the Queens of Archie Bunker. My grandparents lived in the same apartment building for well over forty years; when they first moved there, and throughout my childhood, the Flushing streets were tree-lined, with big, old houses rather than apartment buildings – theirs was one of the first, and originally quite grand, with a doorman and other modern luxuries. Over time, the houses were torn down, other buildings went up in their place, the trees died and around the time the building's land-lord no longer paid for a doorman, a burglar climbed up the dumbwaiter, and so it was boarded shut. A huge convent, a few blocks away, the most beautiful house and flower-filled garden, surrounded by a cast-iron fence was sold, torn down, and in its place a hideous department store – Korvette's – was built, which quickly went out of business.

At the same time, Flushing in many ways grew more fascinating. It appeared that, each year, a different group of immigrants chose to settle in the area, so that one year I would visit and the restaurants were suddenly Indian, the people on the streets were dressed in saris and Indian garb; the next year the new influx was Korean, and then Chinese, Latin American, West Indian, Russian – and with each new group of arrivals the restaurants, shops, churches and synagogues changed, the older immigrants moved elsewhere.

My great-aunt and -uncle lived in Bayside, Queens – this area was quite a long distance away from my grandparents, and here small houses lined the streets, complete with little yards, a whole different flavor and feeling, an area which, architecturally at least, did not change from when the houses had originally been built, in the twenties, thirties and forties. So these were the two parts of the city I knew, a bit, as a child; from my grandparents' house we would take the subway in to 'the city', as Manhattan was known. The subway was some distance away, and it took about forty minutes or an hour to get to Grand Central Station – this was in the days when, remarkably, the seats on the subway cars were still made of something resembling criss-cross rattan, padded seats covered with wicker. Now, of course, the seats in the subways are made of a hideous, hard plastic, built and designed by Japa-nese – who are a great deal smaller than most Americans. The new seats are shaped like tiny bottoms, so each person is expected to occupy his or her little spot – areas intended to hold six or eight Japanese can actually contain only three

Americans, always in a rage when another person tries to wedge their way in on an overcrowded rush-hour car.

But the history of public transportation in Manhattan would take a complete, lengthy essay of its own – the early horse-drawn public trains; the long-gone elevated train of Manhattan's Third Avenue; the open-top double-deckers of my mother's childhood, now vanished; the brief stint, now forgotten, during the 1970s, when minute double-decker buses with closed tops (so tiny they resembled portable enclosed toilets) ran up Madison Avenue and down Fifth; the money spent by the city on public buses costing nearly a million each – which never worked.

In all these years I have seen little else of Queens, though there is Kew Gardens, and Forest Hills, and Queens Park, site of the 1964 World's Fair.

Of Staten Island and the Bronx I have seen even less. I made one trip to Staten Island, by ferry and taxi, to visit Tibet House, a museum atop a hill, containing Tibetan art. My husband, who is English and a golfer, has visited Staten Island (on his endless quest to find the perfect public golf course) a bit more frequently and has described stumbling across a complete nineteenth-century village, with charming buildings, houses and shops, all intact. And from time to time I have seen photographs of the beaches and various houses, grand and shabby, as well as the infamous garbage dump, but thus far I have never made any effort to get there.

And the Bronx (I am often asked by out-of-towners why it is called 'the' Bronx, but for this I always improvise) I have visited perhaps twice – to attend baseball games at Yankee Stadium, and to stroll briefly along the formerly splendid Grand Concourse, where lavish apartment buildings of the art-deco era have deteriorated considerably. Here, too, is the area known as Riverdale, where huge houses abruptly arise from dusty avenues lined with apartment blocks. And it was from the public golf course in the Bronx that, one evening, my husband returned with one of my favorite golfing stories of all time.

'How was the golf?' I asked.

'OK,' Tim said, 'but we had to play around the 14th hole.'

'Why?' I said, not particularly interested.

'Because of the corpse.'

Apparently a murder had taken place on the 14th green the night before and the police hadn't troubled to move the body, but simply roped off the area and asked the golfers to play around it.

Of all the boroughs, I have spent the most years living in and exploring Manhattan. Certainly I did not want to move to Brooklyn. But in recent years Manhattan has become not only horrendously expensive but more and more homogenized, block after block of the same shops – the Banana Republic, the Gap, upscale Italian restaurants and sushi joints – and the people, too, have become less interesting, young people dressed in the same outfits from the Gap and Banana Republic, all with a certain youthful homogenized bland arrogance.

The Manhattan that I first saw as a college student had virtually disappeared. The only people who could afford to live there were either the extremely rich, those subsidized by their parents or corporation, or those who had been there for so long that they had acquired real estate or rental property twenty or thirty years ago and now had to hang on to their valuable hovel for ever, unable to find anything equivalent for twenty times more money. Even in the 1970s, friends had told me, they came to the city and found huge places to live for fifty or a hundred dollars a month. By the time I finally had enough money to buy a place, all I could afford was a tiny one-bedroom; this was in 1987, the market immediately collapsed, and though others who bought earlier could or would still make a profit, I am one of the few who have ever lost money in real estate.

By then I had met my husband, we had a baby – the place was much too small, and the rental that we finally found, inexpensive by New York standards, was far too much money for us to toss away each month. So we began to look for a place to buy. Harlem, up on 145th Street, still had houses for sale in the less-than-half-a-million price range. But to travel from 145th Street, in an area bleak, bombed out, treeless, to get to downtown, seemed to take an eternity; and the brown-stones were mostly dark, run-down places which, built at the turn of the century, were going to need constant maintenance and repair.

I work at home. I knew I would be the one on the phone trying to get plumbers, electricians, roofers, glaziers, to come over; I knew I would wait and wait. I lived on a block of brownstones when I first moved to the city, and at dawn one day after a rainstorm heard a horrendous crash. Across the street the lintel above the doorway – some seven tons – had simply crumbled from the façade, and smashed through the front steps. It was fortunate this happened so early in the day, anyone trying to come in or go out would have been killed.

The Manhattan brownstones are mostly built of sandstone, which is not the most durable of materials. The remaining houses are of brick – they are of an earlier period, generally the 1850s, and tend to be small merchant homes of the era – or of limestone. The limestone buildings are of course very sound, but they were usually built as mansions, mansions which today have been converted into shops (Ralph Lauren) or museums or consulates.

I have been to a party in a limestone mansion once owned and occupied by a single individual, now converted floor by floor and room by room into luxury apartments – what was once the ballroom for the financier is now one individual's residence, purchased for millions and millions of dollars. The Communists didn't need to take over Manhattan – we had the realtors and big business to accomplish that.

My great-grandfather came to New York at the end of the nineteenth century, to a tenement on the streets of the lower East Side. The tenement buildings built there then for the very poor are now occupied by the descendants of those same immigrants, with little change except that what was once an old railroad flat (all the rooms connecting in a line) where a large family might have lived in squalid conditions, is now rented out or sold for a vast fortune.

The conditions themselves have changed only marginally – in these old places a sixth-floor walk-up will always be a sixth-floor walk-up; there is nowhere to fit in an elevator.

Recently I read an article about a couple who bought the top two floors in one of these antiquated places, spending more than half a million dollars on a place that will always be narrow, dark, without elevator and so forth. I had always sworn against Brooklyn. For one thing, any time I had gone to visit someone who lived there (maybe two or three times) I had had to take one subway, then another, waiting an interminable time for each; and though the people I was going to visit always said they lived 'five minutes away from the subway station' inevitably the walk turned out to be twenty minutes or more – in the dark, or rain.

Manhattanites are accustomed to hailing a taxi on the street – we are unfamiliar with the London system of 'radio cabs' – but in Brooklyn there are no street taxis; hence I always felt trapped on a visit. Nevertheless, the thought of buying a brownstone felt, to me, even more oppressive. At last I announced to my husband that the only residence that would suit me would be a penthouse – with a twenty-four-hour doorman, plenty of views, light, and a terrace. I had actually once been in such a place, the apartment of an incredibly famous, successful tennis player, who had purchased it at the bottom of the real-estate crash for well over five million dollars.

This was not our price range. Nevertheless, the following day my husband announced he had found such a place for me. Its only drawback was the Brooklyn location – directly upstairs, however, from a subway line. I still could not visualize myself in the sticks, but, trying to placate him, I came out for a quick look.

We made a bid that day.

After all that time in Manhattan, I had no idea that I would enjoy Brooklyn so much. From this apartment I can see Manhattan, as well as Queens, Staten Island and New Jersey; I can view the entire panorama of Brooklyn, from Coney Island at the tip, with its run-down, antiquated amusement park and strip of gray beach, all the way over to Jamaica Bay. My free afternoons have been spent exploring Brooklyn: by subway and on foot. There is Ditmas Park with its huge mansions and grounds that resemble plantations in *Gone with the Wind* – only each parked on a tiny plot of land. Nearby are neighborhoods of apartments, or other less grand houses, and each area contains a different ethnic group – I've found regions inhabited entirely by people from Haiti, from Guyana, from Russia, from the Ukraine, there are areas of Orthodox Jews wearing dress unchanged from the seventeenth century; there is a complete Chinatown (Sunset Park) and the Italian neighborhoods known as Bensonhurst and Bay Ridge. There is the upscale area in which Norman Mailer lives – Brooklyn Heights – and a poor area, Bedford Stuyvesant, where until recently the film director Spike Lee lived, in a huge brownstone in a once-very-expensive neighborhood.

To have lived in a city for so long and feel I knew the place completely – only to realize that my explorations have barely begun – has both humbled and inspired me. For a writer, mostly alone (OK, so I lie in bed all day with a laptop and a lapdog), continually finding new areas, new people, new adventures, new anecdotes, has made me realize that, ultimately, however ambivalent my feelings toward the city and my residence (OK, so there turned out to be a few problems with this fabulous apartment, like, even though it has four bathrooms only two of them get water) I have found a place in a city that is a microcosm of the world at large.

Art in the Early '80s

I MOVED TO New York City in the early 1980s. SoHo was still a stately region of boarded-up defunct factories in cast-iron buildings, empty at night except for a few artists who had illegally taken over some warehouses and factories as residences. There were no shops or stores, at night the streets were empty.

I lived uptown, on the upper West Side, an area that was then not particularly fancy. Drug addicts and homeless still hung out in Verdi Park, that tiny triangular strip that had been featured by name in the movie *The Panic in Needle Park*.

Each weekend the sidewalks near my apartment were full of the ruined contents of the apartment of some old person, who had been living in the same squalid room for thirty, forty, fifty years. Straw hats from the forties, cracked mahogany mirrors, broken toasters still full of crumbs, lifetimes of papers and photo albums. He or she – unable to pay the rent, hospitalized now, in a nursing home, or dead – wiped from the face of the planet except for these broken bits and pieces, free for the taking, or collected by sanitation trucks at dawn.

In the neighborhood were still cafeterias of the sort featured in the works of Isaac Bashevis Singer, places serving dairy and kosher food where old men would spend the day over a bowl of red Jell-O topped with artificial whipped cream or a rock-hard bagel and cup of coffee. I had no money, though an arts grant paid my rent.

One Saturday afternoon on one of my many lengthy walks that took me across the city I wandered through the streets of

SoHo, admiring the wide, empty cobble-stoned streets and the ornate cast-iron façades of the buildings with their elaborate detail, Corinthian columns, dirty half-moon windows. In front of one entrance a crowd had gathered, maybe twenty people standing in the warm early-evening autumn sun, drinking bottles of beer or plastic cups of white wine.

Maybe it was some party or private event. I knew no one in the city, I had no money, if I did go out, to a bar in my neighborhood or one of the run-down cafeterias, I spoke to no one. I was shy. I looked at the crowd gathered there, hardly a crowd, fifteen, twenty people, smoking cigarettes, chatting, and I thought, I'll just pretend I was invited to this party. So I turned back, walked through the group and up the steps.

The place was a gallery (I no longer remember whose). There were paintings on the walls (I no longer remember whose) and in the back a table set up with bottles of beer on ice in a garbage can and some white wine in plastic cups. I poured myself a glass of wine, wondering when someone would tell me I had no business being here. Then I took my wine and started wandering around the show. 'Hey, you know there's a party tonight at a Danceteria for . . .' Someone was talking to me. He named the artist. 'You can get in for free before midnight – and drinks are free, too.' I was in, without even knowing what realm it was I had entered.

New York in the early '80s and there was a kind of chaos, energy and magnetism in the art scene that was, nevertheless, still small-scale. It would be a decade before there were auctions of contemporary art at Sotheby's and Christie's where the work of youthful painters sold for a million. One didn't have to be invited or even know what shows were on, who was showing where or what. One had simply to wander the streets of SoHo, on a Saturday in season and follow the crowd. The first week it seemed a few galleries had shows; a few people attended. A short time later there were more shows, and the crowds were bigger, a hundred people standing around outside talking and a hundred more inside, not looking at the work but talking and drinking.

In a way I felt I had accidentally stumbled into the equivalent of Haight Ashbury a few years before the Summer of Love – or a scene that was not dissimilar to the rock and roll world of the late '60s. The art, I thought, was crude, vulgar stupid, violent – men, the work of men, 99 per cent of the time, scrawlings on canvas, rough drawings, childlike, testosterone-laden – as if it had bubbled up from the creaky, cracking bubble-gum laden sidewalks of the New York City streets themselves.

Some of it actually had – there were artists, black and Hispanic, who had spent their high-school years drawing graffiti on the streets, who were now being invited to put those same images on canvas. Futura 200, Ramelzee, Daze – the graffiti artists, however, proved to have only short-term commercial success, were dropped from galleries, faded from view. And there were white guys, like Kenny Scharf, Donald Batchelor, James Mather, James Nares, James Brown, whose works seemed, equally, crude and sullen screams for attention, as if they were prisoners in some permanent jail with only the most basic of symbols from which to work.

Gradually I was able to differentiate the style in the men's work. Donald Batchelor painted outlines of houses or flowers or faces, not dissimilar to the petroglyphic paintings of a contemporary five-year-old but without the color. Keith Haring drew cutesy logo-like outlines of babies or people, reduced to simple elemental outlines, like the signs that are able to indicate without words Men's Room or, on the highway, Steep Descent. It was rumored that he had gone out at night to do chalk drawings on empty advertising walls in the subway; gone to work as a janitor at Tony Shafrazi's gallery and Tony had seen his work and given him a show. Kenny Scharf was painting scenes lifted from the Hanna-Barbera TV cartoon series *The Jetsons*, dorky, colorful alien creatures with three eyes.

James Brown was more artistic, his palate more complex, but

even his work seemed to me to be merely lifted from a Western European sensibility of the idea of African art: a white boy painting masks, precious in gold and mauve and brown. And, the flip side, Jean-Michel Basquiat, who first ran around the streets writing 'SAM-O' in silver paint and, when that didn't succeed in getting him attention, turned to canvas, where the work, with its crude voodoo chicken scrawls of skull and crossbones, seemed intent on announcing, 'You may think I'm a good-looking, educated person but I can prove I am really a crazy street tough.'

It was easy for me to be disparaging about the realm of art that I inhabited. Whether or not anybody could paint I didn't know. It wasn't just that the work seemed banal, simplistic, pathetic cries for attention, rip-offs of commercial imagery from popular culture, art history books, a European tradition, television cartoons and product design – beneath the lack of originality there seemed to be no real strength or compulsion, the work did not have the purity of force that I had come to associate with what I considered to be great art. I had the feeling that each painting was something completed to obtain a gallery or for an exhibition. Nowadays I would say that only Jeff Koons came close to completing an antagonistic vision, a pure fascism of hatred, portraying a death and deadness of contemporary culture that these artists, caught in their own egos, were only vaguely able to hint at. But Koons's work to me is the equivalent of a pop group performing in a stadium – slick, commercial, for the masses, destined to be relegated to last year's hit record status when the new thing comes along.

The young male artists had flooded the city streets and had come to the city not in the hopes of being artists but in the hope of making money and being famous. And with the artists came the art critics, who occupied the pages of a number of art magazines and newspapers and wrote in a style that was obtuse, pretentious, convoluted and deliberately, ultimately, seemed to be saying more about how fancy and intelligent the author was than anything of interest or sense about the work.

From one week to the next the paintings escalated in value. A dealer – Holly Solomon, Mary Boone, Barbara Gladstone, Paula Cooper, Tony Shafrazi – would sell paintings for fifteen hundred dollars; soon the paintings of a particular artist were going for five thousand, and then twenty – if a dealer had collectors with enough monetary weight, the work of the painter would go up in value, because the collectors were collecting for investment purposes.

Holly Solomon was one who sold the work of the 'pattern painters' – all of whose work resembled various wallpaper – and rumor had it that, one day, a wealthy Swiss dealer-collector abruptly dumped all of their work, a massive quantity, at auction; the stuff didn't sell and their work (and, apparently, their lives as painters) no longer was worth a dime.

Yet to me the quality of what they were producing was no better nor worse than the same stuff that, at another gallery, sold out, for more and more money, show after show. What made it valuable or worthless? The arbitrary business decision; whether or not someone arbitrarily decided, that week, if the person – the male painter – was going to be 'important'.

In the early '80s a bar existed named for its address, One University Place, run and owned by the same man, Mickey Ruskin, who a few years earlier had owned and run that seminal late-'60's spot, the progenitor of the modern night-club, Max's Kansas City. In the back was a restaurant. Though it served primarily inexpensive hamburgers, I was too poor to dine there. Beyond this area Julian Schnabel cooked, washed dishes, along with writers like Linda Yablonsky, though I did not know them. I was an innocent who sat in the front, at the bar, watching the lively crowd beyond table-hop; they all seemed incredibly adult and sophisticated to me, shy and hunched over my one draft beer.

For fifty cents I would take a bus from my apartment to get down there, at eleven at night; the route took me nearly an hour; I would sit and watch before I had to leave in to catch one of the last uptown buses at around one a.m. (The buses, unlike the subway, did not run all night and I was too scared, this late, to get a subway). At this bar the people were friendly and the atmosphere was as close as I have come to the idea of the Cedar Tavern, haunt of the abstract expressionists in the '50s and early '60s, or those fictitious haunts mentioned in the novels of Dawn Powell – artists, some writers, a drunken scene of people who lived in walk-up flats, subsisting on small trust-fund checks or who worked at the day at some menial jobs – it was still possible, at that time, to exist in New York on not much money – and who at night would meet to drink, fight, talk, fall off their bar stools.

There was the occasional rock star, unknown outside the city, whose pseudo-punk singing paled by comparison to the much earlier Sex Pistols, or whose glam-glitter rock also seemed years out of date. There were painters, struggling to make themselves known for their dabbles – work no more interesting than the accomplishments of a baby left to play with its own feces; and writers for small 'hip' 'underground' newspapers whose precedents from the '60s seemed hip and underground without the quotation marks. Poets who had gone on for fifteen years writing the same poems that had been bad in 1965; jewelry designers whose overpriced junk was supposed to be tongue-in-cheek kitsch but was merely kitsch; teachers from Columbia University who gave themselves extra points for knowing real artists in a realm where there was nothing real; and – though not present, always maligned – Andy Warhol, viewed as a has-been among the cognoscenti.

I was in my twenties and felt embittered that I had missed the Real Thing – the Real Scene – by more than a decade. Around this time I began to date a painter who was vaguely associated with the current art movies – he showed at Shafrazi and painted cartoon characters, rather badly and directly, Mickey Mouse, Donald Duck, Woody Woodpecker and so forth. But unlike Warhol, whose use of a popular current image from advertising or society – Marilyn Monroe, a Brillo box – inevitably said

something more significant and meaningful than the image
itself, the work of this painter seemed, if possible, to say less.
A not-very-well-drawn watercolor of Mighty Mouse not only
appeared to have no meaning but wasn't even particularly
pleasant or interesting to look at, either.

However, the painter's works were part of the present
'movement' and that he showed at Shafrazi, along with
Donald Batchelor and Keith Haring and James Brown, and
that I was going out with him meant that, on occasion, a whole
bunch of us traveled to their group shows abroad and, at other
times we traveled together at the expense of some incredibly
kind art dealer for an exhibition in their gallery.

And incredibly kind these men were. Why or where had the
concept of art dealer gotten such a bad name? Surely it
couldn't all be based on Utrillo's dealer, who had locked
him up and refused him wine until he turned out a new canvas.
These men had a real love of art, an excitement about new
work and the artist (though it was true their concept of 'artist'
never did seem to extend to women). They would have made
more money if they had gone into almost any other business –
they worked tirelessly, unstintingly, without much in the way
of thanks, respect, appreciation.

Tony Shafrazi, Luciano Amelio, Salvatore Ala, an elegant and
sophisticated – yet so nice – Spanish count or grandee whose
name I have long forgotten and who, I believe, died of AIDS
some years ago, a small gallery dealer in Rotterdam; it is hard for
me to believe, now, looking back, how graciously we were
treated – that not just my boyfriend but myself, too, were put up
in luxurious hotels, flown here and there, taken out, nightly, to
lavish meals and that these dealers always spoke to me with
interest, affection, concern, though I was a not particularly
attractive girl from an unknown, penniless background without
any particular accomplishment and nothing of interest to say.

Shafrazi in particular: young, handsome, full of enthusiasm,
taking us in a first-class train compartment to the incredibly

grand Excelsior Hotel in Cologne, all out of his own pocket, to meet with some dealer – whose name I have again forgotten – to discuss the possibility of giving my boyfriend a show; from a proper, upscale Armenian family, he had been in Tehran during the bombing and escaped, I recollect, with only a few of his family's possessions to resettle, broke, first in Paris and then in New York. He had never escaped, however, the oppression of being known not for being one of the city's first and most original performance artists but for the act itself – spray-painting Picasso's *Guernica*, although it was done with non-permanent paint. The act was maligned – I did not approve – but surely others had acted far more reprehensibly and yet were called Artists.

Now he was acting not as artist but in a sense as spokesperson or ombudsman for this new group of painters whose work he hoped or believed would overthrow what had become the twentieth-century art establishment, an establishment that had perhaps been shaken but twice, previously, during the New York City Century – the first time with the 1913 armory show, the second with the action painters and abstract Expressionists of the '50s and '60s. But . . . how sad the acts of pseudo-anarchism seemed to me.

In Venice, or Madrid, or whatever cities we gathered in, the work on the walls – Scharf, Haring, and so forth – seemed to be rather feeble-minded products not dissimilar to some innercity high-school students copying bad cartoons badly. The other artists did not care for my boyfriend; by association, or perhaps separately, they did not care for me. Keith Haring always traveled with one or two boyfriends, who always seemed to be named Juan or known by some street tag name – A1, A2 – kids who had never been out of the ghetto, who whined constantly about not being able to eat unless they found a McDonald's, and if Keith did deign to speak to me – or anyone, for that matter – it was only to say how incredibly important he was, that he had just been to a department store in Tokyo, where he had painted many great works and was mobbed on the street, or had opened some park by painting a billboard or part of the Berlin Wall, and thousands came to applaud him.

He did not open his mouth, at least to me, except to say how famous he was. 'Yeah, I just got back from Tokyo,' he would say, while I, who had never been to Tokyo, had no hopes of going to Tokyo, who had no money, would wonder how someone only a little older than me had gotten so lucky, based, seemingly, on so little. 'I was invited to design a department store, you wouldn't have believed how many kids turned up, some were crying, they had to get the police to keep them back . . .'

For this and other projects he had been paid millions. There were commissions from parks, from schools, from watch companies or ceramic manufacturers, from publishing companies for books. There was no modesty or humility, only a non-stop self-aggrandizing flow of words, and an entourage of interchangeable young men who were on his payroll, each of whom in turn, seemingly, would be involved in a robbery or drugs scam while in his service. And the others, men artists, perhaps of lesser degrees of success, who nevertheless lived in huge lofts, smoked drugs, dined at the most expensive restaurants, traveled like rock and roll stars. It seemed they must never have time to paint – but that was the least part of any of it.

It was true that at these shows in each city hundreds of kids would turn up, kids who did not, normally, go to art openings but might have spent leisure time at nightclubs or rock concerts. Who cared? When I looked at his paintings all I could think was that, at the same time, the cartoonist Matt Groening (who went on to create the hit TV cartoon show *The Simpsons*) was doing work that looked exactly like Keith's, a strip that appeared each week in the *Village Voice*, a 'downtown' newspaper. The only difference was that Groening did not call himself an artist – he was a cartoonist – and his work had text and was funny and made pointed comments about the society in which we all lived.

Over and over Keith painted the same thing – flatly repetitive: the radiant baby who crawled across the surface of a canvas, or a sheet of metal, or a Swatch watch – recognizable, to be sure, but less interesting than the golden arches of McDonald's or the logo for Coca-Cola, advertising nothing, ultimately, but Keith Haring himself. And to see such unabashed confidence and self-love from an artist still, at that time, came as a shock.

Yet Shafrazi, organizing shows, trying to find gallery space, working with other gallery dealers and owners, putting up groups of ten or twelve in hotels, taking them out to dinners, clubs, enthusiasm never flagging, the center of what appeared to be a new movement and fresh excitement in the art world, must have expended tremendous amounts of energy, psychic and otherwise, for what was very little gratitude on the part of the artists (who constantly believed themselves to be ripped off) and, really, not much financial remuneration. While Haring's paintings may have been selling for twenty grand or so, from Shafrazi's 50 per cent he had to pay for gallery space, his own living space and endless support – the dinners, the wining and dining of collectors and other dealers; pampering paranoid, ungrateful painters, all of whom were spoiled white guys who wanted to pretend they were from the city streets; the airfares, the hotels, the advances not just for those paranoid artists who believed, constantly, they were being robbed, or not receiving their fair share, but their equally paranoid, spoiled boyfriends or girlfriends as well.

All of the dealers I met surely had hope that these artists' work would mature, develop, go up in value – they must have hoped but could not possibly know. Investment in stocks or bonds would have had more of a guarantee. I think of the elegant dealer in Spain: immensely refined, his apartment not particularly large, his housekeeper who had been with him

since childhood – he invited us to dinner, in this cramped
space, the silver-framed family photographs, the beautifully
upholstered furniture, the china, the carefully chosen wines, a
kind of old-world refinement . . .

Though no doubt he had his love of nightlife, though no
doubt he had his dark side, he was an educated and consider-
ate man, now dining alone with an American-Italian painter of
woodpeckers from Brooklyn who had never been to college
and his socially inept girlfriend who had grown up eating off
paper plates, a product of the 1960s and two hippie parents
who had never told her to use a napkin . . . Somehow,
perhaps, he hoped to reach beyond or outside the realm from
which he had come, into what he imagined was an exciting
new world, new movement, new philosophy happening glob-
ally, or from across the Atlantic; but of philosophy, of thought,
of idea, I did not then find nor have since found any semblance.
Or perhaps it was that he and the other dealers, all men of
intelligence and refinement, did not have the inner arrogance it
took to call oneself an artist; they were, instead, unthanked
nurturers.

I had only been to Europe once before; it was thrilling for me
to travel, and to see cities and meet people in a way that, had I
merely been a tourist, would never have happened. It was
equally amazing to see the ease with which the pampered
artists seemed to accept what to others would have felt like
winning the lottery. They were like rock and roll stars,
accepting the adulation, without introspection or amazement.

And the hundreds of kids who turned up at these shows – in
Rotterdam, Cologne, Zurich – these were club kids, there not
to buy the work but to attend a cool event. And how sad,
really, the stuff on the walls – not that anyone was looking at it
– a canvas of a cartoon mouse, a house in childlike outline, a
canvas of three heads with one eye each and seven legs. What
could you say about the paintings? You could say whatever
you liked.

Andy, '85

ALL YEAR we had what we called the 'Blind Date Club'. The core group consisted of me, Paige Powell and Andy Warhol. Every week Andy took us to a different restaurant. Each of us was responsible for finding a date for someone else.

It began like this. My cousin Jeff Slonim worked at *Interview* magazine. One day he called up and said, 'Paige Powell has asked me to call you and see if you are free to come to dinner tonight with her and a blind date she's meeting.'

I scarcely knew Paige Powell, then the advertising director of *Interview*. I had seen her in various nightclubs, wearing extraordinary costumes and surrounded by photographers. She was one of those people who always seemed to be in a spotlight, even when, on closer inspection, it turned out there were no spotlights. She generated her own intense radiance. I thought it was very nice of her to include me on her blind date, especially since I barely knew her. 'But why would she do this, Jeff?' I said.

'I don't know,' Jeff said. 'She's just being friendly, I think.' A little while later he called back. He said that Paige had now invited him to come on the blind date. 'Great!' I said. Then the phone rang again. It was Jeff. Andy Warhol, who owned *Interview*, and was a good friend of Paige's, had heard Jeff telling me about the blind date and decided to come along.

It was now me, Paige, Jeff, Andy Warhol and the blind date, all meeting up at the Odeon at 9:00, but Paige had neglected to inform the blind date that the date no longer consisted of just the two of them.

We all arrived at approximately the same time. Andy brought five men with him. The blind date was not at all surprised. He seemed to think it was entirely ordinary. We sat at a big round table, the blind date positioned between me and Paige. To either side sat Andy, the five men and my cousin Jeff.

The blind date appeared to have been sent from Central Casting. He was very short, balding, wearing a gold chain, gold rings and a Hawaiian print shirt unbuttoned to his navel. He had a hairy chest, too. Though Paige and I didn't know each other very well, we worked together quite naturally as a team. First the blind date lectured Paige for ten minutes, and then Paige would flash me a warning and I would distract him and let him bore me for ten minutes.

Andy watched this with fascination. After that night he decided he wanted to do it every week – but each of us should have a date. He didn't want us to call it a Blind Date Dinner, though, he wanted to call them Advertising or Business Dinners. I guess this meant it could be a tax write-off. Plus, I think he found it humiliating to be thought of as a guy who had to be fixed up on a date.

We went to Mr Chow's, all red lacquer and gold and soft carpeting, where I ate lobster and piles of delicious crispy seaweed, salty and better than French fries. We went to Le Cirque and ordered our desserts before the start of the meal: soufflés, one of each, raspberry, chocolate, apricot, which arrived at the end accompanied by a huge nest of spun sugar and crystallized fruit and chocolates and tiny cookies on a tiered platter. Le Bernadin, fifty courses of various fish, The Ritz Café, Odeon, Café Luxembourg, S.O.B.'s, Texarkana, dozens and dozens of restaurants. I grew accustomed to meals that invariably ended with the waiter announcing the chef wished to offer each of us a drink on the house. (Later, without Andy, it came as a shock when this didn't happen.) In any event, Andy always paid.

I was living in a one-room apartment at that time that I

could barely afford. One day I measured my living quarters. It was ten feet by thirteen feet. I had practically never eaten in a restaurant before. My clothes came from thrift stores. When it got cold, Andy and Paige bought me a winter coat. I still have it – Fiorucci's, red-and-black faux fur.

It was bizarre to go from one extreme to the other, picked up and delivered home to my cell in the meatpacking market by limousine or chauffeured Rolls-Royce. Among my dates were a film director, a count, a stockbroker, a journalist, an artist, an anthropologist, a gossip columnist, a fashion designer, an investor, a ballet dancer – Italians, French, Austrians, Swedish, a Mexican. Dozens of men, hundreds of men – I can scarcely now remember any of them.

The tension level of the evenings was extremely high. If one of the invited guests wasn't ordinarily nervous about being on a blind date, he might get nervous about being on a blind date with six people. If that didn't throw him, he might be nervous about being at a dinner with Andy Warhol. Or, even if still calm, the hovering, excited waiters, the eager, clustered bus-boys – anxious to wait on Andy – usually did the trick.

Once, early on, while making a reservation Paige let it slip that the event was a Group Blind Date – with Andy Warhol. That night our table was literally surrounded by a vast group of giggling, snickering staff, all dying to witness the Date. After that we tried not to mention just what it was we were doing.

After a short time we ran out of single people we knew who were appropriate to invite. Then we included another man – Steven Greenberg – who had to provide dates for the three of us and sometimes himself as well. He had to take us all out to dinner; his driver – in one of Steven's huge, ancient Daimlers, Bentleys or Rolls-Royces – had to pick us up and take us home.

That meant, when Steven was invited, there were eight of us on the blind date. We could almost never find a date for Steven, but this didn't bother him: he had friends at a modeling agency and they would send along any new girl in town.

Occasionally we let one or two other men participate in this fashion instead of him.

Sometimes we had a Giant Group Blind Date. One night we had twenty people, ten friends, and ten strangers. Everyone had to procure for someone else. The friends sat on one side and the dates were seated opposite. Unfortunately, that was the night we picked a restaurant with live music and nobody could hear a single thing. Some of the people hadn't been informed what the purpose of the dinner was, and they seemed particularly baffled.

After dinner we usually went to a nightclub, dumping our dates or, less often, allowing them to come along. It was fun going to a nightclub with Andy. The crowd at the door magically parted; we were ushered in and once inside a sort of electrical charge would flicker through the air. 'Andy's here, Andy's here.' Immediately the whole energy level of the place went up, everyone seemed to feel they could now safely assume they were in the right spot – it had just received the most fashionable seal of approval.

I enjoyed watching Andy in public. He went out because he genuinely enjoyed it. It was obvious he wouldn't have kept going out night after night for thirty years unless he really liked doing it. Some people said he went out so much for business purposes, but there was no business to be found in those nightclubs. He simply liked seeing the latest places, and especially young kids. At the time I thought, Gee, doesn't he ever want to stay home? In a way I suppose it must have been intoxicating, having that much attention paid to him. People came up to him constantly. They said things like 'Oh, Andy, my cousin met you fifteen years ago, and you talked to her for a few minutes. Do you remember her – Judy Smock-owski, from Wichita?' Andy always smiled graciously and asked them some questions.

Then, suddenly, after a few minutes, came the cut-off. It was exactly like a curtain falling. He wasn't rude, but the person who had been gibbering on about their cousin would suddenly look embarrassed, stop talking and slink away. Andy never did anything rude, he was always friendly, but then this cut-off point came, his eyes went blank and the person got the message that the audience was over.

He liked to talk about peculiar diseases and psychic phenomena, and by sheer chance one time I fixed him up with a nice Jewish doctor and he was more excited about that date than anyone else who had ever come on the dates before. Unfortunately the doctor already had a boyfriend and it was really sad because I couldn't tell Andy that the reason this doctor wasn't interested in him was because he lived with someone. The rule was, on the blind dates, the date had to be single, not married or living with someone. But I was desperate to find Andy a date and so I just called whomever I could think of, since I never thought Andy would actually want to see the person again. And now I couldn't let him know the doctor wasn't single, or he would have been really mad.

One time I was actually dating someone and I got my date to come and pick me up at 11:30, after the Group Blind Date, and Andy got quite angry that I was breaking the rules by having another date on the same night.

And both Paige and I knew how mad he would have been if he had discovered what we sometimes did, when we ran out of people to invite. Basically we began to call up friends of friends of friends of friends – who were in reality complete, utter strangers – and then we had to say, 'Listen, I know you don't know me – I'm sort of a friend of so-and-so's, who, actually, I guess you don't really know either – but I was wondering, could you come out on a blind date with me, another person and Andy Warhol?'

One time a guy agreed but decided not to come, and sent another guy instead. Since I had never met him but couldn't let Andy know this, I had to pretend I knew Andy's date. It was only later I found out this stranger was not a stranger named

Bill (the one I had invited) but somebody named Dan. I suppose it didn't really matter, though. We might as well have been picking names out of the phone book.

Another time the date cancelled a half-hour before dinner, and I ended up knocking on the door of two men who lived down the hall from me. I had only chatted with them very briefly, while walking our dogs. But now I said, 'I know I don't know you very well, but could one of you please just drop whatever you doing and come to dinner on a blind date with Andy Warhol – in about ten minutes?'

At the same time Paige was frantically scrambling to come up with someone, too. The guys who lived on my floor looked perplexed, and frightened. They decided against it. So I got on the phone, fast. By some miracle, each of us got a guy to show up at the restaurant. Each thought he was Andy's date. Andy was alarmed. He was seated between two men. I don't know why this was more than he could handle. He didn't have the slightest idea who was supposed to be his date. Probably he thought one or the other of them was my date. Or Paige's. Anyway, he knew there was someone extra at this dinner. The rule was, one date per person – and Andy was a stickler for rules. So he completely ignored one guy. He just refused to speak to him. The person I had found was very clever. When he came in the restaurant he came to our table. 'Hi, Tama,' he said, turning his head fast. That way he could fake the fact that he really had no idea who I was or which one I was. I had told him, in advance, we had to pretend we were old friends; there was no way Andy would have tolerated the humiliation of having a complete stranger at our meal.

But the remarkable thing was that this man, a complete unknown, looked exactly like a younger version of Andy. People all over the restaurant were whispering, 'Is that his cousin? Is that his nephew?' He had white hair, pale skin and glasses that were just like Andy's. It was uncanny. And to make matters even better, he was also a doctor, a nutritionist.

Food and vitamins and any sort of cosmetic was another favorite topic for Andy.

It was only the second time that Andy showed a genuine interest in his date. But when he asked him out again, the doctor showed up – with a date. This made Andy furious. His feelings were deeply hurt.

Not a single blind date ever worked out or led to anything else, not even a second date. And we did this once or twice a week for two years.

On New Year's Eve 1986 we didn't have our blind date. Instead, Steven Greenberg took us all to dinner at the River Café. I saw recently in the paper that this restaurant, on New Year's Eve, had a special rate of $350 per person. I had never done such glamorous things before – and few since. It was just us and a few friends, in a restaurant with champagne, and caviar, and balloons, and an orchestra. Afterwards Paige, Andy and I took one of Steven's cars with driver (Andy had to host a party in a club, Steven stayed behind with the others) and headed back into Manhattan. As we crossed the Brooklyn Bridge, fireworks began to explode all around us, directly over the car. It was exactly midnight. On the radio the Rolling Stones began to play 'Time is on My Side' and the three of us began singing along and laughing. I don't know why, it was just such a perfect moment, to be in this luxurious old car at midnight, with the fireworks and the skyline of Manhattan before us.

He died fifty-three days later.

After Andy's death Tim Hunt came from London to help with settling Andy's estate, and – around a year later – Paige invited him to come out one night for drinks with a group of us. He was my blind date. A few years later we got married.

Twenty-one authors who published with Picador were asked to write an essay, to celebrate the twenty-one years that Picador had been publishing. Each was assigned a

*different year to write about – I was given 1985. At first I
thought, 1985? What kind of a year is that? I couldn't
remember last week, let alone something as nebulous as
1985. Then slowly I remembered what I had tried not to
remember. A lot of very stupid journalists say to me, 'I
read that Fred Hughes said Andy didn't like you at first.'
Fred Hughes said that because he was never invited to go
out with us, in that era of Andy's life, at the end, though
originally he had been close with Andy. I met Andy, and
then he said, 'This is fun! Let's go out again next week.'
Then the journalists say, 'I read that Fred said Andy was
only friends with you because you were famous.' When I
met Andy, and we started going out to dinner, I wasn't
famous. And I never got very famous, and nobody at our
dinners was famous.*

The Story of Publishing
as Told by an Author

IN 1986 MY second book, *Slaves of New York*, was published. My agent had gotten me an advance of $3,500 – part of a three-book deal: my next book, *A Cannibal in Manhattan*, was already pre-sold for $20,000! And, when I wrote my next book (which would take me a few years), provided it was accepted, I would get twenty thousand more. Even in 1987 $20,000 did not go very far. And it would take me at least three years of work before I got paid again.

I decided to change agents, although it was thrilling that Andy Warhol, who was a friend, had bought the movie rights to *Slaves of New York* for $5,000, which my agent said I should take since it was unlikely anybody else would ever pay me anything.

Still, I was very excited that for the first time I would not have to worry on a monthly basis how I was to come up with the rent. At that time I lived in one room that measured ten by thirteen feet for which I paid one thousand dollars a month. And now my boyfriend – who was leaving his wife and had no place to go – could live with me.

My boyfriend at that time was an editor at a publishing house that he also owned. He had been living in his co-op – an entire floor – almost a city block – on the upper East Side. He loved the manuscript of *A Cannibal in Manhattan* and wished he could have published it. He had some very good ideas regarding the book, one of which was to hire an art director to

do some illustrations. I was to pay the art director $10,000, so
from my advance (which had dwindled to $14,000 after taxes)
I was going to have $4,000 left over, except for one problem: I
had to pay the original agent of record 10 per cent off the top –
$2,000 – and my new agent who was working with me had to
get 10 per cent as well, so I was now down to zero dollars.
They were also going to get 20 per cent of future earnings, if
any.

In return for getting me an art director and aiding with the
editing and publication of the book, my boyfriend said that he
should be entitled to 10 per cent of the advance and any future
sales.

'But you're my boyfriend!' I said. I was shocked. It wasn't as
if he needed the money. 'Besides, I don't have anything left to
pay you.' I was never very good at math, but in this case it was
clear to me that I would no longer be simply breaking even but
actually going into debt over my own writing.

We split up a short time later. The boyfriend went around
telling mutual friends that I 'was very cheap'. This bothered me
a great deal and continues to bother me. Maybe I really was
cheap but how would I ever find out if I didn't have any
money?

Summer of Excess

I T WAS the summer before the crash. 'I remember seeing a half-naked man wearing high heels running along the side of the road in the middle of the night – either toward Calvin's, or away, I can't remember,' said my friend Miranda.

Oh, that Calvin! In the '80s, in the Hamptons, he was the epitome of . . . something. Class, maybe – style and money. And artistic to boot. His taste was exquisite. He practically represented the Hamptons. Maybe his clothing wasn't quite as perfect as that of Armani – nobody could do understatement like Armani – but Calvin was American. Just his name made you think of perfect blonde girls in black dresses and men, so clean-shaven it was as if no hair would dare to grow on them, wearing crisp white shirts and pleated pants and loafers without socks.

Over the past few years summers in the Hamptons had grown progressively more excessive, until, that summer of '87, the parties, the events, the price of a summer house or a summer rental were so extreme, Gatsby's parties in old East Egg might as well have been a tea-party thrown by your grandmother.

The ubiquitous, penultimate trainer, High Voltage, was in the Hamptons all the time, charging around in glittery sequins and platform shoes, yelling 'Energy up!' at the top of her lungs, full of excitement. Almost everyone invited her to stay, for a weekend, for a week – if they could only drain some of her energy from her maybe they could be that thin, that lean and muscular, that full of excitement about simply being out in the

Hamptons, alive and breathing. She remembered going to a party, that summer, in a house in Southampton, a party thrown by Mary McFadden and R. Couri Hay. 'It was a white party, everyone was dressed in white, the house and garden over the bay full of celebrities, it was so elegant! And those days are over, there's nothing so elegant now, I don't roller skate down the highway.' (It was before the roller-blade era, she added apologetically, as if it was pre-telephone) 'I don't even wear glitter any more.'

Now there are gyms and health spas all over the place.

It was the end of the last genuine Hamptons eccentrics: the Bouvier mother and daughter who inhabited the cat-filled wreck called Gray Gardens, made famous in the Maisels brothers' film, had departed (the mother had died, the daughter at last sold the property), and Gray Gardens was later purchased by Ben Bradley and Sally Quinn. They had to spend a small fortune to rid the place of the smell of cat that even years later, on a rainy day, would sometimes resurface, as if the ghosts of un-neutered cats were able to spray from the Other Side.

Shortly the artist Ross Bleckner would purchase the cottage owned by Truman Capote; the beach shacks in Amagansett were no longer considered shacks. They had become expensive Retreats – without running water.

To Retreat! That was the whole point of the place, wasn't it? After all, even though the days were long since gone when the only way to get out to the Hamptons was via two-lane highway, a five-hour or more journey – it still took practically the same time.

One had to book a ticket on the jitney (which, back in 1914, was the name for the 5¢ horse-drawn bus – the cheapo ride), and then try to remain calm in bumper-to-bumper traffic. Even before cell phones were so commonplace and everyone had one, back when they were still 'mobile phones' and had to be carried in a little suitcase, you could see a small boy, perhaps eight years old, still too young to travel without his nanny, climb on to the jitney and, as soon as he was seated, take the telephone from his nurse. He lowered his voice to a whisper – it was impossible to say whom he was contacting . . . his mother? his agent? his broker?

There was the train – but that was for the kids, the twenty-year-old crowd – or get the Range Rover or Saab out of the garage. Eighty, a hundred thousand dollars – for that price one had a vehicle that would do a hundred and eighty on the autobahn or cross the Australian desert – and lower the top or turn on the air to cross the Queensboro bridge and then sit, stuck behind an interminable traffic light beneath the elevated subway in a gray industrial miasma, wondering who possibly could or would live here.

Even flying – while it had panache – took ages, one's driver taking one out to La Guardia, the plane ready on the tarmac, then another car and driver waiting at the other end to drive one back to Bridgehampton – maybe three hours, total, in getting to and taking off and so forth – just in time to dress and head out to dinner. It might have been simpler to stay behind in the city – but who with any money or desire to have fun would do that in July of 1987? 'I don't like the Hamptons – but I have to have the beach.'

The beach, the beach. Endless, empty miles of clean white sand. Apart from some sort of . . . state park kind of place, out near Montauk, only residents with a sticker could park anywhere near the water. And of course, even if you were just renting, as a summer resident you were entitled to a sticker – for a fee. 'The mountains don't do it for me – I have to have the beach.'

But the beaches – there was a reason they were empty. They were too hot. There was too much sand. It was tiring to be out there for more than, say, twenty minutes, unless you were serious about getting a tan. But that was kind of boring, especially if no one you knew was there – it must mean you

weren't in the right place at the right time, or maybe there was
a party going on someplace to which you hadn't been invited.

For those without money summer shares were found – full
shares, half-shares, quarter-shares, sharing a room for one
weekend a month in a house packed with complete strangers,
young people just starting on Wall Street, who wanted to
return to childhood, when summers were endless and Mom
was around to clean up.

They had forgotten Mom wasn't here – they hadn't wanted
her, she would never approve of the parties that went on until
four a.m., Phil Collins and Aerosmith blaring from the hi-tech,
out-of-place stereo lugged from the city, the traces of coke and
roaches on the faux early-American coffee table. ('God these
people have bad taste,' said every summer tenant in turn.) The
heaps of empty Rolling Rock and Chardonnay bottles that no
one managed, all summer, to take out to the garage – in the city
it would have been, for some homeless person, like winning the
lottery. *

And at the end of the season the rented houses were trashed:
broken mirrors and sinks, filthy bathtubs, beds broken, grease
on the stove; 80 per cent of the deposit was kept by the house's
owner – to pay for the cleaning woman, the ripped sheets, the
dishwasher repair – but who cared, after all? Not the owner,
who had made eighty thousand dollars just for getting out of
town for three months, and certainly not the summer tenants.

It was worth it, to roast in the sun until skin had baked
leathery brown; to drive through traffic to a club and drink
eight-dollar margaritas or hang out at a beach party with a
bonfire until the sun came up over the early dawn gray-and-
pink sand. Days spent in bed, a lumpy bed that basically was
being rented for five hundred dollars a night (five, six, seven
thousand dollars for a summer's half-share, how many

---

* New York State requires a 5¢ deposit on beer and soda bottles,
  refunded on return of empty. If you're rich, you don't bother to
  return them, you leave them for the homeless – or the doorman.

weekends was that? Five hundred a night for a shared bathroom – plus the other twin bed in the room occupied by that
snoring stranger who you thought would be amenable because
you both worked at Bear Stern). Then, wake up with a face full
of sand, hung over – the whole day slept away – just in time to
drink a beer and catch the last Sunday night train back to
Manhattan.

At picturesque roadside stands along the highway peaches
could be purchased by the bushel basket – peaches hard as
rocks and flavorless, which turned out to have been bought at
the supermarket and re-sold for five times as much per pound.
The sign at the stand hadn't said anything, after all, about their
being local. If a person driving by wanted to think that, whose
fault was it? But by then the weekend was over, the fruit-
buyers on their way back to the city, and by the following
week no one remembered to complain.

It was the summer when, on a residential street where locals
actually lived year round, one night a copper-leafed Japanese
maple was mysteriously removed and in the morning the
residents found a gaping hole on their front lawn. A few days
later a remarkably similar-looking tree turned up at a local
nursery, tidily balled and on sale for eight thousand dollars.
Overheard at this same nursery, from a woman with sunglasses
and blond hair, 'Five thousand impatiens, including planting,
five thousand dollars?' She paused. (The same impatiens were
$1.89 per six-pack, do-it-yourself, at Woolworth's.) 'Will they
come back next year?' She was talking to Joe – Joe, forty pounds
overweight, in a dirty baseball cap, face red from years in the sun
– whose nursery had been in the family since 1957.

'No, they're an annual.' He's distracted. The day before
some kid had come by with a bunch of plants in the back of a
truck – said they were from the yard of an old house that was
being ripped down and a bigger one being built in its place. Joe
gave him $200 – put a sticker that read, '80 Year Old Japanese
Maple – $8,000' and by mid-afternoon it was sold, to someone

who had come with their Landscape Architect. He couldn't
quite believe it. These people – for all he knew, he had sold it
back to whoever's yard it had come from.

'Oh. Well, I want them anyway.' The woman contemplating
$5,000 worth of impatiens was getting restless. Obviously she
thought of him as subhuman. 'It'll be so pretty, a border all
pink and white – or maybe all white, do you think? Very Vita
Sackville-West.'

'Definitely all white is pretty.'

The woman paused. Maybe she had changed her mind,
come to her senses? 'No, I definitely want the red-and-white
mix. Half of each, please, alternating.'

At night Joe lay in bed wondering if it was all some kind of a
joke; would he wake up one morning and find it had all been a
nurseryman's dream?

It was a place for gay men to forget, at least temporarily,
about the AIDS crisis.

In the City tuberculosis was on the rise. In the East Village
homeless men built fires in steel barrels and shopping carts as
if, despite the ninety-five-degree air, stale, without oxygen,
they needed a fire to keep warm – or to know they were alive.
And in Riverside Park whole encampments slept in the open,
inhabiting miniature villages built from cardboard boxes that
had once contained refrigerators and washing machines, villages that would be abandoned in a soggy heap after the first
rain.

But none of this was visible in the Hamptons. Elegant dinner
parties, catered, or labored over for hours – balsamic vinegar
drizzled over fresh, sliced, deep-red tomatoes layered with
slabs of mozzarella and fresh basil; the table decorated with
floating candles and tiny bowls containing the sweetest, musk-
iest wild pink roses . . .

People one wouldn't normally dream of seeing in the city out
here didn't seem so bad, you actually had things in common –
after all, you both furnished your place from the same East-

hampton antiques store and Watermill Anglo-Indian store (the one run by that gorgeous Indian boy, with all that great rattan and mahogany stuff, allegedly from the palace of a maharaja?); you both had the same pool cleaning service once a week. You both bought tickets for the horse show, went to the same benefits for that Boys' Camp, and your boyfriend of the summer before was now living with them. And afterwards the whole group headed out (including the neighbor whom in New York you wouldn't have spoken to) for the Swamp, or some other place, and even though you were almost forty, you felt just as silly and frivolous as if you were being sent off to camp – only this time it was a camp where you were accepted. Being successful made you a popular boy.

It was the same summer when a man walking on the cliffs near Montauk at night saw what appeared to be a guinea pig the size of a Rottweiler, gray, with cloven hoofs. The animal came grunting out of the bushes and ran down the trail. It turned out to be someone's pet capybara (a South American rodent which can weigh several hundred pounds) but by then the man, badly shaken, had decided to give up drugs and return to the city.

In August of that year the market crashed and the Hamptons' summers of excess were over, at least for a time. And when they returned they would never be so extreme.

Big City Makeover

Originally the editor asked me to insert some paragraphs containing introspection – about appearance, and the experience. I had to make up fake introspection for the version published in the magazine. But it wasn't real introspection. So I took it out. As far as I was concerned, I looked one way, and then a magazine spent a ton of money to have me look a different way. That's as much introspection as I'm capable of.

How did it happen that I came to have big hair, one attribute for which I became, in a modest way, well known? It may have stemmed from an episode in childhood, when I had two long braids that were always getting tangled. It was decided I needed a trim; my mother took me to a beauty parlor in the small town in which we lived, and, without unbraiding or brushing my hair, despite being told I was merely there for a trim, the hair-stylist took a scissors and chopped off each braid alongside my head.

At age eight this was traumatic, but when the results went on being the same with each haircut I got, I gave up and by the early 1980s decided never to get it cut again. It didn't look any tidier after it was cut – or more stylish. My hair had its own ideas about how it should look and the direction in which it wanted to grow. There was no use my fighting it.

It was some time after my decision that I also concluded the best look for me was white skin, dark eyes and red lips. Why I decided this I don't know – unless it was due to my poor eyesight. At a distance in the mirror, with white skin, dark eyes and red lips, I could easily pretend I was a Warhol portrait. And gradually I felt naked without powder and red lips and black eyes.

I wanted a makeover. I wanted to look better. On the other hand, I didn't really want to look any different. I might have liked to be blonde *, but in a week or so I would have had black roots, and I wasn't the sort who had the time and patience to go and sit in a hair salon, or even do it at home myself. As for a change in makeup, what else was there, besides red lipstick?

Anyway, I didn't mind getting the gray covered. Many, many hours passed while the colorist covered the gray and with some kind of vegetable dye tinted the rest a reddish color. I had only tried to dye my hair once before: a man spent five hours, in his own apartment, putting 'tiger' stripes of yellow, red and black, in horizontal bands, all through my hair. However, two hundred dollars later nobody noticed.

After he had finished coloring another man took a brush, a blow dryer and various gelatins. After chopping off the ends he yanked my hair with all his strength until it was absolutely straight and shone like the kind of hair that is submissive.

I felt completely transformed. I now had smooth, straight and shiny hair. 'I'm a real girl,' I kept thinking as I walked down the street, tossing my locks. All my life I had known girls who had straight, shiny hair; they always seemed like real girls. They also seemed like nice girls. Women with a lot of frizzy, black, bushy hair did not seem like nice girls. I knew that, because whenever anybody looked at me they looked away very quickly.

I thought by now I was adjusted to not looking like a nice girl.

* A recently published statistic said 17 per cent of American women are born blonde. It didn't add that – in NYC, at least – by age twenty, 90 per cent of American women have *become* blonde.

I went to meet Tim. 'I didn't recognize you for a minute,' he said. 'I saw a woman with a flat head, and I thought: could that be you?'

'I'm a real girl now.'

Tim looked perplexed.

On Monday I went to the second half of my makeover: they had brought hundreds of outfits, Christian Lacroix, de la Renta, Donna Karan. There must have been a hundred thousand dollars' worth of clothes. All my life I have shopped at the Salvation Army and the thrift store. 'Why, this stuff looks just like the things I get at the thrift store,' I said, 'only they don't have any stains on them, and they're in style.'

It took six or seven people around five hours to make me presentable. They twisted my hair up into a chignon on top of my head and they refused to let me wear red lipstick. What a surprise, but apparently rich women did not wear red lipstick. They wore beige lipstick. Why bother? was my thought. The stylist strapped me into an Oscar de la Renta plaid sequined jacket and velvet skirt that probably cost six thousand dollars. It was strange to think that people actually wore this stuff. It wasn't that it wasn't nice, but it was so expensive, and what if I spilled spaghetti sauce on it? 'How do you feel?' the makeup artist said admiringly.

'Like I want to go home and change into dirty sweatpants,' I said. 'Don't the rich women who wear this sort of thing rush to get home so they can change?'

'The rich never change,' the photographer explained. 'Even when they're alone at home, they're alone in expensive outfits.'

I wondered why I only felt comfortable in old clothes and blue jeans. I liked buying clothes with stains already on them, that way I didn't feel bad when I spilled stuff myself. It would be hard being rich and always having to feel bad that I spilled food on a six-thousand-dollar outfit instead of a two-dollar-ninety-five-cent one. I like to lie around, eating and spilling food. Of course, the rich never eat, obviously, or they would never be able to keep wearing the tiny clothes without stains. 'I suppose it's all what you're used to,' I said. 'But for me, it's too late.'

The photographer said it wasn't too late – he could easily see me married to a seventy-six-year-old man, spending my days shopping. Maybe it was the look in my face, when the stylist kept decorating me with various jewels and slipping ornate, luxurious shoes on my feet.

Finally I was ready to go out: my friend the writer R. Couri Hay was taking me to opening night of the ballet. Sheer black stockings (my usual is cotton tights with runs), Manolo Blahnik high heels (ordinarily I wear low boots held together with a safety pin), my hair upswept in a bun so tight it kept my eyes open, and the Oscar de la Renta suit. The team crowded around me to say goodbye. 'Whatever happens, keep wearing the beige lipstick,' they said. 'Don't go sneaking off into the ladies' room and putting the red stuff on.'

Tim wouldn't be home until late. Couri didn't say anything but went straight to the refrigerator. Maybe he didn't recognize me? I dumped the contents of my handbag (it had cost fifteen dollars, from a Senegalese on the street) into the expensive black suede clutch they had lent me for the night: scraps of paper, a Woolworth's lipstick, old chewing gum, keys on a tiny pair of handcuffs I had once gotten as a gift. 'So, how do I look?' I said.

Couri was devouring some old chocolate mousse. He didn't seem to know how to respond. That wasn't like him. He looked me up and down. 'I guess you have some cash,' he said at last. 'Strangely, I don't have any money on me tonight.'

So that must be what it feels like to be rich. Nobody else around you has any money.

Opening night of the ballet and the first night of my life when I ever felt that I really, truly fit in. People looked at me, but in such a way that made me feel I belonged. How different that look was than the one I was accustomed to! During intermission Couri whisked me upstairs to the private VIP room. No one questioned our going in. The champagne was borne by butlers who were handing out glasses for free. Everyone in there seemed to know me: at least, I thought I heard an audible gasp when I entered the room. I felt like a character out of an Edith Wharton novel, a mysterious – and wealthy – woman who had just arrived back in New York after ten years abroad. Behind me I heard a voice, *sotte voce*: 'That's Tamara deLampicka!'

Jacqueline Kennedy Onassis opened her handbag, took out a tiny pair of spectacles and gazed at me up and down – approvingly, yes approvingly! – before Couri introduced us. A famous man, who under normal circumstances would never have said a word to me, told me at length about his losing twenty pounds. Another man – a rich entrepreneur, I had read about him in the paper – kissed my hand. These were all my friends! 'Are you going to the Hamptons this summer?' Couri asked.

'Oh, I'll be spending a few weekends in the Hamptons,' the man said. 'But this summer I'll mostly be on the Island.'

What Island? I wanted to say, but in my new guise I kept my mouth shut.

Suddenly a handsome man, tall, Latin and dark, sprang out from behind a pillar and grabbed my arm. 'Where did you get that dress?' he said, almost fainting at my feet.

I laughed and glibly waved my free hand. So this was what the right clothes – and hair, and makeup – did to men. 'It's an Oscar de la Renta,' I explained.

'Yes, I know,' the man hissed. Suddenly I realized he was going to attack me. 'But where did you get it?'

My attacker was Boaz, Oscar de la Renta's assistant, and he was furious. The dress I had on had been borrowed from the showroom and it was a dress from an upcoming collection. Many women in the room had ordered the same outfit I had on, and by getting to wear it now, while the others were waiting for their dresses to be made, I was upstaging them. It was meant to have been borrowed for the purposes of a photo shoot only; it was lent under that stipulation and Boaz never expected to see the dress out on the town.

During the next intermission a man told me that the women he was with had spent the entire second act wondering who I was – and where I had gotten my dress.

I decided that even though it was a lot of work, and even though I could never afford such clothing, and even though it wasn't really me, I wouldn't mind staying permanently made over. The magazine said they were willing to give me one last try. They said they would fix me up again – and I could borrow some other clothes. There was a cocktail party to which I had been invited; an exotic Donna Karan dress and jacket seemed suitable. A photographer from the magazine came along to document. The constant flash of the camera did help in making it appear that I must be somebody important. A giant man approached me immediately. 'Hi, I'm Senator————— of ———,' he said. 'Who are you?'

'People are being so friendly,' I murmured. Maybe he only wanted money from me. What did I care? Never before in my life had a senator rushed over to be in my photograph. In my previous guise he would have fled, probably thinking that spending time with me meant getting himself in some kind of blackmail or extortion situation.

Of course it had to end. There was no way I could keep myself in clean Lacroix and Ozbek; even if I did, I had the feeling that people would still think I got my clothes at the thrift store. It was only when a team of seven experts went to work that I could pass.

Still, there was one element I hoped to maintain: the silky hair that made me feel like a nice girl. I called the salon and wrote down the names of everything they had used on me. Then I went out and bought the stuff. It came to one hundred and eighty dollars.

After several hours I emerged from the shower. I had shampooed with the special shampoo and used two types of special conditioning treatment. My next move was to apply some sort of material resembling Jell-O while combing, tugging and blow-drying all at the same time.

When I finished I looked in the mirror. My hair looked no different than it had looked before the makeover.

The heck with it, I thought, and put on my red, cheap lips.

Tim had said, on my return from the ballet, that I looked like a million dollars. Perhaps it was just as well that this façade couldn't be maintained. It had taken me such a long time to figure out who I was. What would I do if I were suddenly somebody else? 'This summer, I'll be in the bathtub,' I said, practicing a bemused, wistful smile in the mirror, which, I noticed only now, was speckled with powder and toothpaste.

Manhattan Manners

EVERYONE IN New York has a different idea of how to behave; for better or worse, though, all of them have got manners,* and I see a lot of them. People walk around with their manners, large and reptile-shaped, some with beaked heads, others ethereal and seemingly delicate but secreting a venomous poison.† I am the sort of person to whom others apparently like to subject their manners, and almost every day when I leave my apartment to go out to walk the dogs, people come over to me to practice.

In front of my building is a small square of dirt where recently a new tree was planted; this spring I decided to grow a few plants around its base. The first to sprout was a lily, which stuck up its head from the sorry dirt and produced four orange buds on a stalk. This really gave me a lot of pleasure, that I was able to grow flowers in the city, and every day on my way out with my dogs I would stop and look at the buds, momentarily about to burst open, and I looked at the buds and thought nice soothing thoughts at them. I was pleased.

The day the first flower opened I was gazing at it admiringly when a woman headed down the street paused to address me. 'How are you going to stop them from stealing your flowers?' she said angrily. I glanced over at her; she had a sour expression on her face, and I could see she was ready to carry on a

---

* Another thing they have all got is qualities.
† I have no idea what I was talking about.

lengthy conversation. The thing was, I didn't really feel like chatting just then; I felt like admiring my flower and then going to the park with the dogs. So I didn't answer her, I just shrugged. A funny look came over her. She was not going to leave until she received an answer from me. 'What will you do?' she said. I didn't respond. 'Huh?' she said. 'You know, I planted flowers in a windowbox and within twenty-four hours they had all been stolen.' She stood fiercely and it seemed that she was not going to leave until I acknowledged what she was saying. 'What are you going to do?' she demanded.

'Don't know,' I mumbled at last.

'You don't know?' she said. 'You don't know?'

What possessed me to ignore her and move off down the street I can't say. My explanation, that I simply didn't feel like speaking – well, that just wasn't good enough. Life in New York must be treated as if one has entered a fairy tale. Any passerby may prove to be a good witch or an evil stepmother. I felt the woman's ice-cube eyes on my back as I walked away; this made me slightly apprehensive.

When I returned, perhaps a half-hour later, my flower was broken in half. Only a crippled stub remained. The orange lily and three buds were gone. I looked up and down the block. The woman had long since left. Several school children from a nearby school were walking past; I suppose one of them could have stolen the flower, but somehow I just didn't think so.

The woman had had her own flowers stolen; I was unfriendly; therefore, she was going to teach me a lesson. Looking at what had once been my tenderly nurtured plant I felt sick, it was as if something inside me had been yanked out. How I had watched it growing, day by day, stretching out of the stale earth . . .

Of course there are all sorts of manners. The ones concerning which fork and knife to use at dinner, combing one's hair in the women's room and remembering to wipe the sink, not snubbing a stranger who attempts to join one's conversation at a cocktail party. But all these things are mostly common sense, and it doesn't bother me too much that most people in New York don't pay any attention to this sort of common courtesy.

They spit in the streets, slam doors on people exiting behind them, steal each other's taxis. Everyone behaves as badly as they want to, because nobody recognizes them and nobody will ever see them again. The city is too crowded. But these things are excusable.

It's easy to see that the only way to survive, after a time, is to pretend that no one else exists. Probably I myself am guilty of all kinds of rude behavior that I'm oblivious of. I forget names and faces constantly and instantly. Once at a party I spent ten minutes talking to a woman I knew and her boyfriend – whom I had not previously met. She introduced him as Bruce and then left. I asked Bruce all sorts of questions – where he came from, the project he was working on and so forth. After a few minutes I excused myself, went to the bar, and then stood on the other side of the room; a friendly man was at my shoulder, chatting about something and – quite naturally, I thought – I introduced myself and asked his name. 'But we just met!' he said with some surprise. 'We were just talking. I'm Bruce.'

'I thought you looked familiar,' I muttered. He looked astonished. 'Just kidding,' I lied. Actually there was nothing familiar about him at all. He was standing in a different place; he never should have moved if he expected me to be able to figure out who he was. By now I have learned that if a person is wearing a different outfit, if they are in a different setting, or if the time of day is different, as far as I am concerned they are not the same person. I need to have dinner with them approximately 150 times before I can possibly be expected to recognize them.

I'm just as guilty of bad manners as the rest of New York City. I'm sure I've let doors fall on plenty of people, though not deliberately; I've been accused of cutting to the front of a line (though in fairness I only did so because I was sent over to speak to some representative, and wasn't trying to get in) I don't mind not getting thank-you notes after a dinner in my home, although I am certainly impressed when I do receive one – after all, who has time? The days here go by at such a hectic pace, people have so much to do, there's endless waiting in line at the bank, the grocery store, stuck on broken-down subways or in a taxi in traffic. There's no going back to the old days when people had time for simple considerations and gentlemen tipped their hats to ladies and always took the kerb. Which I can live with. No, what offends me is a different sort of rudeness.

A woman I liked very much and had known for quite some time; I bumped into her at a party, I was excited to see her . . . I was chatting eagerly to her in one corner when Tim, who I hadn't been involved with for all that long, came over to join us. I introduced the two of them with some pleasure.

Suddenly J. looked at me oddly. 'You look so tired,' she said earnestly. 'Yes, you really look awful.'

I was hurt. Maybe I did look tired, but why did she feel obliged to tell me so? And why did she wait to do this until the moment Tim, a man with whom I was obviously infatuated, came over to join us? Of course, the next day I thought of what my response should have been; I should have looked down shyly, pointed to my new friend and explained, 'That's because he, uh, wakes me up ten times a night.'

But I was not on guard. I trusted her, even a few minutes later when we sat down at a table and she leaned across me, resting her hand on Tim's thigh and began to tell him, in a sympathetic voice, her theories of baseball versus cricket, a subject Tim was particularly interested in, and, stroking his leg, remarked again, sympathetically, on how poorly I looked, perhaps I should go home?

More forgivable is a man I know, a mildly famous movie actor in his sixties, who insists on telling me, whenever he sees me, about the awards he has just received, the directors who have called him begging him to act in their movies, the fancy places he has been to earlier in the evening and will be going to next.

This is boring, but not malevolent. 'Oh, there you are,' he said, the last time I saw him, quite by chance, at some benefit gathering for an obscure disease. He was standing with a woman who was reading a piece of paper, which he took from her hand. 'Are you still able to read without glasses?' he asked, forcing the paper under my nose.

'Yes,' I said.

'I wanted to show you this,' he said. 'Thought you'd get a kick out of it.'

I had the feeling he believed the benefit party was being held in his honor and I had come to pay homage to him, but I forgave him his delusion and read the piece of paper. It was a letter, postmarked Finland, apparently from a director, although I didn't recognize the name. 'My dear————,' the letter began. 'I can't tell you how wonderful it is being that you will be involved with our movie; you are a fantastic and terrible actor and we are delighted you have agreed to the part.'

I thought I had been handed the letter because I would be amused at the word 'terrible'; obviously the author of the note was not a native English speaker. I forced an amused chuckle. 'Isn't that nice?' the actor said. 'I thought you would like to see it.'

'Very funny,' I said. 'It says you're a terrible actor.'

He snatched the letter from my hand. 'No, it doesn't!' he said, squinting. 'It says I'm a terrific actor.' Cruelly, perhaps, I pointed out the word 'terrible'.

'Must be a typo,' he said. It dawned on me then that I had been shown the letter for no other reason than that it heaped praise on the man's head; he hoped I would be suitably impressed. It was a worn and crumpled letter, too: obviously he had shown it to a good many people before me. But this was so sad! Pitiful! After all, on the one or two occasions when I had received a favorable review or an acceptance from a magazine it never would have occurred to me to take the letter or article out in public and pass it around.*

No, the manners of New York are composed of desperation, insecurity, competitiveness and despair, though not everyone is really evil and there are many people who do good deeds all the time. But while I can forgive the man who needs to brag or talk only of himself, and the person who forgets to pass the fried calamari platter down the table, and the taxi driver who turns to scream at the passengers when he gets lost (and the nasty agent who, having been crushed by someone higher up that day, turns on me to kick in the teeth, knowing that I'm lower down the totem pole) – all these things are part of New York, in the end. What I can't live with is the meanness, the reason why the city has no flowers.

* I still don't understand why so many people think a conversation consists of them coming over and bragging. What do they hope to accomplish? Will I like somebody better if I learn they're successful? Who tells me how successful they are? It's one thing if it's someone very close to you, then you can be excited for them, but to just have someone sashay up to you and start in about their latest success, without any concern for how you are, what you've been doing . . . A discussion of the weather would be vastly preferable.

Some New York Apartments

I HAVE NEVER been lucky with my apartments. When I bought a place the market immediately plummeted, when I rented it was always for some exorbitant fee. Some people are naturally lucky with their apartments, it's a gift, other people can afford whatever they want. One is expected, as a guest, to spend time admiring the resident's place or, if not the place, their taste.

Through one of those New York quirks, I ended up at a party one evening at the home of a lawyer, often in the papers, who always appeared to inhabit that realm in which non-human beings reside. He owned a townhouse, in which everything was beige. There were chrome and beige sofas, beige coffee tables, beige rooms, beige Abstract Expressionist paintings on the beige walls, so much beige I thought I was losing my eyesight. And the worst of it was that obviously it had been done up some years back – maybe five, eight, ten years previously, when high tech was the vogue. Only the designer, or the decorator, or the lawyer who owned the house, hadn't wanted to make the plunge into total high tech, so he just leaned in that direction and now, despite the fact that the furniture – the low beige bed, the sofas, the chairs – still all looked new, it also looked out of date, dated, grim and beige and chrome, like an airport lounge.

Upstairs off the master bedroom, which occupied an entire floor, were the His and Her baths, the His and Her saunas. It was the country of someone who thought of himself as a

Playboy. It wasn't just that the place had been neatened up for this party, it was like a beige person lived here.

And in fact the host was a very beige person, with a scrubbed look, a beige suit, a blown-dry hairstyle . . . Perhaps he was even wearing a gold chain around his neck, though that may have simply been my imagination. In the back was a garden, but it was a garden where nobody ever went, though carefully maintained no doubt by a gardener, with low evergreens, a brick terrace area, a central fountain, a few wooden benches. It was a showplace and not a home, but I did not feel like admiring the place. Still, it was apparent that was the type of party this was, where the guests were supposed to wander from floor to floor. Yet one room was virtually indistinguishable from the next.

Then the shock: the lawyer's girlfriend emerged from some remote room, wearing a low-cut dress, like a parody of a pin-up, acres of cleavage and ditsy blond hair piled on top of her head in a frou-frou sheepdog-meets-Madame-de-Pompadour style. She was all giggles and energy, playing Miss Dumbo (but was she playing? Or was it real?) the Playboy bunny from Ohio or Kansas grown a bit too hip and savvy from her years spent in New York, so that the sleek, wistful look was altered now into that of the girl who has spent a few too many nights in the fast lane and is something less or more than innocent.

So this was the lawyer's girlfriend and she lived with him in the beige house, and though the lawyer was nearly fifty she was apparently the first girl who had won her way far enough into his heart for him to allow her to move in. But, as one of the guests whispered to me on the couch, things had not been easy for the couple, even though said guest hoped it would work. The lawyer, it turns out, was very neat, compulsively neat; he had to have everything his way. And the girl – well, she had arrived with her dog, some kind of giant pooch that shed, and a hyacinth macaw, which shrieked and dropped feathers, and three ferrets. Lawyer had managed to make her get rid of those, though she still had the bird and the dog.

And on this particular evening, the loose-lipped guest next to me confided, that girlfriend had decorated the living room for the party with pink streamers, and sprinkled confetti on the coffee table, and tried to make the place more appropriate for a party – and, why, the lawyer really almost had a nervous breakdown, and wouldn't let her leave the room until she had taken everything down and put it back to the way it was meant to be.

I felt somewhat guilty, going to a party at a stranger's house, uninvited, and yet at the same time feeling perfectly free to be critical, and superior. How awful, to give an event where people attend and sneer. On the other hand, the party, like so many others, seemed to happen purely as an excuse for the host to show off. One was quite obviously expected to enter every room over the course of the evening for no other reason than to admire the spaciousness, the beige museum . . .

Some time after the party I heard the girlfriend had moved out, the lawyer had grown too unhappy with their relationship and moved someone else in. I don't know where the girl went, with her fluffy hair, her buxom farm-girl beauty, her dog and her bird . . . she wasn't beige enough.

Once in Jamaica, Queens, I remember being in an apartment with a friend; it was his grandmother's apartment but he had grown up there, the first two floors of an old brownstone. Probably it had once been a decent, middle-class place; but years of neglect, no money, a landlord who did nothing to maintain the place, meant that now the windows were blocked with cardboard and the floors, ceiling and walls were almost wriggling. When I looked more closely I saw that was because the place was crawling with cockroaches. On the floor a two-year-old baby – my friend's sister's child – was dipping a fat fist into a large tub of Vaseline and eating it by the handful.

Once I lived on the same street as an old lady with legs like two vast tree trunks who had a young energetic dog she could no longer walk. After I got to know her a bit I offered to take the dog out on walks. I went to her apartment. She shared the room with another woman, an even older woman, who was sitting feebly on the edge of the bed, like a little pile of twigs. The two of them lived in what had once been the back parlor of the first floor of a brownstone.

It reminded me of an apartment I used to gaze into at street level, an apartment on a back street of Greenwich Village. Walking past and accidentally gazing in (it never seems right to look directly into apartments, even when the blinds are up and the curtains open), I'd peer through grimy windows to a large room with a high ceiling, the entire apartment absolutely filled to the top of the walls with papers, piles of newspapers, books stacked precariously, everything dark and dusty and old . . . The Collier brothers were not alone, so many of New York's elderly lived buried in objects, in rooms with high ceilings, long strips of bulging paint on the ceiling, sheets of wallpaper nearly black with age, grease, grime, a dense and luxurious texture, peeling ominously from the walls.

Old windows with wrinkled glass in a brownstone off Amsterdam Avenue, a floor covered with old strips of lino and pieces of oriental rugs and cheap carpeting, but which in places revealed an extravagant parquet beneath, puzzle-shaped pieces in various rare, multicolored wood; and an ornate marble fireplace, splendid, sleek, with a frieze of carved cherubs. In the corner of the room was the large double bed, piled with blankets, strips of newspaper, on one edge of which was perched the housebound lady like a pile of twigs, while my friend, the one with the dog, slowly tried to rise from her chenille-covered broken armchair.

Some time later, after I had moved elsewhere, I went back to this street. In front of my friend's building, on the edge of the sidewalk, was a pile of garbage and newspaper and a broken, dirty toaster-oven, and in the center of the heap was the old pink chenille-covered armchair, like a huge bathrobe . . . I walked quickly past.

Now I often list in my head the various apartments I've been in: in the East Village a tiny apartment, one room belonging to friends of mine, an artist-couple. It isn't big enough for one person, let alone two. Yet in this one room the two of them live, along with two large dogs, and a cage inhabited by three huge white rabbits with pink eyes. These friends of mine, they had a collection: what they collected, it was hard to say, but in the room were two worn-out sofas, plaid; a plastic bust of Elvis Presley; a large stuffed hyena, genuine, about three feet high, losing most of its fur and mounted on a set of wheels. On the shelves was an assortment of hats, mostly cowboy; antlers; a large alligator hide complete with head; and a huge stuffed fish (real) with rows of sharp, jutting teeth. It was if some indulged child acquired and acquired and never grew up, until it was imprisoned in a homey nest of chaos, every imagined dream finally realized.

Or another place, this one a top-floor apartment, not terribly large, with glass walls on all four sides, nothing blocking the view, no other buildings with apartments to stare back, like a fishtank mounted in the sky. And in the center of the room was the bedroom – this too was surrounded by glass walls, so that it was like a smaller fishtank inside the large one.

Once I was invited to lunch in this apartment. The hostess actually resembled a goldfish with alarmed, bulging eyes. On a glass table in the dining area, on thin glass plates, she served her guests large pink shrimp and a clean green salad in a clear glass bowl. The leaves of the salad, green and ruby, the oil on the leaves, all were picked up by the light which came down in rays from all directions, rays of light glinting off the glass, bathing the thin leaves in light so that they took on the quality of some unimaginably formed mineral, a thin green crystalline . . . the fat shrimp tails curled and twisted in the light as if we were underwater, instead of up in the sky.

Then there was the apartment of a man I dated briefly, in an old building over on the upper East Side, which must at one time have been a one-family mansion belonging to a family out of an Edith Wharton novel. Now it was converted into apartments, but such apartments! This man's was more like a castle, really, a hideous Victorian castle, with walls hung with satin wallpaper, pale, watery-pink, and over this huge paintings – a naked woman sitting on a mountain, with a dazed, exhausted look in her eyes, and no wonder, for crawling over her naked body (only one pink-nippled breast visible) was an array of huge, fat, naked children, with long, curly hair and fat, petulant faces, crawling up over this huge, naked woman, almost molesting her with their plump, greedy hands.

And the floors of black and white marble. And the bathroom, with its vast pool-sized tub, and a stone spiral staircase leading to the upstairs bedroom with its massive canopied bed. And the collection of nineteenth-century bronzes – men sword-fighting, a deer running from hounds, a giant boar, a hare and a snake. Of course, my relationship with this man could not possibly have worked out, obviously he was stuck in the wrong century, in this dimly lit, cold apartment behind a gloomy stone-fronted façade.

New York is the city of apartments, apartments in modern buildings, tiny cubicles placed one on top of the next, grim as jail cells. And other buildings, the old brownstones, blocks of brownstones set like teeth into the jaw of the street, each with an almost human personality, some stolid, uncaring of the various residents who come and go over the years, others flighty, fragile, worn out from the lives that have gone on inside. Some brownstones have never gotten over their initial grief, the loss of their first inhabitants, a single family with father, mother, children, maids, a cook. Others accepted being chopped into smaller units, enjoyed their years as a brothel or SRO.

And the massive apartment blocks of the '60s, thrown up

along Third Avenue, with paper walls and impersonal appearance, automaton buildings slapped up for residents who were destined to lead lives in gray offices. Or those old apartment buildings along West End Avenue, the last buildings whose halls smell of pot roast, cabbage, Brussels sprouts, a meal of smells in the halls and dark elevators, with the creak of steam heat and the rattle of windows no longer firmly attached to their moorings.

By now I have been in hundreds of apartments. I don't remember all of them, some have blurred into others. There is the memory of bathroom fixtures, old bathroom fixtures, where the hot is on one tap and cold is on the other and it is never possible to get water of medium temperature – one's hands race back from the hot stream to the cold, first scalded, then frozen.

I have seen sad bathtubs in the kitchen, public showers and toilets located down the hall, I have walked up five flights to tiny rooms that rented for thousands of dollars a month. And once, in the past, I found an old apartment, quite huge, with a tiny balcony off the dining room, and little steps and stairs leading to other, spacious rooms, and a garden in the back, which was being rented for only a few hundred dollars. But that few hundred dollars was more than I had at the time.

And in lower Manhattan a tiny house, standing in a yard, with crooked white walls and green shutters, an ancient farmhouse, probably once just a chicken coop, stuck up next to a dusty old brick wall and surrounded by grass. Buildings squeezed between buildings! And the buildings of the newly wealthy, with spectacular views of Manhattan up on the fifty-seventh floor: the twinkling lights glossy and glamorous, the tugboats miles below slipping up the East River. These apartments, with expensive second-rate art on the walls, and gold faucet handles in the toilet, libraries filled with coffee-table books and VCR equipment, stereos, CDs, are the rich cousins to the Third Avenue bunch. Here the wall-to-wall gray carpeting is of real wool, not nylon. Every object appears untouched by human hands. Far below the drivers of the chauffeured Jaguars wait to take the apartment dwellers to a restaurant or museum dinner, all that money can buy is to keep the financier sheltered from the street.

Apartments without heat where the wind whips in off the canyons, one has to wear gloves in the house, the walls seem no protection whatsoever, candles blow out in the center of the room. And apartments that are so overheated the floor is hot to the touch. Even opening the windows does not let in cool air; an evening spent in such a place leaves one feeling infirm, exhausted, ancient, like some artificial nearly extinct species kept in a glass case, a completely artificial atmosphere. The person who lives here has become delicate, fragile, their importance overinflated, while on the couch little dogs snuffle and groan uneasily in their falsely induced sleep, a stupor of heat . . .

Noise in New York

NOISE IN New York is not something most people feel comfortable complaining about. There is plenty that is acceptable to complain about in Manhattan – and the other boroughs – but to complain about noise is a bit like a climber on Mount Everest whining that there's not enough oxygen. If you need oxygen, why the hell did you decide to climb Mount Everest in the first place? And if you can't deal with noise, you shouldn't be in New York.

The other problem is, the levels of noise are not universal. I mean, if a person has a great loft near the Holland Tunnel, but it's noisy from traffic, tough. You have a great loft, so shut up. We live in Brooklyn, on top of a hill, on top of a building on top of a hill, with great views: people come to visit and they say, 'Oh, it's so quiet.' It is quiet, except at certain times of day when airplanes are coming in to land at JFK, when I have to go out on to the terrace to make sure they're not going to crash into my apartment. So it's not really acceptable for me to say, 'Oh no, it's not quiet here – we have noise between seven and nine, when jetplanes come in.' Nobody's going to care – after all, they don't have that jetplane-landing problem.

My mother is extremely sensitive to noise, and even though I think this place is totally silent except for take-off and landing, when she comes to visit she finds it so noisy here that she brings her special noise-machine, which is a machine that makes so much noise you can't hear any other noise. It is called a White Noise machine, and once, when my mother was

staying here and we had a dinner party for a couple of friends
and my mother excused herself and went to sleep, the friends
said, 'What's going on here? What's all that noise, all of a
sudden?'

It was my mother's noise machine, so noisy that no mere
mortal could sleep through the sound.

Another friend who stayed here complained about the noise
of the elevator, which sounds like, well, two people on a
mattress with very creaky springs. She wondered, who could
be so active – all night? But I had never noticed that noise; for
one thing, our bedroom is in a different spot; and, to me, it was
just the sound of the elevator, which is quite elderly and if
anything might be thought of as whining or complaining,
slightly, but certainly could never be interpreted as actively
engaged in an act of abandon.

I once lived in the meat market district – this was years ago,
before that area became fashionable – and between the trans-
vestite prostitutes, who retired to sleep each night on a loading
dock directly across from my window, five floors below, where
they held a slumber party complete with loud cassettes playing
dance music and lots of giggles, gossip and makeup sessions –
and the delivery of meat, on huge trucks, starting at about five
a.m. – it was a noisy place. How was I going to complain about
it, though? What could I say? That the meat being delivered
made it impossible to sleep? Who, really, was going to care?

But apart from that, the thing that made this apartment
particularly noisy was the mice. I knew I had mice, and I
suppose I could have learned to live with them, but these were
fighting mice. The apartment, I guess, was too crowded. There
must have been many families of mice, Jukes and Kalikaks,
fighting generational battles, night after night. Their screams
of rage, hatred and fury were so loud, I became a murderer.
This apartment was only ten by thirteen feet (I measured it),
formerly a locker for frozen food – meat, primarily, I guess. It
was crowded for me and two dogs (and yet, curiously, the

dogs, terriers once bred as ratters, never noticed the mice, even when one scampered across Beep-beep's feet) and I did feel bad after I killed the first mouse, with a trap. I also felt bad about the death of the second mouse, and the third. But by the fourth, I was hardened, and when I had killed seventeen or eighteen mice I knew the meat-market district was not helping the evolution of my karma. I moved a short time after that.

New York Media

THE PHONE rang and a woman asked if I would appear on a show about big hair. 'Big hair?' I said. 'Is that your show?'

'Yes,' she said, 'I know, but that's what the show is, and I was wondering. I would just love it if you could.'

'See,' I said, 'I'm going out of town. I'm awfully busy.'

'Oh my God,' she said. 'Please, please, please.' She sounded desperate. 'I'm the hostess of the show and I don't usually make these calls, but I so wanted to have you as my guest.'

'My hair . . .' I said. 'You know, it just grows like this. It's not something I can help. Are you going to be . . . making fun of me? I mean, I'm used to it, but . . . maybe I'm getting a little tired of it.'

'Oh no,' she said with a shocked gasp. 'No, not at all. Please, if there's any way you can work it into your schedule. It will only take ten minutes if you want to come here to the studio; or we could come up to you; or anywhere, really, anywhere that you want.'

'Oh, gee,' I said. 'You know, I'm—'

'Just ten minutes. It would mean *so much* to me, and I think – I don't know what bad experiences you've had with television before, but this would be—'

'All right, all right. If you can do it tomorrow, after three, at Café Luxembourg, which is just up the street.'

'OK,' she said. 'Great! No problem.'

I went out of the house. When I got back there was a

message on the machine. 'We'll see you there at one-thirty tomorrow.'

I called her back. 'Look,' I said, 'one-thirty's no good. You'll have to make it later.'

'Just a minute,' she said. I waited. She returned to the phone, sounding cold and angry. 'One-thirty is the only time. The crew has to be someplace important at two. It's all arranged. We'll arrive at one, set up, ready to go by one-thirty.'

The next day I went to Café Luxembourg at one-thirty. The crew didn't finish setting up until two-fifteen. 'And afterwards,' the hostess of the program said, 'we'll go out for a street shot, to show you walking down the street with, you know, your hair. Then maybe over to the park, and maybe you getting in and out of a taxi. Do you mind sitting on that stool?'

'I'd be more comfortable in a chair,' I said.

'No,' she said. 'You can't sit in a chair. You have to be at that height so we can show the background and the only thing the correct height is the stool.' She looked at me as if I was being incredibly difficult.

I sat on the stool. 'All ready?' she said. The crew had to make a number of adjustments. There was a delay while a cameraman apparently sawed a table leg using a Swiss Army knife. I wondered if the restaurant, which had always been incredibly kind in allowing me to do interviews there, would ever let me back. I perched precariously on my seat.

'You look fine,' the presenter said. 'Big hair. Ready?'

The lights were bright and hot, the cameras were rolling. The staff of the restaurant gathered to watch. I nodded.

'OK,' she said. 'You think men – when they're with you – they don't want to touch your hair? You think maybe . . . they find it kind of disgusting?' She touched her own hair, which was short and sleek and blond. Then she looked back at me, crinking her nose as if something smelled bad. With a dainty gesture at my head, she said, 'It's so big . . . and . . . bushy . . . tentacles and . . . I mean, I don't know, what do you think, do you think it puts them off?' Like a bird hypnotized before a snake, or a child mesmerized at the sight of something repugnant, she struggled briefly to collect herself and waited eagerly for my response.

Some ten years later I was walking down the street and a homeless person on the corner yelled to me, 'Hey, honey, you having a bad hair day?' I didn't respond. 'You not having a bad hair day,' *he went on, 'I think you having a bad hair* month.' *He cackled at his own joke appreciatively and then decided at last, 'No – you having a bad hair* life!'

A New York Bank

I WENT INTO my bank. It was just before closing on the Friday of a long weekend. The place was packed. I had a check from a foreign country and two Yorkshire terriers with me. The place was really crowded, but I wanted to find out what I should do with the check.

First I waited behind quite a few people in a line marked 'Information'. But there was nobody at the front of the line to help. A woman came up to me. It seemed as if she was trying to push her way in front of me. I gave her a look. 'Is this where they give a cash advance?' she said in a foreign accent.

'No,' I said. 'This is the line for Information.'

There was a woman standing in the Transactions line who also had a Yorkshire terrier. When she saw my dogs she suddenly released some kind of clasp that allowed her dog to run in front of all the people in her line over to where I was standing. I quickly tried to yank my dogs out of the way. One of my dogs was a fighting dog. I didn't want him to go for the other Yorkshire terrier's jugular. The woman's leash, now twenty feet long, pulled by her Yorkie, was getting everyone tangled up. She gave me a mean look, indicating she thought I was horribly unfriendly. There was still no one at the Information desk.

Then a woman came up next to me. 'What a cute dog,' she said. 'That's a very cute dog. What kind is it?'

'Yorkshire terrier.'

'Oh, it is. That's a good dog to have in a city apartment, isn't it, due to its size,' she said. 'It's a small dog, and a large dog takes up a lot of room.'

'Mmm,' I said.

'I was taking care of a friend's dog, on several different weekends,' she continued. 'It was a German shepherd. It shed a lot. Every time it left I had to spend hours vacuuming. I tried to make it stay on a towel, which I put out for it, on the floor, but it wouldn't stay there. And when it got up, it would leave white hairs everywhere, although it wasn't a white dog. The dog had brown fur but the fur it shed was white. My carpet is textured, with various layers, you know, one of those carved carpets, and it was difficult to get the fur out of the carpet.'

I looked into space. It occurred to me that the woman's monologue was particularly loud. I had never seen her before in my life. There was still no one at the Information counter, but the line behind me had grown.

'A small dog like that, it doesn't shed,' she said. 'Does it?' I tried to ignore her.

'Today,' she said, 'I had a lot to do, I was running around everywhere, so before I left the house, I made a sandwich to have for my lunch, and then I realized I had forgotten it!'

I wondered if people thought we were acquaintances. I had been in the bank for almost twenty minutes. Another woman charged to the front of the line just as the Information lady appeared. 'My checks haven't come,' she shouted. 'All I need is a few checks, so I can write a check. It's been three and a half weeks since I ordered them.'

My queue began to make angry noises, and the Information person told her to go and wait in line. For some reason the woman gave me a look and decided to push in front of me. 'All I need is a few checks, there's no reason she can't just give them to me,' she said. Then she turned to my friend. 'I got in here just before they shut the doors,' she said. 'Running, running, running. I was so out of breath I had to sit down once I got inside. They say the economy is down, why is this place so busy?'

'The economy isn't down,' said my acquaintance. 'Although it's very busy in here today. But sometimes it's not so busy.'

'Oh, you think they're just *telling* us the economy is down,' the other woman said. 'I see, I see. That's what they tell us, but it isn't true.'

I was glad the two had found each other, even if she had cut ahead of me. Now maybe I would be left alone. It was the sort of day when people were paying attention to me. I must have had the aura. I looked at the two women surreptitiously. The first one was wearing a gray knit hat with frizzy gray hair protruding beneath and a gray fake-fur coat. The second had on a pale short red wig, pale-red glasses and a pale-red wool coat. 'All I need is a few blank checks,' she said. Her teeth protruded and were covered with red lipstick. 'If I don't pay my phone bills they charge me a penalty.'

'You could send a money order,' the gray woman said. 'You could go to the post office and send a money order.'

'Who's next?' the woman said behind the Information desk.

'Actually, I think I was,' I said.

'What is your sign?' the pale red said to the gray. 'You are a very friendly, nice person.' Then she glared at me.

'I'm an Aries,' the woman in gray said.

'An Aries!' she said. 'So am I. All Aries are nice, *friendly* people.'

I was having a hard time hearing the Information teller. She said it would cost me forty-five dollars to change a foreign check into US currency, and she would have to fill out a lot of forms, and it would take a few minutes. Then she disappeared.

'I bet *she's* a Gemini,' the pale-red woman announced. She pointed at me. 'What sign are you.'

I tried to ignore her.

'Are you a Gemini?' she said.

'No,' I said, as coldly as possible.

'She doesn't want to say what sign she is.' She was almost cackling with glee. 'Are you a Libra? What are you?'

'I'm an Aries,' I muttered at last, hoping it would put an end to things.

'An Aries!' the woman said. 'That's because she's beautiful. All Aries are beautiful, and I'm not embarrassed to say so.' She turned to the gray. 'All Aries are psychic, too. You know, I'm in the art business and . . .'

A fight had broken out across the room and I was momentarily distracted.

'Let me ask you, using your psychic abilities, how many millions does it take to . . .', the pale red was saying to her new friend.

The Information teller came back with a second clerk. 'I need a drink,' the new clerk said to the first. 'If there's one thing you could get me, it's a drink.'

'If you're asking me for a psychic number, the first one that comes into my head is two,' the psychic gray Aries was telling the psychic red.

'Was that your first guess?' the pale-red said. 'Without thinking? Two?'

'Oh, yes,' said the gray.

'That's what *everybody* says.'

The Information lady seemed to have forgotten where she was. 'I'd like a drink, too,' she said to me. There was a high counter between us, almost as if we were at a bar.

'If I had a drink, I'd give you one,' I said.

The teller laughed. 'When you get the charges, on your next statement, bring it back in,' she said. 'You can find out then if you can get the forty-five dollars back.'

'I have to come back and wait again?' I said.

'Sorry,' she said. 'Have a nice weekend.'

I couldn't believe all this chaos was really taking place in a bank. I was about to leave, but the front doors had been locked. There was no security guard with a key to release anyone. A crowd had gathered, impatient, hoping to be allowed to leave. For all we knew, we were trapped here for the weekend.

Suddenly a man came over. I knew him – anyway, I had met him at a movie premiere – he was one of the bank's vice-presidents. 'How are you?' he said, picking me out of the crowd. 'What do you need?'

'I'm trying to get out,' I said. 'But they've locked the front doors, and there's nobody here with a key.'

'You want me to let you out here?' he said. He lowered his voice seductively. 'Or you want to go out the back way? Come with me, I'll take you.'

I remembered when I had met him, at this party, at the bar. Around two minutes into a conversation, for no reason at all, he had taken out his two front teeth and displayed them to me, quite proudly, in the palm of his hand. He was a young guy, no older than me and appeared capable of serial crimes. 'Maybe if you could just unlock the front door,' I said. 'And let me out, with the others.'

It was this sort of everyday occurrence that kept me enjoying life in the city for a long time. Now I no longer find it so amusing, but then I simply went out of the house and loved it – not the cultural aspects of the city, or the restaurants, or social life; what I loved was the people, who seemed so funny and strange.

The Literary Mafia

RECENTLY, ON the street, I noticed men and women selling books at a tremendous discount. There are lavish art books (new) on Van Gogh, the Impressionists, modern photography for fifteen or twenty dollars; five bucks will buy a cookbook by Craig Claiborne or a new hard-cover true crime book by Anne Rule; children's illustrated pop-up books sell for a dollar.

Some of the books are printed on fairly shabby paper and the color reproduction quality isn't top notch. But mostly they are just the same as in the shops. At a lunch one afternoon I was seated across from Paul Gottlieb, a publisher of art books, and I asked him where all these books on the street were coming from.

'Some of them, they print them in China,' he said, 'where they have no copyright laws. The Mafia is involved with this. They tell the printer, "Look, you're planning to print ten thousand copies of a book, print a couple extra thousand and we'll give you a dollar a copy."' He was getting more and more worked up as he spoke. 'And once, I had to send some books to be destroyed, out in New Jersey. And I received a letter, saying the books had been destroyed. But the next week, I saw those same books, being sold on the street. The Mafia is involved with this – they sell them off the back of a truck. Not only does the author not get royalties, but there's no sales figures – and of course the publisher loses money.'

'But ... surely it's not legal. Why don't the police do something?'

'The police? There are no Book Police!'

'I suppose they don't need them. Scarcely anyone reads any more, anyway. George Orwell had things a bit wrong.'

Chairs

I was asked to write a piece on chairs for an auction catalog, a benefit auction of chairs in memory of Jed Johnson. This was in the winter of 1997. Later I realized there were all kinds of Eames chairs. I was thinking of the Herman Miller chair, that big black leather-and-rosewood number with the ottoman. My article didn't make much sense, since it was accompanied by a picture of a small metal chair.

The Eames chair is the daddy chair. I say this, I suppose, in part because this is the chair that my father had when I was a kid, but also because the Eames chair looks like the daddy chair. It's obviously a male chair, and one that nobody would dare sit down in without being invited to do so.

Chairs have personalities and are always male, female or neuter. I like the idea of clothing for chairs, especially little dresses, and anyone can see that chairs bask in the excitement of being clothed or having their upholstery and springs redone.

I sometimes think of the story of the famous and wonderful painter Larry Rivers and his romance with his mother's chair. (You can read a more detailed version in his autobiography, or hear one if you meet him.) Anyway, it wasn't much of a romance, more of a straightforward sexual relationship, but it just goes to show how other people can also get involved with chairs. I've been hanging out at the local upholsterer's, and there's a chair I can't take my eyes off: she has fat, short gold legs and a gold back that resembles a lyre. Her springs are shot and her blue velvet is worn out. Nevertheless, she reminds me of Mae West. I kept admiring her until finally I asked if she was for sale. 'No,' said the upholsterer. 'Somebody found her in the basement of their building.'

That kind of thing never happens to me, although I did once buy – for five dollars – a metal office chair with spindly legs on wheels and a leather seat that resembles a spider, whom I dearly love. This chair is a male, and if he were a person he would be wearing an old-fashioned Homburg hat. One of my favorite chairs (long since deceased) was a canvas-and-tubular-steel chair that had the playful habit of folding up on new occupants and then toppling over on to her side. That was always a source of family entertainment when I was a child. No matter how forcefully the family announced to the visitor that they shouldn't sit in that chair, by her own willful personality she lured guests on to her lap.

I figure if you see a chair you really like, and you can afford it, you should buy it, because then when you walk into your house you have a lot of friends waiting for you who don't need to be walked. And it will never complain, it will just be there with open arms – if it has any.

Pearl River

I ALWAYS THINK it's fun to take out-of-town guests to China-town; but the narrow sidewalks, the tiny shops jammed with handbags and wristwatches, the crowds of people, can be overwhelming – though I have a fondness for the counterfeit, and am always amazed by the most recent styles in Hermes and Louis Vuitton and Prada, the Movado and the Cartier, most of my friends do not share my interest. Pearl River department store, located on the northeast corner of Canal Street at Broad-way, is a bit easier for most people to deal with; its several floors are carefully divided into manageable areas, the place is gen-erally empty and as of late the products are simultaneously more upscale and sweetly antiquated, in some instances harking back to items found in pre-Maoist China – the little round stiff silk hat (I'm sure there's a name for this, but it reminds me of an oversized yarmulke) for children, in the clothing department; hand-made paper in the stationery department; silk brocade mules for women in the shoe department; and so forth. Gen-erally I begin my perusal on the top floor: here is a porcelain department with rows of bowls, dishes, plates, many of which now are being shown in an utterly beautiful luminescent green glaze, beautifully shaped bowls – for cereal, or side-dishes, the outside in a deep chocolate, the innards in a crackled color somewhere between celadon, mint and pea. All range between ten and fifteen dollars; there are other beautiful dishes, too, in soft cherry tones and blue designs, as lovely as if they came from some exclusive artisan's shop. Nearby, in the stationery department, there are bound notebooks with covers in very simple banana-tree bark, resembling exotic wood veneer, containing thick, mottled paper, hand-made in Bali; others have covers with hand-made papers, some containing pressed flowers, all around eight dollars each. The clothing department has pale pink and green cashmere sweaters, robes and kimonos in Japanese-print-style cottons or Chinese print rayon or silk brocade; in this same department beautiful strips of embroidery can be purchased by the yard, if one has a dressmaker able to apply floral or abstract embroidery designs to the edge of a garment. Also available, displayed on paper cards, are amazing Chinese Mandarin-style frogs, embroidered twists of fabric in the shape of butterflies, leaves, geometric designs, with nugget-shaped toggles, which could be substituted for existing buttons on, say, a sweater – these come in various double colors, pink with blue lining, green with pink lining, red and black, and so forth.

If shopping here feels a bit exotic, it's also as close to visiting a department store in China as I've come. In China, one selects merchandise from the department with the aid of a floor-walker, who then takes your merchandise and goes to a cashier. Some time later she or he returns with a receipt. One then must go – without merchandise – to the cashier of the proper department and pay. Then at last your merchandise is tidily returned, wrapped in a bit of paper.

It must be, I've always thought, quite similar to shopping during the Victorian era – when Ladies' Mile, full of stores then like the original Tiffany's – had floorwalkers in every department and pneumatic tubes which slid one's cash to the basement; back would come correct change. Though the method of paying for one's purchases in each department is only somewhat similar to a department store in China, another resemblance is that, in Pearl River, junk products may be mixed in with more upscale or fashionably Western items – in the kitchenware department you might see cheap plastic

colanders, pink or orange, alongside beautiful lacquer chop-
sticks, or rather nice heavy-duty steel woks.

Though I enjoy the experience, there is no one, really, to
assist me here at Pearl River department store. If in an
American department store one can't obtain assistance because the sales clerks are hiding in a closet, here it is as if the
Communist mentality means that workers shouldn't be aiding
capitalist-materialists.

One floor below are more housewares and other basic items –
plain cotton T-shirts and traditional Chinese 'wadding blankets', thick comforters stuffed with varying quantities of silk and
cotton, perfect for a summer comforter or for those allergic to
wool or down, many of which have fantastic covers (the duvet
covers are also available independently): subtly pale geometric
designs, brown on green or pale lavender, resembling patterns
found at Pierre Deux, or those of some upscale Japanese designer
of bed and bath supplies. This department also contains beautiful
lanterns, of pale gauzy stuff, in melon and raspberry and green,
perfect for an outdoor summer party; there are intricate ribbons
like strands of cut-paper banners, quaintly resembling the decorations from some child's birthday of the 1930s, again suitable
for a party, costing anywhere from two to ten dollars. The
merchandise fluctuates, seasonally or depending on, I suppose,
what factories in China are producing items thought suitable for
Western consumption; it is possible to leave the department store
with a feeling of having visited a foreign country, if not China,
somewhere other than Manhattan – and with a sense of having
gone on a mini-adventure, which, as I say, is particularly fun to
inflict on an out-of-town visitor or guest. Afterwards one may
wander over to one of the many fairly decent Chinese restaurants
in the area – Joe's Shanghai comes to mind, as does the third-floor
dimsum palace, The Golden Unicorn and, at the start of East
Broadway, Dim Sum A Go-Go; the best time to go, at least on the
weekend, is either very early, before ten a.m., or around three-
thirty, when there is a good chance of them being fairly empty.

Net Worth

THESE DAYS, it seems like everybody's rich. Even me, who never made much money from writing but saved every penny, I'm starting to think I'm doing pretty good. Thanks to my money guys (George Tanaka and George Loening), one of these days I might even be a millionaire. Which is pretty amazing considering how little I gave them to work with, initially. Believe me when I say there are only two or three writers making a decent living from their books and they are Stephen King, Danielle Steele and the one who writes the Harry Potter books. Otherwise, you get an advance – let's say, one hundred thousand dollars. Agent gets 15 per cent, this equals eighty-five thousand, taxes make it equal, say, sixty-five. Now, this money is not given to you all at once. How it works, one-third on signing, one-third on handing in final manuscript (maybe six months, a year later) one-third on publication (maybe another year or year and a half later). I can't do math, but to me this does not appear to be a living wage such as a Wall Street receptionist might earn. Some writers, they teach; other writers, they write for Hollywood. The best thing I would want to do as a writer is to be a contributing editor, at a magazine, which would give me a few assignments and a salary, and still give me time to write the novels. But, no one has invited me to do any of the above. So you make a choice, I think, when you become a writer and you say to yourself, 'When Herman Melville died, his books were out of print and he was wandering around South Street

Seaport, poverty-stricken and unable to afford even J. Crew.'
One thing that makes me happy, on a bad day writing some
freelance article (as far as I can tell freelancing is the one field
that hasn't had pay-raises in twenty years) is to think about
how rich I am.

Maybe to somebody else having a few dollars in the bank
wouldn't be considered being rich, but hey, it's not a deficit!
So, to me there's a major difference. Which is why, even if I
ever had one million dollars in the bank, what would be the
point of living off the interest? What's eighty or a hundred
grand a year going to get me? Let's say, one hundred grand.
After taxes, seventy. Child's private kindergarten: fifteen
thousand. Buy used car, parking space, insurance; country
cottage; housekeeper; I'd be so tired from all this I'd have to go
out to dinner to eat, or order in – nothing left, I'm poor again,
maybe even a deficit, no time to write – forget the whole thing.
I'd rather keep this fictitious money in the bank. Sometimes I
think, What if I had twenty million dollars? But that doesn't
sound rich to me, not really. What's twenty million dollars
going to get you? To me, being rich would be at least one
hundred million. Otherwise, just forget the whole thing. To
me, twenty million: you'd have to run around, crimping
corners, clipping coupons (like the one in the Entemann's
box, fifty cents off for two Multi-grain bars) to give to the
maid when she goes to the supermarket. Twenty million, you'd
have to keep trying to show your friends that you were worth
something – when the reality is, you're really not. And what
about those poor Steinbergs? They were rich, and then they
had to sell all that stuff, and what a lot of work that must be!
And all your alleged friends, suddenly, who were nice to you
when you were worth half a billion, suddenly snubbing you
when you're down to twenty million. I don't want to be friends
with such people who would sneer at me behind my back for
only having twenty million.

Anyway, to continue. The apartment we bought a couple of

years back – it's maybe almost doubled in value, considering what's happening in real estate. The problem is, I still don't have enough money to buy anything. I've been pricing those Manolo Blahnik shoes, and the Range Rover, and private kindergarten for my kid and I figure, if I cash in my retirement fund it would only be worth about half after taxes and the penalties you have to pay for getting the money out early. I only have this retirement fund because one year, when I did earn some money, my accountant said, 'If you save this money in a retirement fund, you won't have to pay as much in taxes now.' At the time it made sense, because if I became senile, or couldn't write any more books that only a few people want to read anyway, then I would have this retirement fund.

That was before I had a thought. The thought was: I'm saving so I can go in a nursing home? If I do wait until retirement to use the money – and I know this sounds crazy, but what if I didn't use it to go to a nursing home but say, to, buy groceries? – by then inflation will be so steep that it's probably still not going to be worth much, and I'll still have to pay taxes, and after all it's not like the retirement fund of somebody who was earning big bucks, so I doubt it will go very far then, when I'm old. And I won't really be able to count on my daughter to support me, when I'm old, because, after all, I wasn't able to send her to private school for kindergarten, so who knows where she'll end up? Judging by what the parents in my building are going through, trying to get their kids into private schools, if you're five years old and not in private school, you're doomed. I don't know whatever happened to Horatio Alger success stories; but who am I to say? All I know is, I don't want my kid to end up as a writer – which is OK, actually, because she's already said she wants to be a plumber when she grows up, so maybe things will work out, after all.

And the money that's in just plain investment, if I spent it, what would that get me? I saw the other day that one of those

Hermes Birkin bags costs around five and a half grand, and they're made out of denim, trimmed with different color leather. What am I going to do with a five-thousand-dollar denim handbag? What if I suddenly needed some cash and had to sell it, who's going to buy a slightly soiled used denim handbag? And aquaintances who are getting face-lifts say that runs, these days, to around twenty thousand, so I don't know if I should use my savings to get these things now, or let George Tanaka keep making me more money, when the cost of the Birkin bag and the face-lift will probably have tripled, or quadrupled, and the Birkin bag that is supposed to be so timeless will be out of style.

If I had had the money I had now, only it was thirty or so years ago, then I might have been rich. I was reading in the *Times* real, estate section, this one woman bought a loft in SoHo in the '70s for something like thirteen thousand dollars. So I guess now she's sitting on a couple-of-million-dollars piece of real estate, at least. The problem with this is, if she sells it, what can she buy instead? In the same article it described these people buying some raw space, in the same downtown New York area, for more than a million and a half – and spending another six or so to do up the place. So if the woman sold her thirteen-thousand-dollar property at a profit, and then paid the taxes, she probably wouldn't have enough money to buy anything nearly as nice. Which is one thought that stops me from thinking we would ever sell the apartment we're in now. Of course, if a Depression comes along, I'll be one rich lady.

Except, of course, when I think this through and realize that under those circumstances all my investments aren't going to be worth much. No, the only way I'll ever stay rich is to keep it on paper.

This was written before the market crash, fall 2001. Now, I'd settle for the instant lottery that pays $1,000 a week for life.

The Economy of New York

Chapter One

The American system of business and enterprise was founded on what is known as the Economy. It dates back to a long time ago. When the early settlers arrived, they were able to take some seashells, open a store called Tiffany's, and trade the designer shells (wampum) to the Indians for an island.

The island is known as the Big Apple. This name was first mentioned in 1923 in a story by a man named Ring Lardner. In the Indian language, Ring Lardner was called Man-With-a-Hat-on, or Manhattan. Many of the terms used in the United States today are in the Indian language (Native tongue), since the city of Manhattan was constructed by Mohawk Indians, known for their inability to fear heights. And it was at a time when a decent man did not go out without his hat on.

In these long-ago days other men began to work on the Economic System, in order to open up the Gap between rich and poor, otherwise known – in Indian – as the Great Divide or, in German (due to the many Germans who tried to take over the Midwest), the Tectonic Plate.

Work constructing the System was laborious. If the men had some tea but did not want to pay taxes on the tea, they would take the teabags and throw them into a harbor. That is why, in each city, there is a Chinatown near the water. But now, if a man has something and he doesn't want to pay taxes on it, he threatens to move his factory to Mexico or Korea or New

Jersey. Conversely, he may work out a deal with the Mayor, who is lonely and does not want his citizens to leave.

But this way of life did not come easily. There was a price to pay. Many years ago, it was necessary to break away from the cruel King of England, who had gotten away with murder when he divorced his wives at a time nobody believed in divorce. When there was no longer a King to rule the people, it was much better. City government was able to work out deals with men known as Contractors. This led to a great many artistic endeavors in the arts. Otherwise, there would have been many fewer biographies of great men, and movies about gangsters.

In modern times, these gangsters give their companies names such as Acme Renovators and Decorators, but in earlier periods we had men such as Andrew Carnegie and John D. Rockefeller, who were not gangsters, because back then there were no income taxes, so they didn't have to pay any. Nor were there any problems regarding monopolies. People paid their phone bills on time, for there were no alternative long-distance carriers; postage stamps cost one or two cents; and whether or not your computer was IBM-compatible made no difference. Back then, if a man wanted to own everything, that was his right as an American.

Now, if a man owns everything, he has to juggle things around until it looks like he doesn't own everything, or else make it look as if what he owns is so bad nobody else would want it and it might as well be called Junk, which is how he is able to sell junk bonds. But in the chain of Wal-Mart stores, the quality and value of the merchandise are quite high, and the prices are reasonable. And the Walmart family lives simply.

It is thanks to this sort of family, and to men such as John D. Rockefeller and Andrew Carnegie, and Henry Ford, and 'Diamond' Jim Brady, and the James Brothers, Oscar of Delmonico's, Eli Whitney of The Cotton Gin and Sirio Maccione of Le Cirque, that we have all kinds of benefits. We have major foundations that can donate 5 per cent of their tax-free income to put plays on Public Television, there are touring production companies of *Cats* and in addition there are movies and jobs for projectionists. More and more people are becoming aware of Conservation, and if they get enough money they go out to look at it. *Example*: in Pittsburgh, home of the famed Andrew Carnegie, the French, Indians and British, at the start of the French-and-Indian wars (1757, Fort DuQuesne vs. the people's General Braddock) had badly polluted the three rivers, due to the steel industry. (Extra Credit: In what *National Geographic Special* did Jacques Cousteau, a native Francophile, visit the fabled 'Land of the Pink Dolphins'?)

To go back in time, the settlers were able to arrive in this country, and after some shenanigans, break away from the King, which was so easy they decided to start up divorces of their own in this country. If we had a Royal Family today, we would be still less dependent on the British, for after a time we had to invite them back to run the fashion magazines in Manhattan and provide us with someone with an English accent to feel inferior to.

After the settlers broke away from the cruel King, the Economic System was able to blossom. The pilgrims carried with them a quantity of teabags which in New York are taxable by 8.5 per cent, while in New Jersey the tax is only 3 per cent.

From this came the expression 'History Repeats Itself'; but it is thanks to the influence of Zen Buddhism, which began in Haight Ashbury in 1967, the Summer of Love, that the expression 'Those who do not remember the past are expected to keep on keeping on' was popularized. Or, to put it another way, 'Those who do not remember the past will get paid to keep repeating it.'

This led, in part, to the psychedelic era of music and modern techno-pop, in which the same notes are played over and over, and which enabled Philip Glass to put on productions at the

Brooklyn Academy of Music, where one can become a member and support the arts, as well as receive full-season subscription tickets, for what is to some a nominal fee, yet for others might be quite hefty. The Brooklyn Academy of Music is easily accessible by public transportation. A 'patron' might also get to attend a cocktail party to meet the artist.

It was around then that we formed the United States, one of which was Mexico. But the Mexicans did not mind being squeezed south, since we decided to leave them enough land so they could go and live 'South of the Border, down Mexico Way'. For one thing, they were used to sleeping in cramped quarters, and they were pleased to help out in the formation of Texas, because places such as Texas help this great country have fifty-two states.

Even though the Mexicans still – after all this time! – keep trying to sneak up here, with great expense, effort and human man-hours we are able to turn them back across the Rio Grande in order to allow them to make their traditional crafts. If you visit Mexico today, you will find many of the old ways still intact, with fine embroidery, silversmithing, the asbestos tile and – my personal favorite – the bean-and-beef burrito, produced just as their grandfathers and grandmothers before them, from time immemorial, politically incorrect though this may be.

To condense matters even further, some of the Americans got very rich, and some never did get rich, and some got rich and had their money taken away from them, because they were not smart enough to hold on to it. And our Economic System states that this is how it should be.

Nevertheless, the rich people formed what became known as High Society, and ordered lots of flowers from florists, arrangements that changed in style with the period. The Great Victorian Era: moss roses.

A slightly more revisionist way to view this era is to consider that ladies wore restricting corsets, sexuality was repressed and people had hideous taste in Victorian furniture. Yet it was a romantic age and perhaps a more innocent time, for there was no television, and carriages – types include the brougham, phaeton, landau, dog-cart* and cabriolet – were pulled by horses that ranged in color from matched bays, chestnut, roan, palomino, dappled gray all the way to black with a white blaze. The proudest horse of all was the racehorse Man-o'-War, from whom the modern thoroughbred is descended. The cobbled streets of the city were littered with manure and apple vendors plied their wares. It was another time.

If a rich person had enough money, he would try to arrange for his daughter to marry dissipated European aristocracy, large in number, in order to provide Henry James and Edith Wharton with material. And while some prefer Henry James' rather dreary, endless novels, others feel that Edith Wharton never did get her fair shake, since she was a woman of the fairer sex. Both writers dealt with themes: how, for example, the *nouveaux riches* might buy a yacht or other material possessions such as Period art works, which for a time went out of fashion but by the end of the twentieth century were sold at Sotheby's, unless even to begin with they were reproductions of old masters, painstakingly painted by starving art students whilst studying at the Louvre.

At night these students, returning home to their garrets in Montparnasse, drank quantities of Absinthe, made from wormwood. And though today Absinthe is in many places no longer a legal beverage, Absinthe glasses and ashtrays have become highly collectable, whilst the jolly French courtesan, considered so decadent by American standards, lifted her petticoats high. And, it is a known fact, if homosexuality had been popular back then, Henry James would have been out there having a good time, probably with Oscar Wilde.

---

* What exactly was a dog-cart, anyway? Why did they call it a dog-cart if it was pulled by a horse? This has always troubled me.

Then came the twentieth century. People were able to buy stocks on margin, which meant that they didn't actually have to have the money, only enough margin. Having enough margin was just as good as bread 'n' butter. When the Crash came, many did not have enough to cover their margin, and it was a horrible thing and a horrible time. People's grandparents never got over it. For years, at restaurants, my grandmother used to tip the contents of the bread basket into her handbag, and even if there was only one teeny-tiny spoonful of chicken chow mein left, she would ask for it to be wrapped up so she could take it home.

'Ma!' my father would shout. 'There's only a tiny spoonful left, either eat it now or leave it. You put all this stuff in your refrigerator, then you forget what's in there and it gets moldy.'

Now my grandmother is dead. The conditions in the Depression were so dreadful, only one thing is certain: whether the person was rich or poor, eventually they died. And for those who are not dead, they will be.

Back then, people foolishly took things seriously. Nowadays if a man did something, and then the Government and the People decided that what he had done was very, very bad, and mean, and illegal, and sent him off to jail as a lesson to others, the man would not kill himself. He would know that with his knowledge and expertise, he would easily find a position when he got out. And he would know that his real friends would still care for him.

The Crash and subsequent Depression did, however, provide a boon for the movie industry. For the people were so depressed, and there were so few jobs, there was little for the people to do but to go to the movies. Cecil B. De Mille, Alphonse Daudet, Shirley Temple – how the movies were able to make folk laugh!

One is reminded of Lamarck's Theory of Evolution, in which he stated that if a giraffe kept stretching its neck to eat leaves off a tree, when that giraffe had a child (whether legitimate or not) that child would have a long neck.

Of course, Lamarck was not entirely correct. We now know

that giraffes have longer necks because they are taller than other animals. But if many youngsters want to get into films, and become directors and actors, and say that motion pictures have always been in their blood, there is little chance they can break into the industry – unless their mother or father was a famous movie star or mogul.

Alas, few child stars go on to have happy, productive and fulfilled lives as adult actors, either, though nearly every one is working on a screenplay. (Extra Credit: Can you name two child movie stars who, as adults, were pure and good? Hint: remember the sultry pint-sized siren who sang 'On the Good Ship Lollipop'.)

Chapter Two

It seemed the way to emerge from the great Depression was to have a war, which would give everyone something to do besides going to the movies. During this time our enemies were the Germans, who were a bunch of Nazis. Although in any country there are some good people, and some bad, that is not how the Germans were. Then we added the Japanese to our list of enemies. Then the Russians, for they were pinko and Communist. Many of them were out to spoil the American way of life, and even a hint of this caused McCarthy, during his era, to ban them from writing movies.

There was a lovely Tsar, perhaps a bit slow mentally, and four lovely daughters and a hemophiliac son, all of whom were shot, although this happened much earlier. Yet it was unforgivable. One of these daughters, a bit wounded, due to the heavy jewelry sewn into her hem, tried to pass herself off as Anastasia; however, DNA testing proved this to be an impossibility.

Thus a Broadway musical was born and was made into a movie starring Yul Brynner and then into an animated film agreeable to both children and their parents, featuring the voice of the fine actress Meg Ryan, married to actor Dennis

Quaid,[*] scheduled for release in the holiday season of 1997, only three years before the end of the century. This was the fault of the Communists. (Extra Credit: Which animated film for children starred a hunchback mentally retarded dwarf, and why are so few hunchbacks seen publicly nowadays?)

However, these Russian people began to see the error of their ways in the late twentieth century, when the first McDonald's was built in Moscow. McDonald's was a great achievement, showing what one man could do, and if not for McDonald, whose real name was something quite different, there might very well still be Rusky Commies in Russia today. (If you would like to write an essay about Ray Kroc, Millard Filmore or Maynard G. Krebs, the Founding Fathers of McDonald's, subtract ten points.)

Much happened in the development of the economy during the Years After the War. In the fifties, momentum was kept going by the Cold War. This might best be described as a marriage that was kept intact by a couple who dealt with their problems by sulking, only on an international scale.

Then came the sixties. The government was able to distract the majority of the population who were not on drugs by a) organizing an exciting trip to the moon, and b) having a war in Vietnam, where at least they were able to try out various bombs and munitions that they had built to keep the Economy going but which they hadn't had a chance to detonate yet, not even for fun.

The seventies were a time of introspection. As the young country matured, so did its people, for as Herbert Spencer stated, ontology recapitulates phylology. And that is why, when we think of the 1970s, we think of the beloved Disco, short for 'Discothèque', from the French, with such wistful appreciation, humor and a certain tragic longing, as if it were possible to return to the Womb.

---

[*] Alas, since writing this piece the golden couple have divorced.

Then, during the 1980s, came what we now know as the junk bond (see Chapter One). To buy stocks on margin was no longer legal. But if a man wanted to be important, he could still strive, as men have always strived.

First he had to find a company that was struggling, or could struggle. Then he had to find someone else who wanted to fight him for that company, or what kind of fun would it be?

Let's say a man wanted a cookie company. This company had all different kinds of cookies – some with marshmallow and chocolate, some ginger, raspberry, mocha-walnut, crème-filled and low-fat vanilla, perhaps a bit dry and bland, but healthier than the others, nevertheless. This company was more like a family than a company. Its executives wished only for the employees to be happy, and employed. Then other men – cruel and greedy, without values or morality – began to think, 'Gee, we want that cookie company too.'

The question arises, how were the men going to get the cookie company?

Well. One man, if he acted quickly enough, could acquire that cookie company, before anybody knew what was happening. And if it turned out he didn't have enough cash to buy that cookie company, what he could do was, once he had acquired it, he could sell what amounted to the idea of that cookie company.

Once he had sold the idea there was little reason to keep the cookie company afloat. For one thing, the cookies tasted terrible. They were not tasty cookies. Lacking in flavor, perhaps a bit stale. Artificial color and flavoring, high in calories – the American consumer has to be educated to read not only the ingredients but the nutritional value listed on the side of the packaging.

In addition, these particular employees were not happy and grateful. They were obese and ill-educated, given to crude innuendo, their clothing garish and unattractive. The fashion magazines, run in New York by English people, had little effect on such miserable subhumans who cared nothing – nothing! – about Donatella Versace. Finally, cookies could be produced in Korea for one-tenth of the cost.

Hence the term junk bonds, from the more formal term junk Food bonds. For it was the same with sugary cereal, and potato chips, tasty hot dogs and French fries. Hundreds of grams of fat, and sodium, might be consumed by a person who, for breakfast, devoured in three bites a delicious, hot, fresh jelly donut, the surface crusty with sugar, the interior soft and fluffy, with a center filled with jelly that simply exploded in one's mouth. Crisp slabs of bacon, bright sunny-yolked eggs – and meanwhile the poor chickens were fed hormones, fish-and-meat by-products, and kept in tiny, overwrought cages.

And if you bought a junk bond for one dollar, if twenty million other people did so, then you would be part of a twenty-million-dollar company. And using that money, the man who first had the idea could buy other things, so that everybody would be rich – or at least feel that way.

Sometimes, however, it didn't work and the whole thing fell apart. This meant that everyone would lose their money, though of course not the man who had first come up with the idea, who was no doubt entitled to compensation. And then people would say, 'People who buy junk bonds are greedy, and it serves them right for taking cookies from Girl Scouts.'

This is also what they said to justify buying Manhattan off the Indians for a few pieces of wampum. Those poor indigenous peoples of the forest and plains! There are, to this very day, few starring roles for Native Americans in first-run movies. To name but a few tribes who have been denied this right, Pequod, Shoshone, Arapaho, Delaware, Perce Nez and the gentle Navaho tending his sheep in his happy buffalo-hide wigwam. And to make matters worse, many of these are not the tribal names that the Native Americans called themselves, but are names given to them by the White man.

And it would be hard not to notice that, whenever the spirit of a Native American is channeled, it is almost invariably by a white woman in her mid-to-late forties. But this is a topic best left to post-modernism and deconstruction.

In the future years we can look forward to many more developments in the Economy. Only one thing is left to say: whatever happens, as we have learned from experience, it will either go up or down. This is our System, one full of Beliefs.

I always try to record the exact moment I wrote something, ever since a reviewer trashed me by claiming I wrote A Cannibal in Manhattan *before* Slaves of New York. *As far as the reviewer was concerned, this was a major crime, though I couldn't see what difference it would have made even if it were true.*

I mean, novelists don't necessarily go on improving with each book. Maybe some things are better, some are worse. In any event, though there was no way I could 'defend' myself, the way I work is by revising. Some of the stories in Slaves of New York *were written in 1979 (and never revised and not published until 1986), while some of* A Cannibal in Manhattan *was written in 1979 but revised many times all the way up until its publication in 1987. So there, Mr Reviewer!*

I was doubly furious about the whole business because a friend who worked for the magazine where this review was published had called me personally, asking for the manuscript before publication in order to publish a chapter or two or excerpt it. This lured me in, as it would have been fantastic. Instead, he immediately slipped it to the magazine's reviewer, even though I had begged him not to show it to anyone, at least – if he decided not to excerpt it – until closer to the book's publication date. At that later date even a bad review might have tempted some readers.

Half a year before publication the reviewer had his chance to announce what a bad writer I was. Why? At least I was trying to survive as a writer – I wasn't even thirty yet and had written book after book without hope of publication. One of the reviewer's primary objections was that I mentioned The Dinah Shore Show *in the manuscript. For some reason this proved I was a lousy writer. But how was I supposed to know that program was off the air? Besides, Dinah Shore had always been my favorite, along with Merv Griffin. One of my biggest sorrows was that I never got to on Merv's show.*

When the newspapers called me to ask how I felt regarding my thorough, lengthy trouncing, I simply announced that I had gotten a bad review due to my unwillingness to sleep with the reviewer.

Movies

J UDY GARLAND in *The Wizard of Oz* is a totally different Dorothy than the one in the book by L. Frank Baum. But which Fagin came first, Alec Guinness in the movie, or the character in Dickens's original? And is Peter Sellers Chance Gardener in *Being There*, or the cipher in Jerzy Kosinski's novel?

If you see a movie based on a book (before you've read the book), it seems as if the movie actor is pretty firmly cemented in your head as the leading character. Since I saw *Gone with the Wind* before reading it, there was no way to read the Margaret Mitchell book without picturing Vivien Leigh and Clark Gable in the leading roles. On the other hand if you read a book first, it's very difficult to adjust to the actor or actress in the part; for me Edith Wharton's *The Age of Innocence* was miscast.

It wasn't that the acting was bad, but Michelle Pfeiffer could never be, for me, a returning member of a decadent aristocratic European world. The character in the book was sophisticated. Winona Ryder as a wholesome American heiress just didn't work, either; the character in the book was a sort of bouncing field-hockey type, loud, no-nonsense. I don't know what it would have been like to see the movie if I hadn't read – and loved – the book first. But I suspect that both actresses were chosen for their sympathetic qualities – qualities that they brought to their portrayals of two characters who, in the original novel, were not so sympathetic nor likeable.

The only time for me that the casting (after reading a book) has been perfect was in the TV show made from Olivia Manning's *The Balkan Trilogy*, a three-volume novel about the Second World War; the TV series starred Kenneth Branagh and Emma Thompson, who seemed so right for the parts that I very quickly forgot the people I had envisioned in my head while reading the books.

The House of Mirth, another of my favorite books by Edith Wharton, has also been released as a movie; it's a wonderfully grim and depressing novel about society and hustlers in New York City at the end of the nineteenth century.

This is not a happy book, nor, really, romantic. One feels constantly enraged and at war with the heroine, Lily Bart, for her lack of values and poor choices – though she is, apparently, or at least to most people I know, a sympathetic character as she sponges off her aunt, expects a married man to make investments for her because she flirts with him, tries to woo an oaf because he has money, rejects one suitor because he's vulgar (read, Jewish) and another who is decent but poor. Women in this era without money did go out, get jobs – Lily Bart is unable to abandon the world of glamorous New York society.

Nevertheless, finding the heroine to be an anti-heroine is not, for me, a problem as a reader. A book is no less interesting to read because you don't like the main character.

But while an anti-hero has always been acceptable in fiction by men (I'm thinking of Donleavy's *The Ginger Man*, Knut Hamsun's *Hunger, Portnoy's Complaint* by Philip Roth, *A Fan's Note's* by Fredrick Exley and the writings of Henry Miller), it's never been permissible to have a heroine who drinks, screws around and is generally amoral. Traits that are tolerable, even charming or amusing, in a man are cause for grave alarm, even hatred, when shown in a woman.

At least in *The House of Mirth* Lily Bart is redeemed – for the readers of the time, for the readers of now – by committing suicide through accidental overdosing – at the end, just after realizing the error of her ways. Actresses in the movies today must be heroines or villains – the motion-picture industry seems unable to accommodate anything else – and whatever actress portrays Lily Bart will, no doubt, be expected to provide the movie with a lovability quotient that the character in the book never did have.

Still the movies chew up the past, the conduit – novels: *Pride and Prejudice*, *Jane Eyre*, *Tom Jones*, *Sense and Sensibility*, *Wuthering Heights*, *Tess of the d'Urbervilles*, *The Great Gatsby* – female characters reduced to villains or goodness incarnate, and with the visuals intended to show us what it was like to live then. But the visuals are almost always filtered through the present. Movies made in the '60s generally show actresses ostensibly living in 1850 yet with blue eyeshadow. Even the most careful 'period' movie made today would not have a single actress without eyebrows heavily plucked in the current style. Soon the films will come to look dated – 'period' films of a certain 'period'. But the novels will always be of their time.

Movies often – generally – reduce novels to plot outlines. The novel has room for description, psychology, pages of interaction to demonstrate character traits. A book can linger over a meal; can describe to you what it was like to live in a certain time and place. A movie is like jam, the original shape of the fruit boiled into pulp. Nevertheless, what a movie can do is *show* – the clothing, the rooms, the cars of the era – and can show the viewer quickly, concisely, *visually*. The correct shot (I'm thinking now of a brief flash, on screen, in the movie version of Henry James's *The Golden Bowl* in the Merchant–Ivory production, in which the characters climb into a horse-drawn omnibus) can make you feel and see what it was like in a way that a novel perhaps can't.

In a hundred years, a line from a novel 'He got into his car' will not mean as much to the reader as it will to the movie-goer who sees what will be, to him or her, a shot of a man (dressed in period garb) climbing into an incredibly antiquated 2000 Jaguar. What will be lost from the scene is what the man was thinking; a good actor might be able to show his *feelings* while turning the key in the ignition, but the *thoughts* have vanished – left behind on the page.

One hopes that *The House of Mirth* shows what it was really like to live in New York City one hundred years ago – even if the actress playing Lily Bart is lovely, sympathetic and (unlike the novel) without a thought in her head.

Years ago I was invited to attend a dinner in Washington, DC, for the press corps and the actress starring in the movie was also a guest, at my table. I had never seen a desperate actress before and was astonished to watch, as the only time she seemed to come to life during the evening was when a photographer appeared. At one point a photographer asked to take my picture and for the first time she acknowledged my existence by actually pushing me out of the way to get into the picture. To see this sort of hunger was highly entertaining.

Cross-town, Cross-culture

I WAS STANDING on the street on lower Broadway, and I was so late that I decided I had to take a cab to pick up my child from school. It would have taken me ten minutes to get to the subway, walking, and then waiting for the subway, and walking from the stop at the other end. She is four and her school gets out at five-thirty; it's a public school, Shuan Wen Academy, way over in Chinatown, so far east that I'm not even sure it's Chinatown, just opposite the Henry Street Playhouse. There are a lot of kosher butchers and restaurants nearby, but Chinese shops, too. My daughter is Chinese, adopted from China, and one reason she was in the Shuan Wen Academy is that half the day is in Chinese, which I'm hoping she'll speak, even though I don't.

It was one of those days where there weren't any taxis and everybody else was looking for one, too, and there were women – far more aggressive than I – perching on every corner, hailing the empty air and glaring at the other hailers. A man came by on a bicycle rickshaw and said to me, 'I'll take you if you can wait two minutes.' He whizzed down the block. There were still no taxis, but a couple of minutes later he came back and stopped and asked me where I was going. 'Get in,' he said. The seat part of the rickshaw, behind his bicycle, was a two-seater and had large advertisements on either side for Altoids, the Curiously Strong Mint. It looked like one of those heavy-duty rickshaws made in India or Pakistan, not too common over here.

'How much is it?' I said.

'What does it usually cost?' he said.

'Five dollars.'

'OK,' he said. 'I'll do it for six.'

He was a black man and he pedaled the bicycle using all his strength through Chinatown. He must have been in very good shape, although apparently it was difficult to stop and start the bike with the heavy seat behind it, because he didn't like to stop, which made him go through red lights if he didn't see oncoming traffic, and pull around non-moving cars into the opposite lane. Many people in Chinatown kept looking at me in the rickshaw, maybe because I was laughing so hard. 'I hope I see somebody I know,' I said.

'How far is it?' he said. 'Is it all the way east?'

'Just where East Broadway meets Grand,' I said. 'Just beyond Henry Street. Do you do this all day?' I couldn't really hear his answer because he was breathing so hard and facing the wrong way. I pointed out where my daughter's school was, and he let me out. I had had such a good time, and also I felt so bad for the man, having to work so hard at pulling me in a rickshaw, that I gave him ten dollars. Plus, he had gotten me there in time. When I went in, my daughter was walking with her fellow students (the teachers made them line up in pairs) in two straight lines, sixteen small Chinese kids (mine was the only one with non-Chinese parents) and the one Hispanic girl – Chandelise – and the one black girl, Beanca. They were all dressed in their school uniforms and singing the song that they had been practicing all week, '*Dreidle, Dreidle, Dreidle, I made you out of clay*', at the top of their lungs, badly and out of tune as they were led to the lobby.

After Ms Chen handed my daughter over to me, I tried to explain to her that a black man had taken me to get her in an Indian rickshaw through Chinatown, but it was hopeless. We had to wait for a bus, and in front of a store that repaired shoes and framed pictures, run by an Orthodox Jewish man, there

was a metal duck that children could ride for twenty-five cents
– one of those electric things that rock back and forth. I felt so
ebullient that I told Willow today she could ride the duck,
which she had been asking to do almost every day. The kids in
her class all wear big plastic backpacks – with pictures from
Pokemon or other Japanese characters – and she didn't take
off her backpack before she got on the duck, so maybe she felt
a little crowded. I put the quarter in and the duck, which was
wearing an old-fashioned conductor's hat, also of metal, began
to rock back and forth. She sat on the duck for quite some
time. 'How long is this going to take?' she finally said with
some irritation, as if I had forced her into taking a duck-ride
and, though not in her teens, already thought she had a
rickshaw-riding lunatic for a mother.

The Same but Not the Same

(title thanks to Roald Hoffman)

The magazine editor called up and asked for a piece on 'Return of the '80s'. I find this kind of thing really difficult. I have a literal mind. If someone calls and wants me to go somewhere or do something, I can. But something like 'Return of the '80s' – the way I think, I just don't get it. How could it be the return of the '80s, when it's the '90s? I keep thinking over and over, 'What are they talking about? It can't be "return of the '80s". It's the '90s. Or did something happen that I just don't know about, like putting the clocks back?'

So it's a struggle for me as a journalist.

I was walking down an upper West Side street in New York and coming toward me was an extraordinary-looking couple: the woman was swathed in a huge, black velvet cloak, while the man wore what appeared to be a white zoot suit. At his side was a black Great Dane, almost as large as he. As the couple got closer, I heard they were speaking Russian.

These days the city is filled with Russians – seemingly rich ones. They're in every shop, buying food, electronics, clothing, cosmetics. I suddenly realized that they had taken over the city in the way that the Japanese had back in the early and mid-1980s. Then, the Japanese wore black, streamlined clothes and carried cameras, snapping pictures everywhere as if they came from another planet and we were the most peculiar creatures they had ever seen.

Now the New Yorkers were all wearing black and carrying cameras, while the Russians were dressing flamboyantly and didn't carry cameras, as if they had just descended from the sky.

The '80s died in Manhattan in 1987, along with Andy Warhol. For me, New York's last gasp of '80s extravagant decadence came on New Year's Eve, 1986. I remember a group of us were taken to New Year's Eve dinner at the River Café. In a room full of black-tie strangers, surfeited with caviar and the best champagne, looking out across the East River to Manhattan, I felt as if I was balancing on a bubble. Shortly before midnight Andy had to leave to host a party at another restaurant, and we hopped into one of our host's chauffeured cars – an antique Rolls-Royce. As we crossed the Brooklyn Bridge, New Year's Eve fireworks bursting overhead, while Mick Jagger sang on the radio 'Time is on My Side', it seemed as if life was always going to be perfect. Less than eight weeks later Andy was dead, and shortly thereafter the real-estate market crashed, and the stock market, and even though a lot of people still had money they decided not to spend it.

For years after that people looked on the '80s with contempt and talked about how terrible it was, all that conspicuous spending in a city where there were homeless people, and people living in slums, and terrible public schools. During this time people were still living in slums, so I didn't really see that things were better or worse when the rich were spending their money conspicuously or inconspicuously.

Even though I didn't get rich during the '80s, I did get to have a great time. Almost every night there were parties – mostly business events – where companies would throw a celebration for, say, a new perfume or a watch. As the guests left, everyone got a bottle of Beautiful or a Swatch watch or an

Armani scarf. When Villeroy & Boch, the manufacturer of
expensive plates and crystal, opened a shop on Madison
Avenue, they invited me to attend the party and presented
me with a thousand dollars' worth of the most beautiful plates
I had ever owned. Since nobody at the party knew who I was, it
was quite a surprise. Orrefors crystal presented me with two
champagne glasses and a large paperweight engraved with my
name. I felt like Sara Crewe in that book *Poor Little Rich Girl*,
when her drab garret is mysteriously transformed into a
splendid and warm palace.

After a while I started to expect that I would get a present
every time I went to a party. Then usually a group of us would
go to dinner, invited by our buddy Steven Greenberg; afterwards he would send us home in his chauffeured Daimler or
limo.

The most fabulous event was going to Sweden (via privately
chartered Concorde) for three days with Michel Roux. He was
then the distributor of Absolut vodka, and had made it
Sweden's largest export. To celebrate he took ninety-nine
liquor distributors and some artists and friends to Swedish
Lapland, hundreds of miles north of the Arctic circle. It was the
first time Concorde had ever flown to Stockholm. Customs
agents came on board to stamp our passports; we were
escorted down a red carpet laid on the runway, past folk-
dancing Swedish girls and fire engines, to shake hands with the
mayor. There were parties and balls, meetings with the Queen,
then a smaller charter up to Lapland, where it was light
twenty-four hours a day. By helicopter we were taken to
the base of a glacier, in the remotest Arctic tundra. Suddenly
there was a noise overhead. We looked up. Descending from
the sky – attached to another helicopter – a fifty-foot bottle of
glacial ice, carved in the shape of a bottle of Absolut, flew
overhead and landed at our feet. Michel presented each of us
with a small glass in the shape of an icicle. Then he smashed
the giant ice-bottle with a hammer and from inside it took a

frozen bottle of vodka, which was poured around to loud cheers. How the bottle had been carved in such a remote spot remained a mystery.

For a long time in the early '90s in New York things were quiet. Oh, there was plenty going on – new openings, and galleries, and shows, and restaurants – but the place wasn't charged with energy the way I remembered it. I had gotten so spoiled I was miffed to attend events where I didn't get a gift-bag when I left. 1994 . . . 1995 . . . 1996 . . . the century was drawing to a close . . . Suddenly, almost overnight, the city once again became insane in the way I had remembered it ten years earlier. The stock market began to soar. Apartment rents shot up; and those who had rent-stabilized apartments began to panic at the thought that shortly the stabilization program might be ending. On my upper West Side block, buildings that had sold for twenty thousand dollars only twenty years ago were now selling for a million and a half dollars. Houses up in Harlem – some of them virtual wrecks – rose in value from less than a hundred thousand to half a million. Bergen Line Norwegian Coastal Voyages invited me to take a trip – a reindeer safari in Norwegian Lapland, followed by a winter cruise in the Norwegian Sea, all expenses paid. Bottles of perfume – party gifts – began to line my bathroom shelf once more – Tuscany per Donna, Lancôme's Poème, Cartier. To celebrate new flavors of vodka (now Stolichnaya), Michel Roux gave a party at the Russian consulate, a lavish mansion on the upper East Side.

Nightclub owners arrested for drug-dealing, professional party-givers accused of murder, a gossip columnist publicly slapping and cursing a cab driver.

'We got thrown out of a club last night,' a male friend told me cheerfully.

'Why?'

'For taking coke in the bathroom. I didn't know it was the ladies' room.'

I hadn't heard anybody say anything like that in a long time.

But if one thing happens, there's usually a lot more, like ripples after a stone. The power-suit is coming back into fashion – not the padded-shoulder primly trimmed 'ladies-who-lunch' of the '80s, but something a bit more swaggering (even Rifat Ozbek did one in bright green last season).* And who attends fashion week is as widely publicized as going to the opera was a hundred years ago. Who gets to sit where at the shows, who feels they have been treated badly, round-ups of what each designer is doing in all the papers. Meanwhile many designers have begun lines that are more 'exclusive' than their regular ones. Instead of a dress costing three thousand, there appears to be a market for dresses costing twenty grand or even more. This might be because fur coats are no longer so popular for the wealthy, so there's extra money in their fashion budget. But a fur designer recently gave a party attended by a great many well-known women who have decided they no longer care if they are politically correct: they want their fur coats back. And, as we all know, political correctness wasn't all that important back in the mid-eighties.

Less pricey designers are at last able to open their own shops – Vivienne Tam, for one, whose SoHo store opened in May of 1997. Two surly security guards refused to admit anyone without an invitation. Inside, at a gigantic bar, Stolichnaya vodka in every imaginable flavor (peach, coffee, pepper) was being poured into cups by harried bartenders. And what's this a sign of? That Michel Roux (who is now the distributor of Stoli) has his finger on the pulse of what's going on. Back in the '80s, it was Roux who used art work by up-and-coming as well as already famous artists in the Absolut ad campaigns. Somehow, having his presence back makes me feel something is happening once more.

Kids starting up arty magazines, like Stephen Gan with

* This was in 1997.

Visionaire, sold by (very expensive) subscription only. Other designers as well – the quirky shoe designers Sigerson-Morrison opened a store on Elizabeth Street. Galleries – Paul Kazmin, Paul Judelson – have started up, and are thriving, with shows of younger, unknown artists.

To me part of what New York City was was that it was a place that lured the talented. But for a ten-year stretch it seemed the talented – unless rich to begin with – were not going to be able to survive here. Then, too, AIDS seemed to wipe out so many talented and creative people. It was almost as if the essence had been bleached out of the city. Now it's been ages since anyone I know has died of AIDS – quite the opposite: the people I know are all looking wonderful.

At the same time, the *New Yorker* published an article about sending one's child to private school (it can cost more than fifteen thousand dollars a year, and I'm talking about grade school), while the papers reported that Donald Trump, visiting a public school, offered twenty pairs of sneakers and a child wondered why Trump couldn't provide books or scholarship money instead.

But the Donald is back, after allegedly having nearly gone bankrupt. In front of the former Gulf-and-Western building a sign has gone up announcing 'Trump World'. A metal globe (seemingly as big as the one that still survives from the 1964 World's Fair) has been erected in front and somehow looks like something out of the '80s film *Wall Street*.

In the past few months I've been attending some swanky events: a wedding at the Pierre, where waiters carried platters of tiny cherry tomatoes stuffed with piñon nuts, and caviar heaped on blinis. It was quite lavish – though I suppose not as lavish as the one recently held down in Kentucky (to which a number of my New York friends and acquaintances were invited), where, at the moment the bride and groom were pronounced man and wife, thousands of butterflies were released into the air.

There was a party at the Metropolitan Museum for the Cartier jewelry exhibitions. Hundreds of men dressed in red suits like those worn by bellboys lined both sides of the grand staircase and seemed about to burst into a song-and-dance routine out of a Busby Berkeley musical. A birthday party at the restaurant Balthazar, a new McNally-boy enterprise (the two McNally brothers were in charge of all the most fashionable restaurants of the '80s). The restaurant hadn't yet officially opened, but the host and hostess booked the place for the evening. Heaps of oysters and shrimp studded the bar before the sit-down dinner for several hundred. A week or two later *New York* magazine published an article devoted entirely to this restaurant – where the best tables were located, and so forth.

Even Le Cirque is back in the press again. The location and decor have changed, but the crowd – the old rich, the new rich and a smattering of celebrities – are the same, as if they'd never left.

Yesterday I was walking down a street on the upper West Side and an elderly woman stopped me. 'Nice building, huh?' she said, pointing.

I looked at the building and shrugged. 'Probably expensive,' I said.

'Very!' The woman's face lit up as if she had been waiting for me to say this. 'My frien', he live there, he pay one thousand dollars a month for his room. And this is half price, because he a veteran. Even one thousand, too much.'

Across the street, in a senior-citizen center, a bazaar was being held: elderly women were fighting over used clothing and complaining that two dollars was too much. And a brief article in the free neighborhood paper asked people to drop off baby food and formula at the Children's Museum for people in need.

This has always been a city of extremes – the very rich and the very poor – and these two worlds, so close together are what made the extravagant lifestyles of the wealthy seem so decadent during the '80s.

New York City, One More Time

S OMETIMES I think of the city as a huge organism, a kind of living beehive. People have come here from all over the world. Some are very poor, from Haiti, Mexico or Dominica, hoping to find work or a better life. Others are desperately ambitious and want to succeed as high-paid lawyers, or stock-brokers, or Broadway stars. Others were misfits, perhaps from small towns – the ones who weren't the football star in high school, or the most popular cheerleader. Perhaps they were homosexual, and came to New York in search of a community or support system of similarly oriented people. Some came wanting to become artists; for others this is a place to be anonymous: you could live a lifetime here in complete isolation, never speaking to anyone, in a way that wouldn't be possible even in the most remote wilderness, where chances are that, sooner or later, someone would knock on your door. Or maybe some came who simply craved excitement, excitement and a certain artificially speeded-up way of existence.

Everything is faster here. There are too many people, jammed on to a tiny island where buildings and streets are crumbling and everyone is in a hurry. Often I hate it here. In summer the city is sweltering, the air is stale and used up, recycled millions of times by others who have gotten to use it first. Only the poor are left in the city in summer: anyone with money tries to escape.

But in some ways the hard core of humanity who stay behind are the most interesting. They camp out in the parks

– whole enclaves of homeless, complete with shopping carts, giant empty cardboard boxes, mattresses, television sets. Many are truly crazy. Years ago, with the development of new psychotropic drugs (which, supposedly, enabled the mentally ill to function in society) it was decided to shut down the huge, antiquated and decaying mental hospitals and reintegrate the mentally ill back into society. But, with few halfway houses, and little supervision, many of these former patients simply stopped taking drugs, refused to enter shelters and now wander the streets, talking out loud to themselves. (For a while, after everyone started carrying mobile phones, I was shocked to see so many people – who appeared perfectly normal – talking out loud to themselves. It took me a while to realize they were all speaking into tiny telephones. Then I thought they were really crazy: it must be very expensive to have one of those phones, and the majority of telephone conversations I eavesdropped on were things like 'I'm on my way to get my hair dyed blond, and then I thought I'd go shopping.')

Others who live out-of-doors are drug addicts or alcoholics, who once had jobs, families or ordinary lives, but who lost everything. And some are regular people who, for one reason or another, no longer have a home. I often worry that some day I may end up on the street. I see how easily it could happen: to a person working in one of those huge, anonymous skyscrapers, perhaps someone who works in a secretarial pool or at a switchboard (if such things still exist). They live outside Manhattan, in one of the boroughs that make up New York City – Brooklyn, the Bronx, Staten Island or Queens. Unable to pay the rent one month for some reason – or perhaps their apartment is destroyed by a fire – he or she might miss a couple of days of work and lose their job. It wouldn't take much time to use up any savings. And if a person's family is poor, uninvolved, dead, far away – it's not impossible to imagine – the trip from a job and an apartment to the streets might be only a few short weeks. One is told not to give coins to the begging homeless: 'They only spend the money on drink or drugs.' But getting a drink would be the first thing I would do if I had to beg for money on the streets. Once I went with a lawyer to a clinic for the homeless; this took place after a free meal at a soup-kitchen. I couldn't even begin to understand his explanations to the waiting crowd as to how to get on Social Security disability.

'Where do you live?' my lawyer friend asked one man.

'On the street, in the park,' the man muttered, embarrassed.

'How do you get money?'

'Collecting cans.' He traded them in for their nickel-deposit return.

'The first thing you have to do is to get a mailing address.' My friend explained how to go about getting a post office box-number. That was only step one, and already it was well beyond me.

In the winter the wind whips down the city avenues and they become giant funnels or canyons, shooting icy air in off the Hudson and East Rivers. When it snows, the city is briefly pure and perfect, it might have become an ancient, dust-shrouded preserved city on Mars, the inhabitants vanished millennia before. But almost immediately the snow turns gray, and as heat rises from the sewers, from the subways and infrastructures beneath the streets, the pristine white turns to liquid sludge. My great-great-grandmother died of pneumonia one winter when snow blew down from the skylight of the tenement she lived in – the snow remained for weeks.

When it rains, quite often the drains don't work, and within minutes one is struggling to get through a puddle of water three feet deep just to cross the street. The homeless go through the garbage, looking for food, or whatever, and strew the contents of the bags along the sidewalks, while the heaps of newspapers tied up for recycling lie swollen with water, uncollected, gray lumps.

And of course there are broken water mains, friable collapsing buildings and building parts, constant hazards. One time, late at night, I came home to find my street blocked off. A metal manhole cover had had enough: pressure from below had sent the metal disk, weighing hundreds of pounds, shooting straight into the air, like some primitive, decapitating weaponry from medieval times.

I can think of nowhere else where such a huge range and variety of human beings, at their most pressured, most crazed, most ambitious, have come to squeeze themselves into such a tiny place.

We live on a rather nice block in a rather nice, middle-class neighborhood, the upper West Side. It's an ordinary block, a mixture of small buildings and large, with a public elementary school across the street, a pocket-sized park with some broken playground equipment, a restaurant and a grocery store.

I went out to do some errands, and on my way left a bag of garbage in the alley. When I returned, a half-hour later, a disheveled man was holding up a suspiciously familiar object. 'Hey, look!' he said. 'This is a nice box. Want to buy it?' I looked more closely. It was my box – a box I had just thrown out – which was now going to be sold back to me.

Because we live in a basement and across the street is a supermarket, occasionally a truck parks outside, just in front of our tiny window. The first time this happened, shortly after I moved in, I looked up to see that giant vegetables – broccoli, mushrooms, corn and tomatoes, maybe eight or ten feet tall – had apparently taken over Manhattan. It wasn't until quite some time later I figured out the conquering vegetables were simply the photographic billboard on the side of the delivery truck.

Things are being dumped down our stairs. Once I opened the door to find two brand-new cans of coffee and a bag. I opened it. Inside were twelve brand-new pairs of men's underpants. How mysterious, I thought. Was this meant to be a gift?

As I stood there, quite perplexed, a man suddenly dashed over to me, snatched the bag and the two cans of coffee from my hands and yelled, 'These are mine!' before bolting.

Once I opened the door to find a brand-new box of lighting fixtures, perfectly useless to me. And another time I found a man's briefcase, leather, no doubt stolen, loaded with papers. With great difficulty I tracked down the owner. It turned out his car had been broken into. I think, initially, he expected me to return his things to him in New Jersey. When I balked, he finally decided to come and collect his bag; when he arrived, at an inconvenient time, he proffered a twenty-dollar bill (which I wouldn't accept) with a sneer on his face as if he thought that I had stolen the briefcase myself and that I should be very grateful he wasn't handing me over to the police.

There is a man who lives on our block who is always dressed like Popeye the Sailorman – bell-bottom pants, peacoat with collar upturned, and a little white sailor's cap perched on his crew-cut head. All day long he swaggers up and down the street, but why, or what it is he does or is doing, I have never discovered.

New York may seem cold and unfriendly, but over the years I have come to know many of the people who work in my neighborhood: Michelle at the pharmacy is from the West Indies, I heard all about her wedding when she got married. Mrs Jin is the Korean seamstress. Rob works at the dry-cleaner, owned by his uncle. He wrote me a letter to say how sorry he was when my dog died. Mr Miles at the bank, Hassan at the pizza parlor, Jennifer the coffee-shop waitress – everyone within a block from my door. Though Manhattan is not a big island and it is only a question of a couple of minutes' walk or a short subway or taxi ride from one neighborhood to the next, people are very particular not only about what neighborhood they live in, but what neighborhood you live in. 'Where do you live?' is often the first thing people want to know after they find out what your job is. The answer –

whether the person says they live on the upper East Side, or the East Village, or Chelsea, or Tribeca – seems to provide information about that person above and beyond just a simple address.

'The upper East Side.' One generally assumes that this person has a lot of money, wears a mink coat, goes to society charity benefits and so forth. 'Just off Third Avenue – in the 30s (or 40s, or 50s).' This seems to represent a sort of non-area, a limbo; one will be stared at and then perhaps ignored, as if to imply that one who lives in this region simply doesn't, can't, exist. 'SoHo.' This is an area – South of Houston – that once contained large factories on various floors of cast-iron buildings. In the late 1960s and '70s artists moved into the abandoned factories and took up residence (mostly illegal) until at last, ten or twenty years later, the area was designated by the city as an artists' neighborhood. Certificates of occupancy were granted, the spaces became legal as residences, but though the requirements stated that only artists (who were able to prove they were artists) could buy or sell one of these lofts, now the area is occupied primarily by non-artists – who have enough money to get around the ordinances.

Tribeca is the TRIangle BElow CAnal street, and here, when I first moved to the city, the streets were rich with the smell of roasting coffee, with cheese and spices. But now – though the streets are still wide and empty at night – there are few working factories left; once more a neighborhood has quickly become home to the wealthy . . .

In the East Village old tenement buildings once housed poor working immigrants. Now, a hundred years later, the grand-children of these immigrants (whose only dream was to escape the foul, overcrowded city streets) have moved back, renting out their ancestors' tiny rooms at prices so exorbitant it would have killed their grandmother if she hadn't died already.

I used to live in the meat market district, the Northwest village. My apartment was in a building that had originally been refrigerated meat-lockers, converted now into living space. The walls were very thick, but there was something rather dank and foreboding about the apartments, despite the renovations. The meat market was one of the last real working neighborhoods in Manhattan. Here, each day at dawn, on the cobbled streets, huge open trucks containing slabs of meat came rumbling along to deliver carcasses of sheep and cow. At five or six a.m. the slabs were unloaded and hung up on hooks that swung from awnings over the sidewalk, to be deftly slashed and sliced by butchers in white coats covered with blood.

At night, when the butchers had finished and the streets had been hosed down, prostitutes began to prowl. Many – most – of them were men, dressed as women, as beautiful and exotic as tropical birds. Sometimes in the summer months a group of them gathered on an unloading ramp across from my apartment and all night long they fought, played music and at last curled up alongside each other to sleep, twittering and fluffing feathers . . .

On this same block there was a woman – obese, with masses of white frizzy hair and a cheerful, if annoying manner – who spent all day on the stoop. She knew all the local residents. Each morning when I went out with my dogs there she was, sitting on the front steps. She always found something to say to me. 'A young woman like you – you're always alone. How come you don't have a boyfriend?'

She was a nuisance. And yet, her insidious, invidious conversational tactic could not be taken seriously – it was too typical a New York style. I couldn't help but appreciate her for the type she was.

Years passed, I moved away, and one night I turned on the TV to find that she had been murdered. I never knew her name, but I recognized her face at once. They showed the stoop where she sat, and her apartment, filled with old papers piled up to the ceiling. Someone she knew had crept in at night and, for no reason, for unknown reasons, stabbed her not once but many times; her bloody corpse was found the next day.

There are more stories in this city than I could ever write, more unbelievable things occur than anything I could make up. A person was walking down the streets in the East Village when he found a cardboard box, which he opened. Inside were two human heads. ('Both heads had mustaches,' the TV newscaster said, which I thought an interesting, if peculiar, detail to include.)

The man who had found the heads was upset. But almost immediately a doctor came forward to claim them. The doctor's car had been stolen after the doctor had put the box in the trunk – he claimed he was transporting the heads (for research purposes!) from one hospital to another. I suppose the car thief opened the trunk, found the box, opened the box (did he ever steal another car after this?) and then decided to get rid of the . . . evidence . . . by leaving the heads on the sidewalk for someone else to stumble over.

Harlem – my grandmother grew up there. Morningside Heights – where Columbia University is located, where I went to college. And then there are the other boroughs, which many people don't realize are a part of New York City. But it was only a hundred years ago that the boroughs were incorporated. Each has innumerable diverse neighborhoods – little Russia, Egypt, Armenia, India, Korea – for new immigrants have always liked to settle with others of their background, and Manhattan, for the most part, is the most expensive borough of all in which to live.

The problems that people have here are no different than the problems of people anywhere, at the end of the twentieth century. Yet everything here is speeded up, intensified. So many have crowded together in a small space, from every part of the globe. And while some may find it difficult – and certainly I do, more often than not – recently, at twilight, in a taxi going down Fifth Avenue, the sky abruptly turned the most intense shade of blue I had ever seen. All at once millions upon millions of lights came on; and people with bright, crisp faces, dressed in expensive cashmere coats, walked briskly past the glittering shops and horse-drawn carriages. The ballroom visible from the street in what was once a privately owned limestone mansion – starched, pinched waiters in white scuttling to prepare for some sparkling event . . . My taxi sped faster, the curtain snapped up in the window of an elegant hotel, the lights in the shops illuminated gold wristwatches, ivory Japanese netsukes, Dresden china shepherdesses and a green Fabergé egg . . .

A New York of speakeasys and jazz dives and swirling transvestites flying above the crowd in a long-defunct club from the 1960s, yes, I could almost see it, the ghost of the Gilded Grape, a club which contained a flying trapeze up by the ceiling, where drag-queens dressed in white and purple ostrich feathers, gold paste and gilt, performed for an admiring, jaded, sophisticated New York crowd, who, by today's standards would seem quite innocent.

And for that short taxi trip, all of Manhattan, past and present, came together for one shifting, bumped-together moment.

I was in the subway yesterday and at the end of the platform an elegant if shabby-looking man was standing beside a shopping cart full of equipment. I couldn't understand how he had gotten the huge shopping cart – from a supermarket – down all those stairs, there are so few elevators in the New York subways. Laboriously he unloaded the cart, removed a piece of newspaper which he carefully spread on the ground and then set up speakers attached to a microphone. I thought he was going to sing, but instead he began, in a rich, eloquent voice:
'Ladies and Gentlemen, there is a conspiracy against

*the musicians in this city. The musicians are mysteriously
disappearing, in a holocaust of musicians, they are being
kidnapped, blackmailed, tortured, mutilated, given elec-
troshock, abducted and, in some cases, threatened. The
people who are doing this are in league, to a degree, with
the police. And nobody knows—'*

*Just then on the subway intercoms overhead, in a
static-crackle, the voice of the subway station manager
began to speak. 'If you wish to take an uptown B train, I
suggest you take the D or the A to 168th.' The explanation went on for some time. Wearily, knowingly, the
musician put his speakers back into the shopping cart
and carefully folded up the piece of newspaper. He didn't
speak but everything about him indicated he knew that
They were on to him, that the announcement was a ruse
to stop him from telling the world about the holocaust of
musicians.*

Looking Out

W E WENT out on Monday night – 10 September – to an awards ceremony, a black-tie dinner at a very fancy restaurant called Le Cirque. I had often eaten dinner there with Andy and Paige when it was located at a different address and had always looked slightly out of place. OK, I always looked wrong, totally wrong.

Years ago, at the end of the meal a giant tower of spun sugar and glazed fruits would arrive at our table and I always wondered, how do they make those fruits look as if they're dipped in ice? Later I read a recipe that said it was egg white and then confectioners' sugar, but when I tried it myself at home all I got was grapes and strawberries sticky with egg white and they never looked right and when I tried to spin sugar it was only burned lumps.

At that time very fancy society ladies dined in Chanel suits and padded shoulders and I never wore the right thing but now, at the new Le Cirque, I had on a long green shimmery dress with a train that was like a dress a mermaid would have worn, or else it was like a mermaid, and I felt perfect.

We didn't stay out that late but I drank quite a lot and the ceremony was very long and in order to look glamorous I wore mascara to which I am allergic and which gives me, in addition to my regular hangover-of-existence (which, I find, I wake up with whether or not I have had anything to drink), a mascara hangover.

So the next morning, after Tim and Willow were out the

door – Tim takes Willow to school by car service and then he continues to work – I went back to sleep. The phone rang a few times – one call sounded like my mother, then there were a couple of calls from Tim – but I didn't pay any attention and slept through their messages on the machine.

When I finally woke it was late and I wondered why Tim and my mother had been calling me so early. I looked out the window. The World Trade Centers were on fire. That seemed peculiar. I would never again wear mascara. My head throbbed. All the windows on that side of our apartment face Manhattan. I went and got a cup of coffee. It was terrible, very weak, I had made it myself the night before and not put enough coffee in the pot. I winced and went back to the window.

The first World Trade Center collapsed. It was the southern tower, the one marginally closer to us. Even though I was alone I said, 'Oh my God.' It seemed strange to speak out loud, to myself. The words just blurted out of me, as if I was speaking to someone else. The coffee was terrible and the World Trade Center was collapsing or it appeared to be. It was the most beautiful thing I had ever seen. It happened in slow motion and the clouds of smoke and ash were like the eruption of Vesuvius or Krakatoa. Then another building, perhaps fifty stories, just north of the second World Trade Center, went down too.

'Oh,' I said. Because I was alone I could not think it was real. I believed my grasp on reality to be tenuous at best. I turned on the television. 'The World Trade Center is collapsing,' the announcer was shouting. That did not seem real, but in a different way.

Now there were two unrealities, a) out the window, and b) on the television. I went back to the window and the second World Trade Center went down. The coffee was terrible and real life was like a movie and the television was like the radio, only with fake pictures, and the sight of a building collapsing was the most beautiful thing I had ever seen in my life. I could not quite register what was happening.

All over Brooklyn people had gathered on the rooftops to watch. Our building was the tallest and on a hill. I looked over at Manhattan and all over Brooklyn.

For one day lower Manhattan seemed shrunken, dinky. By the third day I could no longer remember what it had looked like when the towers were there. There were people in the buildings but I could not imagine it, nor them. There was only this terrible beauty on remembering the event, and a sense of disbelief.

Only one time before did I have this feeling of being hit in the stomach with a baseball bat, and that was when I lived in Princeton for the academic year 1986–87 and a woman I knew called me early on a Sunday morning and said Andy was dead, she had found out from a lawyer. I called Paige in the city and said, Andy is dead and Paige said, no he's not, he's in the hospital for a minor operation and she hung up and then called his house and Fred answered the phone. So she knew Andy was dead and she called me back and said, 'Oh, Tama, come quickly.'

When the smoke blew in this direction it was the smell of an electric fire, like when you plug in an old toaster and it blows up, or a defective hair dryer, electricity and burnt rubber and burning toast and hair. Electrical fires smell the worst of all, like something being ripped in the fabric of the universe, and later I remembered when the towers collapsed you could feel it, physically, as if men had torn the atom without knowing what they were doing and now all the pieces were being, wrongly, rearranged, as if the planet was having an allergic reaction. And when Andy had died it seemed like something had left New York, too, and that kids had come from all over the world hoping to be an artist like Andy, and that anyone walking down the street of Manhattan might pass him and say, 'Oh, hi Andy!' or 'There goes Andy Warhol.'

Part Five

Animals

Why I'm a Little-dog Person

I'VE ALWAYS been a little-dog person. Even if I didn't live in a city (where apartment space is at a premium and you're responsible for cleaning the sidewalk after your dog) I would still be a little-dog person. I don't understand these golden-retriever types, one of whom would be my husband. A lab or shepherd mix can be nice enough, sincere, earnest, playful, but as far as I'm concerned a real dog should be timid, feeble, neurotic, snappish, picky, babyish or a combination of all of the above – like me, I guess.

I don't know where my theories on what a dog should be like came from. When I was a kid my best friend, Clivia Pittore, had a mother who raised and showed champion chihuahuas, and they lived in a house with sixty or seventy free-roaming dogs; I thought visiting Clivia was like heaven, and this might have affected me. Later, in grad school, a fellow student brought her tiny Yorkshire terrier to class, where it would sit at her feet gnawing on a pencil, which appeared gigantic between its tiny front paws. I thought it was the cutest thing I had ever seen, and my only desire was to have a little dog like that, even though later, while passing the other student's parked car (she had run into a shop, briefly), I saw the tiny and docile pup ripping up the seats and screaming bloody murder, that it had been cruelly abandoned for five minutes.

As soon as I made a bit of money from my writing I ran out and bought a Yorkshire terrier. I fully believe in adopting dogs.

In New York City, more than sixty thousand dogs, abandoned, homeless, abused, are put to death each year. Most of these are dogs my husband would love to have. Big, happy, grateful mutts. No doubt they are intelligent and unneurotic.

My first Yorkie, Lulu, I bought from a home breeder. Six weeks old, while the other puppies played and romped on the floor, Lulu, the runt of the litter, hopped on my lap and sat prissily, with a smug expression on her face that seemed to say, 'Get me out of here, away from this riff-raff.'

I lugged her around for the next eleven years. Her personality was not pleasant, but very strong.

She had more than a few unpleasant character traits, one of which was to bite anyone who even inadvertently touched her with their foot.

No foot, according to her, was ever supposed to touch royalty. Idiotically, people often assumed a little dog might be stroked with a foot – certainly family dogs when I was a kid didn't mind being used as a footrest – Lulu taught everyone otherwise.

As she had a habit of sleeping at my feet while I wrote at the typewriter, for many years I was extremely jumpy; as the hours passed I would forget about her presence, eventually I would shift my feet and then with a hideous roar she would spring and sink her teeth into my ankles. And on more than one occasion my husband, getting out of bed for an early departure, would come around to my side of the bed to kiss me goodbye. It was on this side, on the floor, that Lulu often slept and sprang up to scare him witless in the dark.

It was my belief, after I got her, that she needed companionship and after a few months I got her a friend, Beep-beep. In no undecided terms she spent the rest of her life – and Beep-beep's – letting me know I had made a mistake. Each morning on rising he would kiss her good-morning and she would return his pleasantry with a growl. Nevertheless, they did love each other and during the times when Beep-beep had to spend a few days away, at, say, the veterinarian, she seemed curiously diminished. Without him to loathe and lord it over, her life was without purpose. They were like an old married couple, possibly from an arranged Victorian marriage, who didn't know how dependent they were on one another.

Beep-beep, though small, was tough, macho and neurotic in his own way. On the street people walking big dogs would often approach and I would do my best to yank Beep-beep out of the way. 'Don't worry,' the other person would say. 'My dog is very gentle.'

'Yeah, well my dog isn't,' I would be muttering just as the other dog began to bend gently for a friendly sniff. At this point Beep-beep, who had previously appeared innocuous, would launch straight up into the air, without warning, to sink his teeth into the unsuspecting dog's snout.

Sometimes while visiting my mother up at Cornell University, where dogs were allowed freely on campus, I watched him chase some huge terrified hound across the grassy quad. He only weighed about five pounds but had no idea of his own size, only that he had plans to beat the hell out of the other guy. Fortunately his legs were too short to ever catch the intended victim.

Of course this led to disaster; one year, visiting friends at Christmas, he decided to attack another dog – a big unneutered Chesapeake Bay retriever – who Beep-beep felt had dissed Lulu's honor. (The reasons for this are too complex to get into here, but the terrible and embarrassing incident occurred at Christmas dinner, at a table for twelve set with beautiful crystal and candles, a formal setting.) The other dog, Max, picked up Beep-beep in his jaws and gave him a shake before Beep-beep could be prised loose.

I thought Beep-beep had suffered internal injuries. He couldn't move, lay near death. He refused to eat, would scarcely drink. Trips to the veterinarian included exams, X-rays, blood tests and so forth. There was nothing physically wrong, it transpired – only that Beep-beep was depressed because he had lost the fight.

Eventually he recovered; but after Lulu's death he fell into a profound state of grieving. Her last act – her body riddled with massive tumors – the day before her operation, was to consume a large portion of Roy Rogers fried chicken, snatching bits away from him. Neither of us could believe it when Lulu died on the operating table. It was months before I was able to get a new dog, this time a hairless Chinese Crested who looked like a whimsical character from Dr Seuss. At first he had no use for the new puppy; she adored him and he was unaccustomed to this. In his cranky old age, he beat up his new concubine, Nike, if she happened to be frolicking too close to him while he slept. He would jump up and give her a sound thrashing. Once, though, my husband sat down near him on the bed and Beep-beep was so soundly asleep he didn't realize it was my husband, not the new puppy, and he sprang up and sank his teeth into Tim. He didn't have many teeth left by then, but still managed to leave a couple of dents in my husband, who was left traumatized, with feelings badly hurt. He grew more demanding, too, as he got older (Beep-beep, not Tim) and each day stood in front of the refrigerator barking for dinner earlier and earlier, with a hurt and angry expression on his face. 'You see how I'm treated?' he once told my mother when she visited, and, after eating, he would sometimes shoot me a look of gratitude that seemed to say, 'Well, the woman can cook, after all.'

Nike did prolong his life, however; in time he came to appear to be quite fond of her, even going so far, one day, while we were on a hike in the woods, as to run back some distance to help her cross a little stream. (Nike had – has – her own set of neuroses, one of which is that under no circumstances can she get her feet wet; another is that she is far too tiny to jump off or on the bed or even walk up a step, though she is quite large enough to do both of these.)

After almost twenty years of having small dogs, I know what I want: something small, peculiar, petulant and spoiled that will sit on my lap and punch me angrily with a paw if I stop petting it. Something that weighs only a few pounds and thinks of itself as royalty. Something with picky eating requirements and an expression on its face that says: I am Lapdog, Queen of the World, and this is My Person.

I'm not alone in my sentiments: recently I was visiting a friend who had just gotten a tiny Maltese pup. While she sat cooing to the tiny fluffy creature, a group of men – her two grown sons, her husband, my husband – sat watching with horrified, sickened expressions on their faces. I was deeply appreciative of this scenario. I'm thinking, Next, maybe Japanese Chin? There's something about that cunning, pompous little squashed face with buggy goldfish eyes . . . or maybe Italian greyhound, long ballerina legs, shivery, prancing . . . Oddly, each of these suggestions provokes my husband to whimper and mutter, 'Mutt. Mutt. Mutt.'

A New York Squirrel

WHEN MY Yorkies, Lulu and Beep-beep, were still puppies I took them to Central Park and let them off the leash. There was a baby squirrel nibbling a nut on the grass and Lulu made a half-hearted lunge at it and caught it. I let out a yell. Lulu was startled. She dropped the squirrel, which ran to a tree. Apparently the squirrel wasn't a very good climber yet, because it couldn't seem to muster the ability to get up the trunk, so it just started to run around the base. Lulu chased the squirrel to the tree. She was running after it but didn't realize that all that was happening was that she was chasing the squirrel in a circle. Still shouting, I chased Lulu around the tree before she could catch the squirrel again. Beep-beep, who didn't know what was going on, decided to join in, chasing me chasing Lulu who was chasing the squirrel around the tree.

So for a long time the four of us ran around and around the base of the tree, the young squirrel, Lulu, me and Beep-beep. Finally I managed to get close enough to fling myself on top of Lulu. I threw my jacket over the squirrel (I didn't want to get bitten) and put it in a hole in the crotch of the tree. It didn't appear hurt, only angry.

For the rest of her life Lulu had an obsession with chasing squirrels, although she never caught one again. I always thought it was sort of sad, to have had her peak experience as a puppy.

City Squirrel No. 2

H E WAS the sort of squirrel who slept late. He didn't usually bother to appear until around eleven o'clock, sometimes noon, and when he started to hang around the garden of my city apartment I had to get up from my typing to give him peanuts or he would get very angry.

While my dogs were visiting my mother for a few weeks, one afternoon the squirrel came in the back door of my apartment and stood staring at me balefully. As usual I got up and gave him a peanut. The difference was, this time he was inside. He was so arrogant he didn't even trouble himself to take it out, but left the shell on the floor.

I took a break from work. I went into the kitchen to make a cup of coffee. When I returned I found that the squirrel had climbed up on to my desk. Then he crapped all over my manuscript. 'Get out!' I said. He paid me no mind but followed me down the hall. In the kitchen, while I poured my coffee, he lay down. His legs were sprawled. He had a demanding expression on his pinched face. I thought perhaps I might placate him by giving him an almond for a change, instead of a peanut, even though almonds were more expensive and he had just shown what he thought of me by defecating on my work-in-progress.

He picked up the almond in his front paws, gave it a bite and spat it out.

Later in the day I went out. I didn't bother to shut the back door; I just assumed the squirrel had other things to do in the afternoon. When I returned, a couple of hours later, I had been vandalized. He had ransacked my desk, tossing objects and papers to the ground. He had gotten into my bed – a fact I only discovered that evening, when I found his little presents. Most appallingly, he had taken the entire bag of peanuts with him when he left, bag included, leaving a trail of shells in his wake. What a pig! I went into the yard, half expecting to see a giant squirrel with a tremendous belly, too bloated to leap from tree to tree.

When the dogs came home from their vacation, Lulu went out into the yard. From high above her head came the most tremendous sounds of rage and fury, a shrill, chattering scream, and then a long period of almost humanly mournful baby sobs. The squirrel couldn't believe Lulu had invaded his territory.

He never came into the house again, but Lulu's life was infinitely changed for the better. She had a purpose now, a reason to exist. There was always a chance, she thought, if she waited long enough the squirrel might topple out of the tree and into her paws. A dog with an occupation – a hobby, at least – even if it is not a working dog, is a happy one.

I don't remember when exactly I wrote this, but while I was retyping it another incident came to mind. Shortly after I moved into that apartment I went away on a book tour and in Los Angeles Susan Magrino, my publicist from the publishing company at the time, came to my room to tell me not to worry, but my neighbor, Gerry Mack, had tracked me down to say there had been a break-in in both our apartments. 'The police said they don't think anything was taken,' Susan reported. 'They caught the kids on the street and put back whatever they had. Apparently they drank your orange juice, though, and trashed the place. It's destroyed.'

Of course, I was worried; when I got back to the city it

was late at night and, it transpired, the front lock to my apartment was broken and I was unable to get inside. I hung out with Gerry until the locksmith arrived. 'The police said your apartment was vandalized,' Gerry said. 'But nothing was taken. Here are your tapes that the kids dropped in the alley.'

I looked at the tapes. Marais and Miranda – South African folk singers of the late 1950s and early 1960s. Some zydeco. Françoise Hardy, the French chanteuse. 'These aren't my tapes,' I said. 'But they're just what I wanted.'

Finally the locksmith came and apprehensively I went in the front door to find what decimation had taken place. I looked around. Nothing I could detect had been touched. Everything was exactly how I had left it: half-unpacked boxes, books heaped on the floor, newspapers, piles of shoes. If anything it seemed that some attempt had been made to tidy up the place. 'The police said the place was vandalized?' I said to Gerry, who I had asked, out of nervousness, to accompany me.

'Um, I guess they didn't know you had just moved in,' he said.

I was the only person I knew who ended up with more stuff after being robbed. The empty carton of orange juice was on the counter. I couldn't remember whether I had left it out or not.

The Dog Without a Personality

W HEN I was scarcely old enough to walk a giant St
  Bernard knocked me down and stood over me to lick
my face; all I did was laugh uproariously. I've always been a
dog person, though as a child I had cats, as well as rabbits, a
goat, a sheep, and – for a brief time – a raccoon and a monkey.
But ultimately, I'm a dog person; more specifically, a little-dog
person. At present I have two Chinese Cresteds, a toy breed
that is supposedly hairless except for the head, the feet and the
tail, except that both of mine grew some hair on the body, so
that they are basically small hairy dogs with bald sides.

I do not recommend this breed to anyone, though they are
amusing to look at, akin to a miniature, prehistoric ancestor of
the horse, or a whimsical drawing from a child's book. It's true
that, though their brains are the size of walnuts, their personalities are as large as that of any human being, at least to me, and
herein is the fact I find so fascinating: that personality is
unrelated to intelligence. A dog can be smart – at least for a
dog – but without much in the way of expressiveness, quirks,
sense of humor and all the other attributes that make up what we
know as personality; or – like one of my dogs – exceptionally
stupid and yet a vivid, colorful character. As I write these words,
on a laptop computer, Nike has jumped on my lap (where the
computer should be; I've had to shove it toward my knees) and is
happily punching me with one paw, demanding chewing gum.
At an early age Nike found a piece of chewing gum (still
wrapped) on the street and carried it in her mouth, proudly,

until she was able to remove the wrapper and devour it; the dog is a chewing-gum addict and will go through available pockets or pocketbooks in search of the stuff. One of my previous dogs, Lulu, a mean little Yorkie whom I dearly loved, had a carrot fixation and would stand in front of the refrigerator, growling, until a person got her a carrot – which had to be peeled and sliced before she would eat it. When I went away for a few weeks the dog-sitter discovered Lulu liked carrots because, she said, Lulu carried a piece of carrot in her mouth and spit it out when she reached New Jersey (the dog-sitter's home) and then looked from it to the refrigerator, until the dog-sitter realized what she wanted. I wouldn't have believed this story except that the lovely dog-sitter was lacking in personality and wouldn't have had the ability to make the story up or figure out on her own that Lulu wanted carrots. Another of Lulu's quirks was to insist on being held up to the sink to drink fresh, running water – another need she was equally able to communicate. She was a spoiled, fat, petulant little thing, so much so that once while I was walking her a derelict lying on the pavement lifted his head to point to her and announce in a gravelly voice, 'That one – she's a shopper.' Which was perfectly true; had Lulu been a human she would have been one of those rich upper East Side matrons who spend every day in the American equivalent of Harvey Nichols or Peter Jones. That, to me, was personality – a series of traits so readily identifiable that even someone who didn't know her could instantly see what she was all about.

Beep-beep was supposed to be Lulu's companion.

He never seemed to be present, during his lifetime. It was Lulu who had all the zest, the wit, the demands, the need for interaction. In Beep-beep's case, years went by yet he remained a blank. His interactions with me were limited to the occasional barking demand – to go out, or to come in – or a prod on my arm with his paw for me to rub him behind the ears. He otherwise was not affectionate, did not want to sit on my lap, would get up and move away if I petted him at a time other than when he wanted to be petted. He was glad to see me when I returned, yet I felt this was an act, in imitation of Lulu. I thought perhaps Lulu had caused him some brain damage when he was a puppy. From the beginning she despised him and thought of herself as an only child – a child who did not like dogs. *She* certainly was not a dog. Whenever she could she picked him up by the ear and tried to shake him to death until one day some months later I came home to find a chunk of fur dangling alongside Beep-beep's head; it was his ear. At some point Lulu had bitten his ear, clamping down on a blood vessel so severely the blood supply was cut off; the ear developed dry gangrene and eventually the upper half died. Beneath the fur I had not noticed this progression.

Nevertheless, Beep-beep continued to worship her. Each morning when he awoke he would go to her and try to kiss her. Each morning she would snarl at him. It reminded me of how I had treated my younger brother when we were children. After several years, however, it suddenly dawned on Beep-beep that when Lulu growled at him and lunged, he could bite her back, and after that she didn't attack him any more. This also reminded me of my relationship with my brother. Beep-beep thought of himself as a much larger dog, perhaps a Doberman Pinscher, who had inadvertantly gotten trapped in a mouse-sized body. He only weighed five pounds, but he was determined to teach other dogs a lesson. On the street he would snarl and leap for the nose of any dog who dared to get too close.

Other dogs he would hate on sight, snapping and snarling a block away; some he appeared to like, sniffing and letting himself be sniffed – but then abruptly he would change his mind and his black rage would descend. In these instances I always had the feeling it was because the other dog had announced, in dog language, something along the lines of 'Why, you little runt!' or another provoking comment.

He didn't discriminate: large or small, bitch in heat or neutered dog, he wanted to kill – except for his one weakness, small white bitches. These he loved, and he would go into his little dance, bobbing his head and sneezing, black lips pulled back in a grin of infatuation.

His interests were few. He had no playful instinct, he did not chase balls, he did not pursue squirrels. He liked to sleep, eat, lift his leg, stop to smell every single inch of sidewalk so that walking with him was infinitely slow. When he was a few years old he and Lulu went to stay with my mother for a time while I traveled, and though he had been content with dry chow, my mother felt sorry for them and began preparing meals: a cut-up hot dog, Brussels sprouts in butter sauce.

At first the meal was served at five o'clock; the next day at quarter to five Beep-beep was standing in front of the refrigerator, barking. 'Oh, you want your dinner,' said my mother. The next day he was there at four-thirty, and so it went. We both found it remarkable that he was able to figure out the time so immediately and accurately. Within a short period my mother was feeding him at three o'clock, then two. He ate richly and eagerly, snuffling and snorting until he had finished the contents of the bowl.

With Lulu it was a different story – she always acted as if she never ate. But around midnight she would rise, stagger off, and from the kitchen would come the sounds of her secret snacking. Had she been human she would have insisted that her inability to lose weight was metabolic ('I never eat a thing!'), and the vanished quarts of ice cream she no doubt would have attributed to someone else.

After the Christmas dinner where he attacked a Chesapeake Bay retriever under the crystal-laden table and was rescued by Cyrus Jhabvala, whose quick actions saved his life, he couldn't walk, couldn't move, wouldn't eat. He had lost the fight and it took months for him to recover.

Nevertheless, this did not stop him from attacking every dog he met after that. Let loose from his leash on the campus of Cornell, where my mother taught, he would take off in hot pursuit of any other dog he could find. Mostly they ran from him – big mutts, black labs, fleeing across the grassy lawn, in fear for their lives, followed by a teeny dog whose legs moving at top speed could not keep up with theirs.

When sleeping his snore was louder than that of any man.

In Ithaca his days were spent in pure delight, tied in front of my mother's house, where he would hide under the bushes and wait until the mailman or a student on foot passed by, when he would spring like a dog in a cartoon, bouncing off the end of the string with a vicious yodel of hate. Inevitably the mailman, the student, caught unaware, would also leap into the air, terrified, surprised. What satisfaction, what bliss, Beep-beep experienced then.

He had, as I say, no hunting instinct and in a mouse-filled apartment I once saw a mouse promenade right in front of his nose and be ignored. However, in Ithaca, there was for a brief period a field mouse who must have come right out and punched him in the face, for an occupation that took many hours was for him to stand in front of a particular closet, waiting for the mouse to emerge.

After Lulu died, his grief was so severe it seemed he would not live much longer. I got Nike, then a puppy, and though he had little use for her – except to beat her severely when she tripped over his sleeping body while she was playing – he slowly emerged from his depression. Though he never felt the same about her as he did about Lulu, in time he grew fond of Nike, who adored him. In his old age he became quite gentlemanly; while walking in the country, when Nike got left behind (too frightened to cross a half-inch-deep stream) he ran some distance back through the woods to aid her. He led her across the stream and back to me.

I had thought it would be Lulu I would miss most of all, but over the years my memory of Lulu and her petulant, spoiled demands has grown weaker. I think of him more and more often – his attempts to drive the car, either from the back seat, where he would pant and pace nervously for the hours it took to complete a trip, or when, while on the front seat, he would try to climb on to Tim's lap and put his paws on the steering wheel. It was obvious he didn't think anyone was a better driver than himself.

What I find interesting is that the traits that display each of my dogs' personality are usually not visible to anyone else, at least not immediately. If I visit a friend with a dog, it is, to me, just an animal – something large or small, hairy or not hairy, snuffling or barking. And I can't see the dog's personality, any more than I could go into a room at a cocktail party and see the personalities of the guests – they're just a bunch of people in a room, until you get to know them.

But as soon as you get to know a person, or an animal, you can attempt to describe them – their personality. For this reason I had to give up keeping tropical fish. As a kid I had an aquarium in my room and there was one fish in particular, a large striped angelfish, who slowly emerged as the dominant figure. He (I assume the fish was a male) watched my every move, swimming to the end of the tank and back if I crossed the room, staring at me with a loving expression. He took food from my finger, he waited for me to get home. When, later, he died in unfortunate circumstances, I was devastated and still can't bear to think of keeping a pet that has to live in a tank, no matter how large.

If it's possible by careful observation to discover a fish's personality, what about ants? Or bees? They live in a hill, a hole or a hive; they are not supposed to be individuals, are supposedly each a part of a larger whole – and yet, is that so very different than the millions of inhabitants of New York, all crowded together, taking subways to work and returning to sleep in tiny cells? It may be that, if one really spent time with ants, one might distinguish specific personality traits in each: a thought rather horrifying to contemplate, if one considers that ants might very well appear to us the same as we would appear to a horde of freshly arrived aliens, without much time or interest in us, but with very large, trampling feet.

The Difference between Dogs and Babies

Y EARS AGO, as a kid in Israel, I was taken to see a visiting reverend. The minister told the story of a desperate family, living in overcrowded conditions, who went to the rabbi for advice. 'Get a goat,' the rabbi said.

For some reason I've been thinking about this fable recently. My husband and I just came back from China, where we adopted a baby. My mother kept telling me that having a baby wasn't going to be any more difficult than having a dog, and any time I got nervous I reminded myself of this. I've always loved dogs, and when I learned that the word for 'little baby' in Mandarin sounds something like 'chihuahua', I knew that a baby was meant for me.

The two dogs we already have are Chinese Cresteds, which is a hairless breed, except that they kept growing a lot of hair, so they only have hairless (bald) patches, and it's occurred to me that one of their ancestors may have been raped by a chihuahua. A lot of people ask me on the street what's wrong with them, same as always, and never even mention the new baby, who is glaring at them, although the adoption agency told us to be prepared for this.

Of the two dogs, Lily is a better specimen, except that the veterinarian was quite upset on our last visit at the number of her pimples, which he said was unnatural, and that she was going to need two hundred dollars in dental work. The baby only has one tooth – so far – but she knows how to use it.

Mentally Lily has some problems, such as anorexia, and a

vicious streak which causes her to blame all of her problems on Minky.*

Sadly, Minky, although fatter (actually overweight) is much weaker than Lily and has lost all her teeth (something else the breed is known for). Lily attacked her every time the doorbell rang, or a plate dropped, or if she was just feeling a little anxious. Minky was losing so much blood that I had to put Lily on Prozac, which is working – to a degree – although first I went through Buspar, an anti-anxiety drug; a personal dog-trainer; and the female hormone Ovaban, none of which had any effect, on Lily, I mean, not me.

My mother said maybe I should put Minky on Prozac, too, for being depressed about her weakness. The Prozac only costs a dollar a day, and I administer it in oral form, which is no problem, I just post notes on the door to remember. The only side effect in Lily was a slight increase in her anorexia, which was solved by buying her delicious, expensive ready-cooked roast chickens, although she is still a skinny dog. But another possible side effect of Prozac is weight-gain, which would probably be the side effect that Minky would get.

What I do to try and keep Minky's weight down is add brown rice and fresh vegetables to her dog food, something my dog-sitter, who is into natural foods and holistic medicine, taught the dogs to love. My mother taught them to love chopped liver, but only from Fairway's or Zabar's.

The dogs really aren't much trouble at all. Now that we are back with the baby, who has no inner resources and seems to need very little sleep, I feel really sad for the dogs, who were completely unprepared to have their lives disrupted by some-one in diapers.

We were told to take twelve disposable diapers per day to China, which is the one thing the Chinese don't have, because

---

* Not her real name. Her real name, unfortunately, came with her: Goddess of Victory, Sneaker – Nike.

the children there have slits in their trousers. Twelve diapers per day comes out to one an hour, and while our baby doesn't need that many, she has had terrible diaper rash, although she appears healthy. Perhaps too healthy, because she needs five bottles of formula, one every three hours, and the bottles have to be just the right temperature, almost like a cup of cappuccino.

The Chinese babies are trained to take their formula hot, and they get angry if it is not just right. It has to be mixed with instant rice cereal, which, although not nutritious, does stop them from being constipated. Constipation for a baby is the one thing you don't want to have happen, as I learned on the trip to China, although diarrhea is equally bad, and it's not like having a dog, because when one of my dogs gets diarrhea, say, in the middle of the night, she will cry until I get out of bed. She knows that I'll wipe her rear end off with an aloe-softened Handi-Wipe or else she'll retaliate.*

A baby is a lot more work. Since I'm back at home now with the baby full time I can't go out unless I get the baby, tie her in the stroller, carry the stroller up the steps, put on the brakes and then get the dogs. Then I put Minky in the basket (Minky refuses to walk, since a) she is very lazy, and b) Lily still tries to kill her occasionally) and shorten Lily's leash so that she can't bite anybody on the ankles. Lily doesn't like anyone who is physically challenged and Chinese messengers distributing menus. But at least since I rarely have the strength to go out now I have a lot of time to think.

All these years, I realized, I incorrectly remembered the story that the minister told us in the ulpan about the rabbi. How it went was, the family came to the rabbi and said, 'We're too crowded.' And the rabbi told them to get a sheep and keep it in the room with them. So the family came back a while later, and the family said, 'We're still too crowded.' So the rabbi told them to get a cow.

* You don't want to know.

The list of animals went on and on, and finally, when the family was having a collective nervous breakdown,* the rabbi said, 'Now get rid of the goat.'

I guess the story probably originated in New York City, once upon a time. The thing is, the baby really is cute, especially when she's sleeping and isn't pulling out the dogs' few hairs. And she is getting me pretty well trained, although I don't serve and entertain her as quickly as she would like.

It's the dogs who are suffering. I can tell that they're bored. They won't play with each other, because they hate each other. I'm thinking of getting 1) a ferret, which I think would make a good companion for a dog, even though they're illegal in Manhattan and some say have a strong odor; or, 2) a chinchilla Persian cat, which weighs only four pounds and couldn't kill the dogs or the baby, though Persians do shed; or, 3) a Japanese Chin or Belgian Griffon which my husband isn't too happy about because he hates snouty-faced dogs.

I would only get one if I could adopt a shelter animal, however. There are so many creatures out there who need homes, and I'm sure it wouldn't be much trouble at all, at least not until our baby needs a sibling.

Commissioned by and rejected for the back page of New York Times Sunday Magazine.

Recently it came to me that the only difference between dogs and people is that dogs don't worry about their weight.

---

* If 'nervous breakdown' is politically incorrect, 'psychotic episode' may be substituted.

The Catlady

W E WENT to a woman's apartment in the Bronx who rescued cats. When we got off the elevator there was a powerful odor so we figured we were on the right floor. The Catlady opened the door. She was attractive, with dark bobbed hair, little or no makeup, maybe forty and conventional in appearance.

She started to talk rapidly and non-stop about a crisis in an abandoned post office where she had found and trapped more than thirty cats, some of which had been tortured. Every night she would go out and rescue more cats. Her eyes were darting, almost frantic, as she spoke and it didn't seem to matter whether we were listening or not.

Sometimes cats were used for bait to train pitbulls. She had found one cat with its intestines hanging out. It cost almost one thousand dollars to treat at the vet. Then it died. Some of her cats would never recover from what they had been through, and these she would never allow to be adopted. All the cats had to be neutered or spayed and given shots. She hoped by appearing on our public access television program. 'Its a Dog's Life'* she would get some donations, and maybe some people who wanted to adopt a cat. But she preferred to find good homes for her older cats, since she didn't like to see her kittens go out too young, and, after all, a lot of people liked kittens and then got tired of them when they stopped being so cute.

---

* Paige Powell and I had this show on public access television – it was about adopting stray animals.

She said she had a hundred cats and kittens just now, and some dogs, but she would never let anyone adopt a cat of hers unless she went to their apartment and made sure all the windows had screens. I tried to think if I had ever been to an apartment in New York with screened windows. I could never remember having been in one. New York apartments don't have screened windows.

At first I didn't think there were a hundred cats and kittens in the apartment, just a few who smelled bad. Then my eyes adjusted to the gloom. On the top of the bookshelf were some cats. On the table were some cats. On the chairs were some cats. On the sofa were some cats. A tail protruded from under the sofa. There were some cats on the back of the sofa. On the windowsill were some cats. There was a big cage, full of kittens. On the counter that divided the kitchen was a cat. There was a big spaghetti pot on the stove and a cat's face peeped out. 'You have a lot of cats,' I said.

'We have three bedrooms. The other cats are in there,' the Catlady said.

There were some dogs, too, a sort of chihuahua-type, a black and white mutt and a beagle-ish one. They all looked tired and stricken, as if they couldn't understand how they had gotten into this situation. Maybe the cats had beaten them up too often.

A man was standing in the doorway to one of the other rooms; he was good-looking in an embarrassed, chagrined sort of way. He held a big dog on a chain.

'My boyfriend,' said the Catlady.

'Are you involved with the cat rescue too?' I asked.

'Oh yes,' he said. I had the feeling his look of embarrassment was due to his circumstances. Somehow he had gotten roped into an existence he wanted no part of. 'This is Duke,' he said wearily. 'Duke is a nice dog. We found him. I'm hoping we can find Duke a home.' Duke pulled on the chain and slathered. 'I don't think Duke would be good in a home with children, though,' he said.

'Why not?' I said.

'He bit me. But he's a good boy, aren't you, Duke?'

The dog growled and lunged. I tried to step away but things were rubbing against my legs and I almost fell. 'Oh look,' said the Catlady, who seemed to notice me – and her cats – for the first time. 'They like you.'

Ferrets

ALTHOUGH THERE are a number of different species of ferret, the kind that is kept for rabbiting has been domesticated since ancient Egyptian times and I've wanted one for around ten years. I'm not sure why or how this obsession came about. I never knew or saw anyone with a ferret – growing up in western Massachusetts nobody I knew ever had one, although according to my books early settlers kept them for rat-catching.

Domestic ferrets (unlike the European and Siberian polecat and the American black-footed ferret) are not able to survive on their own in the wild – though they are related to otter, mink, weasel and ermine – but, despite the fact that they would die if abandoned in city or forest, it is still illegal to own a ferret in many places.

Recently Mayor Giuliani announced that no ferrets – or iguanas – were allowed in New York City. I still wanted one, though, and just around the same time the Mayor said that he was going to cut off all city funding to the museum across the street from where we live – the Brooklyn Museum – due to the fact that he didn't like the upcoming art exhibit (part of the Saatchi collection of British artists) I accidentally went into a pet store and accidentally bought a ferret.

'It's illegal!' my husband said.

Over the years I had collected various true stories about peculiar animals in New York: a couple who kept a massive crocodile in their apartment; a woman I had visited once who had a hundred cats (though she advertised they were available for adoption, so far no one had ever met her strict criteria); my cousin, who lived in a loft filled with literally hundreds of parrots, hornbills, toucans, cockatoos, finches and even a quail, hedgehog, peacock, turtles and a couple of monkeys (one of whom eventually died from onanism).

There was a news story about a person's pet silver fox, which escaped – in Manhattan's fur district – and ran down the street pursued by hundreds of Hassidim. And another about a woman who opened her oven to find a ten-foot boa constrictor curled inside; it had come up through the pipes.

Somewhere up in Harlem a shelter, operated by the police, is full of pitbull terriers who have attacked and been captured – a kind of death row for dogs. In Washington Square Park I saw a group of men with nets trying to capture a huge hyacinth macaw that had landed in a tree; and a girlfriend was once attacked by an angry squirrel when she pretended to give it a nut that was actually a rock.

And then there was the time a woman told me about living in a basement apartment with two small children. After a massive rainstorm one of the children climbed into her parents' bed one morning and announced there was a mouse in the toilet. They thought the child had an overactive imagination, until one of them got up and lifted the toilet lid to find a gigantic rat had swum the wrong way up the overflowing sewer system.

That's not really a story about an exotic pet, though.

So when I got home from Rochester with the ferret, even though I was slightly nervous, I figured in time my family would come to accept it. I wasn't quite sure, walking in the door, why I had wanted one in the first place – it had long claws and a peculiar musky smell.

I was supposed to get a ferret while I was in England over the summer – in England, apparently, almost everyone keeps a ferret, because everywhere I went when I expressed my interest in obtaining one, people kept saying that hundreds of them lived just down the road, and I could take my pick. A friend of my husband's even got on his cell phone, like a drug dealer at a party, and put me on the line with someone who sounded twelve years old who said he had fourteen babies – priced at two pounds each.

In the States they cost one hundred dollars, but are maybe less vicious, since nobody I had ever heard of in the US actually used them for rat hunting.

In England I was taken to Slough to look at some ferrets. Nobody could believe I was going to Slough on my free day during my book tour. Apparently nobody had ever gone to Slough before; apparently it was like saying you were going to Newark, New Jersey, for some fun.

But I do think going to Newark, New Jersey, would be fun – even though I've never been. I have gone to Union City, New Jersey, though, to look at some Mexican hairless dogs called Xoloquintlis, in the home of a woman who was a manicurist and her husband. They had ten large Xoloquintlis, which resembled dogs who had been parboiled; some Chinese Crest-eds, and a parrot. I didn't go home with a Xoloquintli, since I was holding out for a ferret (besides, my dogs didn't get along with other dogs). I did offer to baby-sit some dogs who were looking for homes and later baby-sat two Xolos for two weeks. They had been rescued from a pound in Las Vegas, and were named Vegas and Delta. I changed their names to Bacon and Derma, temporarily, but with a new baby and two other dogs who didn't get along with them it was too much for me.

In Slough I met a man named Mike Ferris, who lived with his wife and baby in a small house, similar to the one with Xolos in New Jersey, only he had many ferrets in the back yard, which is where people in England keep them. I thought they were sweet – the ferrets – and Mike said in the interest of international diplomacy I could have my pick of the new litter.

Unfortunately I found I couldn't take them on the airplane (from May to September airlines don't allow animals) but he promised me when the time was right he would get them to Heathrow.

So far I have my American ferret, my English husband and my Chinese baby (we adopted her a few years ago) but Mike Ferris has been incommunicado. I don't know whether it's because he's afraid of Mayor Giuliani, who has been so public in his anti-ferret sentiments and anti-British art, or because the things Mike Ferris told me about ferrets simply weren't true: that some of them would come when you called their name, and that in England a popular pastime is to put a ferret down a man's trousers.

I figure I can always try this out when my husband gets home. If it goes over OK, I might take it to the Mayor, to demonstrate.

Obsessed with Ferrets

I WAS OBSESSED with ferrets. Almost every night I had the same dream: I was visiting an animal shelter on top of a hill in a strange city that had a lot of ferrets in a pen who needed homes. This dream went on for years. I had only seen a few ferrets, one in a pet store, another at the home of some people who lived on a ranch in the Oregon desert. And when I was a teenager I volunteered at a zoo that had a rare black-footed ferret, but I had never spent any time with any.

I think it was the way they smelled. Some days I thought I had to smell a ferret or I would go mad. It was even worse than the six months or so that I was obsessed with eating sand. I had sand shipped to me from the Oregon coast and drove everyone crazy by crunching all the time. I even chipped a tooth. It was a bizarre compulsion so intense I even went to a psychiatrist, who suggested that clean, good-quality sand was probably available in bags at the florist. Later it turned out I was anemic and after I began taking an iron supplement the craving went away.

This time I was wiser and knew what the shrink would say and figured I would save money by either finding a shelter ferret or simply purchasing one. I loved how ferrets smelled, not a dirty ferret, just a nice healthy clean ferret, a little bit musky. After all, they use musk, sometimes from a civet cat, or a deer, in perfume.

We had two dogs, and one of them, Lily, was crazy and each time the doorbell rang or a plate dropped she would try to kill

Nike, the weaker dog. My husband didn't want a ferret and he despised Lily. Finally, reluctantly, I sent Lily to live with my mother (my mother was quite reluctant, too; even though she loves Lily she wasn't exactly anxious to have a dog). Somebody should do a survey on how many parents end up with their children's dogs. To me these parents belong in the category of saints.

I thought now that the dog was gone Tim couldn't object if I adopted a ferret. People I spoke to involved with ferret rescue groups said under no circumstances would I be allowed to adopt a ferret: I had a small child, I lived in an apartment with a terrace, ferrets are illegal in Manhattan, various other reasons I was an inappropriate adoptive ferret parent.

I kept thinking, there must be so many people out there who buy ferrets in pet stores and then the kids or family loses interest, I could give the ferret a good home. But no one emerged.

One day I was giving a reading up in Rochester, New York, and the guy driving me back to the airport to go home said, 'We have a few minutes. Is there any place you'd like to stop?'

'If there's a big pet store, I can't always find supplies in Manhattan,' I said. 'Besides, I'd like to see if there are any ferrets.'

We stopped at the pet store and there was one ferret, six months old, all alone, in a cage, obviously a bit forlorn. The kid who worked there kept talking about what a great guy this ferret was, how they had all played with him since he was a kit and how lonely he had been since the last of his playmates was sold.

It was sort of an accident but I bought him.

Then I bought a carrier and put him in it.

Then we got to the airport and I had a nervous breakdown. I hadn't bought a ticket for ferret, I hadn't informed them I was taking an animal on the plane, ferret had no papers indicating he was vaccinated, health certificate, etc., all the things re-

quired to fly an animal. Husband did not want a ferret. I said
to the guy who had driven me to the airport, 'Listen, if they
don't let me on to the plane, you're going to have to take this
ferret until I can figure out what to do.'

The poor man looked even more frightened than I was.

I quickly dashed into the bar and bought the man and myself
several drinks.

Ferret was in the carrier on the floor. If I put my fingers in to
pet him, he bit me. Not hard, fortunately, but it was still rather
traumatizing.

I went through security. 'What's in the box?' the man said.

'Well, um, gee, that's a ferret,' I said.

'Oh, really? My daughter has two, a silver and a sable,
they're very cute, very nice.' He took the box from me and
carried it to the other side. Then he called over a few other
airport workers to show them the ferret. The last thing I
wanted to do was draw attention to ferret, but I had no
choice. I kept smiling, feebly, perspiration dripping down. I
tried to get on to the plane as unobtrusively as possible and
quickly popped the carrier under the seat.

By the time I got home I had my story figured out. 'Hi,
darling,' I said. 'Guess what? Somebody . . . ah, unexpectedly
. . . gave me a ferret.'

'Nobody gave you a ferret,' Tim said. 'You bought a ferret,
didn't you?'

'Well, yes,' I said. 'But it was . . . an accident. I couldn't help
myself.'

He was dark brown with a little mask. Willow, our daughter, aged four, named him Totoro after a Japanese video. He
seemed perfectly happy but three weeks later I decided he
might need a companion. I went to a pet store with Willow and
her pal Obie Odom out on Long Island. There was a cage full
of older ferrets. I put my hand in and several sprang up and bit
me very hard. I went to another cage with tiny ferrets. I picked
what appeared to be the gentlest of the bunch. Then I put her

in the carrier. On the way home Willow realized she had lost her stuffed dog and suffered a major breakdown. Obie, who was also aged four, had a reputation for being a difficult traveler but suddenly he blossomed into a helpful fourteen-year-old, comforting Willow, offering to carry things. By the time I got home I was shattered. I couldn't understand what or why I was doing, coming home with another ferret. My life was surely difficult enough. I had an awful feeling: every time things didn't go smoothly for me, I would end up going out to buy another ferret. What if this really happened, and I couldn't help myself? I would end up living with thousands of ferrets.

I hadn't realized that Totoro had really been very lonely. He was so excited to see the other ferret, whom I put into the cage (I ordered this by mail after I got Totoro, who at first had to sleep at night in a large dog carrier), he circled the cage endlessly, trying to get her. This one Willow named Scamper, after a penguin in another video. Finally I let him go to her. For days he dragged her around the room while she screamed. He was like Neanderthal man. But she didn't seem to be suffering, though sometimes I separated them. When I at last let them stay together they slept in the same hammock. Totoro would wrap his arms around her and hold her all night. Sometimes if I turned on the light in that room I would see them entwined. In the morning when it was light outside and I went through to let out the dog he would already be awake and would stare at me with such love I was astonished; I couldn't remember any animal staring at me quite so lovingly.

He was never a lap animal, would lick Tim but not me, he had the soul of a gentleman apart from one terrible habit of gnawing the underside of the sofa. He only did it when I was sitting there, as if to torture me; I would shout, 'No!' and he would turn on his back, so that his face looked up at me, before grinning with an expression that seemed to say, 'Lady, you're going to need a whole new transmission.' There was obviously an imaginary cigarette in his mouth. Then he would roll back the other way so his back legs were sticking out; he looked for all the world like a fat car mechanic.

When Totoro's coat changed for the winter not only did it get paler but two remarkable eyebrows developed, giving him an even more mischievous, Charlie Chaplinesque look.

When he was young he was thrilled to try everything in the way of food; after six months of his life on nothing but dry kibble he was ravenous for new experiences; enjoyed Indian rice, peas, bits of sausage, raw mushrooms, cabbage, peanut butter. But abruptly all this stopped and he then liked nothing other than his dried food, cucumber and melon. He was a strict vegetarian, by choice, apart from the dried food; on the other hand Scamper was only mildly interested in vegetables, mostly because she saw him eating them, and loved chicken. I knew kids who kept ferrets in England and fed them mostly on road kills, raw chicken, etc.; under such circumstances Totoro would not have survived. (These kids, children of friends, all go to a boarding school – Milton Abbey, I think – where each boy is allowed to keep ferrets. After class each day they all go out to hunt rabbits with their ferrets. The school is not exactly known for its academics, but it certainly sounds like one I'd like to go to, though it costs a fortune.)

The following November, when Totoro was about a year and a half old, I saw he was spending a lot of time lying around, breathing heavily (I had thought at first he was simply overweight) and at the doctor the diagnosis was almost immediate: lymphomatic sarcoma. I opted to put him on steroids; he survived until New Year's, mostly thanks to my friend Ashton, who stayed up round the clock to feed him Ferretone mixed with water.

Watching him suffer was terrible. He had been so joyous and full of life. After his death Scamper grew nastier and more depressed. It dawned on me that she was deaf. It was always Totoro who came when he was called or when there was some kind of noise, who ran to the door to greet us; Scamper continued to bite, hard, she ran for cover as soon as she saw a person, she seemed uninvolved. It made sense when I realized she couldn't hear; and Totoro had been her only connection to any living entity.

She was unpleasant. The only personality trait she had was her habit of stealing stuffed animals, which she collected – swiped – from Willow by the dozen, as well as certain shoes. Really, I had little use for her and it seemed to me a typical New York story, that the good one died and the nasty one lived.

In late January I brought home two babies (Mole and Rat, from *The Wind in the Willows*) from Parrots of the World. The animals in that place are so beautifully kept and, because they are handled by customers, seem exceptionally relaxed and gentle. Even though I now know a large percentage of ferrets with white markings on their head are born deaf, and there's not really much way to tell if they are when they are young, I didn't want to go back to the store where I had purchased Scamper.

Mole was six weeks old, light brown, Rat was ten weeks old; I picked him because he seemed so gentle (I had had it with being bitten) and Mark Morrone said that the bigger one would teach the smaller one to be gentle. Scamper had never bitten my daughter; but then, my daughter knew enough not to handle her. I thought, with all Scamper's love of stuffed animals, she must have a strong maternal instinct and would be glad for the new babies, but instead she tried to kill them. This went on for weeks. I thought she was deranged and I would never be able to keep the animals in the same room. I tried to let her be with them for a couple of minutes each day; it always ended in a violent attack. One day, though, it was five minutes before she attacked, and then next day ten, and finally she began to beg to come into the room and when I let her in she pretended to ignore them. That was the breakthrough; though it took two months.

Getting ready for a trip, I left my suitcase on the bed and

Scamper came and crapped in it. She was always a tidy animal, much tidier than Totoro, and I knew she was somehow marking my possessions, or telling me not to go away. I know this sounds peculiar but that was the first time I felt some feeling on her part that wasn't malicious. She did know who I was. Suddenly my heart went out to her.

The sour expression left her face, she slowly stopped (mostly) biting me and Tim. Remarkably, the other night she sat on my lap for a long time and when Tim got home from a trip she came and rested her chin on his arm.

This behavior was so unlike her previous actions that Tim said, 'Is there something wrong with her?' She was more than a year and a half old and had finally connected to – or with – us.

Last night I put all three in the cage to sleep (I don't let them out at night, they tend to get into wild mock fights, complete with screams, or else break into the room and climb on me in my sleep) and I saw, a bit later, the ferrets crowded into the same hammock. They didn't have their arms around each other, nobody would replace Totoro, but they did look like three overgrown baby birds in a nest, peeping up sleepily.

Seven Favorite Sins of Ferrets

Violence. World Wrestling Ferret Association: watching ferrets play has got to be one of the greatest things on the planet. They are such gleeful, happy animals and their methods of wrestling resemble ballet dancers asked to guest-star at a wrestling match. They use every trick in the book, the pile drive, the body slam, the four-point pin, strangulation neck throttle. Nobody ever gets hurt, they drag each other around, it's like those old Peter Sellers movies where Kato, the house-boy, suddenly leaps down from a hiding spot with a chortling war cry. And Scamper, formerly the most vicious, lets Mole drag her around by the neck.

Theft. Stuffed-animal thief: Scamper is obsessed with stuffed animals and since I have a five-year-old daughter, there is an ample supply in our home. Once I looked up to see a giant stuffed chicken moving across the room, apparently of its own accord. Scamper was behind this chicken but so much smaller I couldn't see her. She had a special hiding spot, unreachable, behind a radiator and when the cover was finally removed I found twenty missing toys. Another favorite spot was under the kitchen sink; when I finally checked back there I found heaps of stuffed slippers, rabbits, chickens, penguins, etc. They often like to break into the dollhouse, through the windows or sometimes the door, and ransack the place, much to my daughter's fury. Alas, it always makes me laugh, rather unsympathetically, as there is something so outrageous about the sight of a giant ferret trashing a suburban ranch house.

Lust. OK, so they're all neutered, at least here. Neverthless, Totoro had a thing for Barbie, and I found him many times fondling her in what I could only interpret as a lascivious manner.

Greed. Totoro would climb into any grocery bag placed on the floor and begin to frantically rip open packages, particularly if they were covered with plastic – meat, mushrooms, lettuces, whatever he could get his teeth into (eventually I learned never to put a bag on the floor). He would also hoist himself into the refrigerator as soon as the door was opened and begin to try and pull open the vegetable bins. If he could accomplish this, his task was to leave tooth marks in every bit of food or fruit, without eating it.

Slovenliness. If there's a way to strew a dish of food, or find a place to go near the litterbox but not in it, that's my ferret. If there's a wastebasket full of trash, ferret's main task is to tip it over and remove contents.

Opportunism. If you try to get something done that requires focus, a ferret senses this and immediately appears to use the opportunity to a) bite your toes b) leap on the paper gleefully c) test computer skills d) harass the dog or child, who starts to shriek with rage.

Death threats. A ferret must take great pleasure in hiding somewhere so long you think he or she is dead. If I let them out in the day they are capable of pulling open the cabinet under the kitchen sink, no matter how I've fastened it shut, crawling around behind the cabinets and passing out until three a.m., when you've given up hope of ever seeing them again. Usually I figure they've eaten something poisonous and are dead. I call, bang, shout, get out special food treats – no ferret. Once when Scamper was a baby I opened the garbage room and found she had opened all the bags of garbage and was lying dead, on a heap of rubble. She must have snuck in when someone was throwing out a bag of garbage. Rigor mortis had set in. I was devastated. I called Tim, crying, to deal with the corpse. 'What are you talking about?' he said. By the time he had gone to look she was wide awake and frisking merrily.

Feral instincts/Hunting ability. Three ferrets in the room and a mouse ran across the floor. Not one ferret showed the slightest interest.

A Trip to the Veterinarian

I N THE waiting room of an upper West Side animal hospital
a tall, thin man with metallic glasses was sitting holding the
leash of a brown-and-white bulldog of the sort generally
associated with Winston Churchill. After a few minutes a
woman came in with a large brown-and-white bulldog that
looked almost exactly like the other bulldog, except that the
brown part of its coat was a little bit brindled and it had a cuter
face, slightly more pushed-in and bulldoggish. The two people
could not get over the fact that they had matching dogs, and
then after a minute or so it turned out they had acquired them
from the same breeder. The man's bulldog was named Muffin
and the dog was seven years old; the woman's dog was named
Simon and he was six.

The man said that Muffin weighed fifty-eight and a half
pounds and he asked the woman how much hers weighed.
'Simon is fifty-five pounds,' she said.

'I'm trying to get Muffin's weight down,' the man said. 'He's
on a vegetarian diet and one day a week he fasts.' The bulldog
looked morose. But he did have a glossier coat than Simon and
seemed more youthful.

Simon tried to climb on the chair to sit next to the woman
but his legs were too short.

'I'm not going to help you, Simon,' she said. 'And you can't
do it by yourself, so forget it.' Simon shuffled restlessly on the
end of his leash. The two dogs were not very interested in one
another. 'He's your cousin, Simon!' the woman said.

'Can you believe it?' the man said. 'The same breeder. I had another dog; when he was nine years old he developed a cancer on one side of his stomach and was given six months to live. Well, I started him on the diet, I had him getting acupuncture, and after nine months I brought him back to the doctor and the tumor was gone!'

'That's wonderful,' the woman said. 'I'll give you my phone number.'

'Sure, I'll call you,' the man said. 'We can dish.'

Then a woman came in with a very large Alsatian named Murray. She wanted Murray to sit next to her on the chair, but after she helped Murray up he jumped back down. Murray weighed eighty pounds, but she said to the bulldog owners, 'He's going to fill out. He's a slow developer.' Murray was two and a half years old and had an ingrown dewclaw that wasn't healing properly. It was easy to see that neither of the bulldog owners – nor the bulldogs – thought much of Murray. The veterinary technician came out to look at Murray's dewclaw. 'Hi, Murray,' she said. Apparently Murray had spent quite a bit of time at the doctor's office. He looked like the sort of dog who was always getting in trouble. The dewclaw had been clipped but Murray kept licking it, which caused it to scale instead of scabbing and healing over. The technician went away and came back with a bottle of Gentian Violet, which was supposed to be painted over the dewclaw. Murray's visit to get the bottle of Gentian Violet (which cost two or three dollars at the drug store) had probably cost Murray's owner $75.

Then a vet came out and said to the woman holding Simon, 'Is this Simon Hartman?'

'No,' the woman said. 'They keep doing that. It's the wrong file. There's another Simon Hartman. You have the wrong file.'

'I didn't think Simon was a Labrador retriever,' the vet said. He went and got the other file. Then he led Simon away to have an abscess between his toes lanced. 'I'll definitely call you,' Muffin's owner said. 'We can dish.'

Riverside Park

A SIGN IN Riverside Park, neatly printed and coated in plastic, hung from a fence, warning people to be on the lookout for a man stealing pigeons and squirrels from the park. The sign said the man was middle-aged, a businessman in appearance, and usually wore a beige raincoat and drove a beige station wagon. Anyone seeing him was advised to call the police.

I never saw the man, but the sign did make me take a closer look at the squirrel and pigeon inhabitants. Many of the squirrels were missing the fur from their tails, though whether this was a mutant strain or simply due to some squirrel disease I could not be certain. On a daily basis various squirrel-lovers placed walnuts, pecans and cashew nuts around the base of trees, and if the weather was dry for a day or two I sometimes saw a man or a woman pouring water into a receptacle on a rock for them to drink from.

In this section of the park a number of men slept beneath an old highway exit ramp. On nice days they wheeled their shopping carts filled with possessions up to an embankment where they would arrange lawn chairs and blankets covered with oversized cardboard refrigerator and washing-machine boxes that served as their tents.

Once I saw two men get into a fight. One was carrying a bag of cans collected from the garbage pails. 'Give me those cans,' the other man said. 'This is my territory. Don't you come collecting cans around here or I'll smash your head open.'

The pigeons were perhaps a bit more hardy and suited for city life than the squirrels. In addition to the cracked corn and birdseed that people spread on the sidewalk for them, they pecked at bread-crusts, fried chicken and Chinese fried rice. There was a lot of food in the park, not only from picnic take-out lunches, but the scraps and purchased food that people brought to feed the birds. With its silvery gray feathers, ringed with luminescent purple around the neck, one pigeon might have been beautiful, but many pigeons altogether had greasy red beaks and feet and mealy eyes, and I hated the way they landed together in a hunched, sordid group on the grass or sidewalk.

I kept looking for the man who stole pigeons and squirrels, but all I ever saw was two women discussing the best balanced diet for wildlife. One was carrying a lot of stale bread, but the other thought that cracked corn provided the most nutrition.

Around six months later I noticed a tiny article in a newspaper, about a man who was arrested with seventy pigeons and squirrels in the back of his station wagon; he was taking them to sell to restaurants. I have seen roast squab on various city menus, but never squirrel, though I suspect that there is some place here that serves game or a Cajun/Southern stew containing squirrel meat. The sign in the park was removed shortly after that, but I never learned what kind of sentence the man received.

The New York Birdman

W HILE WALKING her dog, Paige got friendly with a man who each day took huge sacks of grain to the park to feed the pigeons. He complained a lot to Paige, since he was always getting arrested for feeding the pigeons, an illegal act. If Paige found a bird she would take it to his house, since the Birdman was always rescuing birds. Once I went with her. In front of his townhouse, at a fancy address, were many pigeons and parakeets feeding on grain in the small front garden. I guess the parakeets were escaped pets. They looked a bit peculiar, green and blue and yellow, pecking beside the gray pigeons on a New York sidewalk. Paige would ring the bell and hand the bird to someone who opened the front door a crack, or else she would leave the sick bird in a box on the step. She never went in, though she found a lot of birds.

There were many sick birds in New York. At that time we were doing an animal-rights and rescue program on cable television (well, actually Paige was doing all the hard work, I would just show up and speak on camera) and Paige asked the Birdman if he would talk about birds.

At first he was reluctant but then he agreed. We went to his house. He owned the entire mansion at this fancy address. It was much wider than a regular brownstone. It must have been done over in the '60s. Inside the front door, to the right, was a closet made of shoji rice-paper screening and though at one time it might have been used for coats, now it was heaped from floor to ceiling with sacks of birdseed. Paige said the

Birdman fed the birds fifty or seventy-five pounds of grain every day.

The Birdman was wearing a denim workshirt. Feathers protruded from the front pocket, and in various places it was spattered with bird droppings. He was a stout man, balding, maybe in his mid-to-late fifties, the sort of man you might not want to sit next to at the counter in a coffee shop.

I looked around. Apart from the sacks of birdseed, there was nothing particularly interesting about the ground floor; gray wall-to-wall carpeting, no furniture to speak of or that was memorable, a lot of junk lying around, but I could see it had once been quite a splendid place. 'We'll have to take the elevator,' the Birdman said. 'I'm afraid the stairway has too many things on it.'

So the three of us squeezed into the tiny elevator and went up to the third floor. To the right, in the back, was a huge glassed-in atrium with a door of chicken wire. We followed him. It was two stories high, with a rear staircase that perhaps led to a roof garden. There was a Jacuzzi in the center, long since defunct. Poles had been placed up high, horizontally, and I could see the poles were covered with perching pigeons; there were birds everywhere, and the floor and the Jacuzzi were covered with droppings.

As I looked more closely I saw there were hundreds and hundreds of pigeons in this room, the quarry-tile floor was complete covered with the lame, the limping and the halt, birds missing their feathers, beaks, wings, legs, feet, eyes. There was that queer, sweetish smell of birds that always reminded me of Milk of Magnesia and reptiles. It was the sort of stench that got up in my nostrils and made me feel I was going to go home with mites or scabies or something under the skin that itched and couldn't be gotten rid of. The sound was also alien and hateful, that muttered cooing and clucking, a sickly group symphony. The walls were rusty, water had been leaking in from outside for a long time.

'These are the birds that I can't rehabilitate,' the Birdman said. 'They can never be released. My babies.' There were a lot of cardboard boxes on the floor covered with chicken wire and he pulled the wire off the top of one and took out a pigeon that had no feathers and no eyes. He began to kiss the bird. 'It's very sick,' he said.

Then he led us from the room and closed the chicken wire door. He was still carrying the sick bird. We followed him down the hall. There were many cardboard boxes, covered with chicken wire, and from time to time he would stop to open the lid and show us the bird inside who had no legs or was missing a wing. A baby-grand piano in the front room had some pigeons standing on top of it and a seagull was in the middle of defecating a vast quantity of greenish-white stuff. On the floor were more pigeons and seagulls and a baby crow was in the process of opening and devouring an egg that one of his colleagues had laid. After a while we went to the second floor, where Paige was going to video the Birdman and his views about birds for our program.

'I'm not supposed to have my birds up here,' he said. There were a few really fabulous Asian antiquities on this floor – a huge bronze Japanese samurai, a fourteen-foot-high Buddha, a stone Hindu dancer – but I could see that probably these were only the remains of what had once been a massive collection. Even though the Birdman said he wasn't supposed to have any birds on this floor, one or two or maybe more must have been here, because there were quite a few feathers and bird droppings around, and in the front near the curtained bay-windows something was fluttering.

The Birdman removed some cardboard boxes and their inhabitants from a couple of Chinese rosewood chairs and we sat down. 'Ready?' Paige said. She was holding her fancy video camera. 'Oh no,' she said. 'It's not working. The battery is screwed up. I'll run home and get my adapter.'

I looked at the Birdman. He was holding the blind, naked

pigeon and sitting with his legs apart in front of the bronze Samurai. 'Don't go, Paige,' I said. 'We can come back another day.'

'I'll just be a couple of minutes,' Paige said. Then she left.

The Birdman told me that he had once been an art dealer. He had an Asian wife, but she went away and then he decided to dedicate himself to his birds. Now the bank was trying to foreclose. The walls were leaking on this floor too, the parquet floor was ruined, furniture that must have once been lovely had watermarks and mildew. We sat, waiting for Paige, for quite a long time while the Birdman nuzzled his pigeon.

Queen of the Brooklyn Rodeo

I T WAS late summer when I wandered out to take my kid, who would shortly turn four, to the swimming pool. The pool was just up the block in a gym I belonged to but whose facilities I never used apart from taking her swimming; it was upstairs, above a synagogue, occupying the top floors. When I did use the gym I figured a workout was costing me five hundred bucks, averaging membership and fees. It was in one of Brooklyn's oldest synagogues, maybe the oldest, on a block of buildings that must once have been quite grand, lavish old apartment blocks built in the late twenties, shortly before the crash. All the original tenants had long since died. Now the neighborhood was run down and the buildings were like old ladies who had gone to the beach and stayed out too long. We had been living in our apartment for almost a year; you could tell it had once been grand, it had four bathrooms, but only two of them still had running water.

Willow was excited about going swimming. It was hot, an August day, she was naked under her dress; in a bag I carried towels and her swimming suit. A street-fair was in progress below. I hadn't heard it from where we lived, on the sixteenth floor; there were balloons for sale, and toys, and the library had some performers, dressed up, doing recitations on the main steps, and little rides for kids were out and so forth; the weekly farmers' market was taking place, so I bought tomatoes and zucchini and a lot of stuff the farmers bring down from upstate New York and New Jersey once a week – peaches and apples, and more. The truth was none of it tasted very good, and it was expensive, but it was still better than what you could find in the neighborhood shops, of which there weren't many. Then Willow said she was thirsty, so I bought a large cup of lemonade which she didn't drink, but since it cost two dollars I held on to it, in case she changed her mind.

As we were heading over to the pool I saw a man holding a big horse and a little horse by the reins. 'Can I have a pony ride?' Willow said.

'I guess so,' I said. I staggered over, holding Willow's hand and all the bags.

'Are you giving pony rides?' I said. 'How much is it?'

'It's two dollars, if you can wait a minute,' the man said. He was wearing a cowboy hat. Other people seemed to be coming close; now that I had approached, I could see they wanted pony rides, too. I quickly got out two dollars and gave it to him. You have to be aggressive, in Brooklyn.

'My . . . colleague has just gone to get a lemonade,' the man said. 'He has to come back so he can hold the horse, if your daughter wants to ride on the pony.'

'OK,' I said.

We waited and waited. The colleague showed no sign of returning. 'You ever been around horses?' the man said.

'Yes.'

'I tell you what,' he said. 'You hold my horse and I'll take the little girl on the pony.'

'Oh.' I thought about it. 'OK.'

He took Willow and hoisted her up on the pony. I was sorry now I hadn't made her wear something under her dress. Then he handed me the big horse's reins. I only had one hand to hold them in; I had transferred some of the bags, so now I was holding the reins in one hand and everything else in the other – the toys we had bought and tomatoes and the bag with the towels and swimsuit and the cup of dripping lemonade and a few books that the library had sold from a tent.

'There's just one thing,' the man said, starting to lead away his pony, with Willow on top. 'My horse, he's real fond of me, when he sees I'm leaving he may try to . . . take off after me, so hold on.'

'Oh.' I thought for a moment. 'OK.' I stood with the horse for a minute. He did seem to be looking, longingly, a bit desperately, at his owner. I was looking anxiously at him, too, as he led off my daughter. Then I heard a honking. A man in a big car was trying to get out of a parking space; my horse and bags were blocking him in. With the reins in one hand and the towels, tomatoes, balloons and other stuff, I shuffled across the street. It really was hot and it wasn't that easy to get across the street, there was traffic and the horse was very big and the tomatoes had been expensive, at the peak of ripeness. Finally we made it across, though. Then a group of people gathered around. 'Hey, lady, can I pet your horse? Does your horse bite?' 'I don't know.' I didn't know how to explain, it wasn't my horse, I just happened to be here, holding it. What if this group of people was just trying to distract me and planned to steal my tomatoes – or the horse? More and more of them clustered around. I didn't know if my horse kicked, either. The man and his pony – and my daughter – were gone, vanished, down the block, out of sight. I had thought a pony ride would be, I don't know, a circle or two, within eyesight. What was I going to do, if he didn't come back? I could just see myself, leading the horse and the tomatoes and trying to explain to the police that my daughter had ridden off with a stranger, to whom I had paid two dollars, and what was I supposed to do with a horse in Brooklyn?

Sweat was pouring down my face, and not only because it was hot. The horse was pleasant, but even he was getting anxious. Finally I saw the man and the pony returning, my daughter still seated on the saddle. She was talking. I couldn't hear her, but she was chatting non-stop, and since I could never get her to say two words to me, let alone to a complete stranger, I couldn't imagine what she was saying, but she looked very grown-up and serious, chatting away, with the man leading her on the horse and from time to time nodding or asking her a question.

As soon as they got back I handed the man the reins and grabbed my kid.

'Your daughter was telling me all about your dogs, Nike and Lily, and how Lily attacks Nike – she says they're Chinese Crested dogs? I've never heard of that. She says she goes riding a lot. Where are you from?'

'Massachusetts,' I said.

'Oh, I'm from Maryland,' the man said. 'I'm a rodeo performer, with the Black Brooklyn Rodeo. Listen,' he said. 'Here you go. Here's a dollar, I'm returning a dollar to you, for holding the horse.'

That sounded pretty lucrative. So I asked him if he wanted me to keep holding the horse while he gave some more pony rides, since his colleague still hadn't returned. I think he thought I was just kidding. A few months later on my way to the airport I passed a bunch of trailers and a dusty little horse paddock. I thought maybe that was where the Maryland cowboy and his horse and his pony lived, right there next to the highway on the way to the airport, but the taxi was going too fast and I didn't really have time to look.

Some time later I saw in the paper that many horses died and the whole stable burned down when a kid set fire to the place to get revenge on a girlfriend who kept a horse there. It was all very sad, and I hoped the man's horse and pony were all right. After that I did once see a man on a horse riding on the median strip of the highway, an odd sight in the middle of all that traffic, and I wondered: How has he gotten to the center of the highway on horseback? My taxi was going so quickly, however, I didn't have time to see if it was the Brooklyn Cowboy.

Raped by Butterflies

ONE SUMMER we rented a cottage a couple of hours outside New York City. I had a driving phobia so severe that I was almost unable to drive. It was the country, though, so we had to rent a car. The first week I went with Tim to the train station since he was going back to the city for the working week. I was sitting next to him at the station and I started to cry.

'Why are you crying?' he said.

'Because I feel so terrible, that we'll be apart all week.'

'No,' he said. 'You're crying because you're scared to drive home alone.'

This was true. Every time I got in the car I broke into a cold sweat and my head hurt so much it felt as if someone was right there utilizing a mallet. But I found that I could drive provided I knew the exact route and someone had driven that way before, so I knew exactly where to turn and where I would be able to park and so forth. I found it astonishing that other human beings, who seemed subnormal in so many ways, got into a car and drove it and their heads did not hurt. I was certain, however, that I would probably murder someone.

My mother came to visit me for a few days and during that time whenever we sat outside a large cloud of Swallowtail butterflies would gather around my head. Each time it would start out slowly, one would come along, and then two and fairly soon ten and then twenty.

The butterflies were very aggressive and I felt uncomfortable. On the one hand butterflies look attractive, and objectively it must have been a charming sight, Woman Surrounded by Butterflies, but these butterflies seemed to have something else in mind. I don't know what the sex life of a butterfly consists of, exactly, but I knew that during this time I was part of it. I didn't even want to go outside any more, I was so desirable to these very masculine butterflies. So my mother and I stayed in until she left, and for some unknown reason after that my butterfly season seemed to be over.

At the end of the summer, on our last weekend, Tim was driving and I was the passenger; by then I didn't cry any more and my head didn't hurt, though I still wasn't comfortable with driving, and on a Sunday afternoon, antiquing on a two-lane country highway I told Tim there was an antiques store up ahead and he should pull in. He began to slow and signal for a turn but just as we were about to make the turn our car was suddenly rear-ended and spun around a hundred and eighty degrees; it wasn't all that forceful a blow but enough that when our car came to a halt, Tim leapt out. He was about to go to the driver who had rear ended us and ask what she had been thinking, when we realized the entire back end of our car was totaled and the woman's car was now in the middle of the highway, completely destroyed, and so was another car, oncoming, flung to the far side of the highway with people inside screaming and crying, unable to escape. I got out and watched Tim going to the middle of the road to try to help the woman who had hit us. There was blood and gasoline everywhere.

Suddenly from nowhere another man appeared and peered into the woman's car. 'I'm a doctor,' he announced, 'A heart surgeon. Go and try to help the others. This woman is dead.'

We were there for many hours and the other people had to be prised from the car with the Jaws of Life (a sort of giant tweezers) and the hearse came to collect the woman in the middle of the highway and tow trucks and ambulances and fire engines, and traffic slowed to a halt in two directions and blood and parts everywhere that had to be washed away and an emergency medical technician who grabbed Tim and held him down and said that by law he was not permitted to release Tim unless Tim signed an agreement that he didn't need treatment, which was difficult for Tim to do since the technician was holding Tim by the head from behind.

We never did learn what had happened – had the woman been drinking? Was she having a heart attack? – that she had sped up while we were signaling to turn and slowing. I have never driven since then, but later I realized that for a short time that summer I had used some unusual kind of shampoo, briefly, something fragrant and herbal, that had made me sexually attractive to butterflies. So it wasn't even really me the butterflies desired.

A Monarch in Manhattan

I N THE windows of the Labels for Less store was a large topiary made of artificial leaves and flowers in brilliant shades of pink, yellow, red and pale purple. Somehow a butterfly, mistaking the arrangement for real flowers, had found its way into the shop and was now circling without pausing to land. The poor butterfly, a Monarch, tigerish orange and black – circling, dipping, unable to quench its thirst for nectar yet at the same time seemingly unable to bring itself to leave. How long is a butterfly's lifespan? I thought when I passed the shop.

Butterflies, I knew, were attracted to certain colors of the spectrum, but whether it was the red and pink flowers, or the yellow, or the blue, I no longer remembered. But it was obvious that this butterfly, while attracted to the flowers, was for some reason simultaneously repelled. It could never quite bring itself to land. Trapped behind the glass storefront, no other flowers in sight, flying around and around – I wondered how the sales clerks could bear to watch. Couldn't one of them open the door and shoo it out to freedom? But perhaps those who worked there thought it was an amusing performance, the baffled real butterfly on the imaginary flowers.

How had it gotten into the shop? I wondered about it that afternoon and felt depressed. The real butterfly circling the artificial flowers seemed to represent something terrible about New York City. It reminded me of all the talented and creative people coming from all over the planet to the city and then getting caught up in the most mundane, materialist desires – the quest for a bigger apartment, for a husband, for the latest fall fashions, to get their name mentioned in the newspapers, to go to the 'right' restaurants, to be famous . . .

I told Tim about the butterfly. 'I should have gone into the store and demanded that it be released,' I said. 'But I guess I was afraid. Plus . . . I didn't have a net and if you catch a butterfly it's usually so damaged it can't fly.'

'Don't feel bad,' Tim said. 'If the butterfly found its way in, I'm sure there's a way for it to fly out.'

He was probably right. I tried to put the incident out of my mind.

A few days later I found myself walking down the same block. The butterfly was still there – a bit battered now, flying a bit more wearily, still circling in an endless loop, hoping against hope that on its next downward dip a flower would actually contain nectar instead of dust. How could it have survived for days without food? I felt awful. I should have helped it to flee days ago, when it still had a chance. I pushed open the door to the store and stormed in: I wasn't going to be afraid, I would insist that the butterfly be set free.

A few smiling salespeople were standing toward the back of the shop. I took a step toward them, then hesitated. I didn't want to seem like a complete idiot, after all, and I didn't have any constructive suggestions for how the butterfly might best be released. Maybe they had tried innumerable times; maybe I was the 189th person to burst in demanding the Monarch's release. I waited a bit, then turned and walked over to the window.

In the center of the top of the topiary was a tiny box containing a motor; from this box a delicate black wire emerged; and at the end of the wire – amazingly lifelike – was the butterfly, twisting, darting, circling endlessly.

I had been in New York long enough, I thought, but where else in the world could I go? Wherever I went, I would still be there.

A NOTE ON THE AUTHOR

Tama Janowitz lives in Brooklyn with her wonderful
husband Tim Hunt, her wonderful daughter Willow
Hunt, age six, her Chinese Crested dog Nike (a pathetic
wretch of an animal) and the five ferrets: Scamper (deaf
and mean); Mole; Rat; Weasel; and the loving and rare
angora ferret Badger (given to her by Mark Marrone of
'Parrots of the World' located in Rockville Center, L. I.
on celebration of her appearance as cover girl in
Modern Ferret magazine). She has attended Barnard,
Hollins, Columbia and Yale. This is her first collection
of non-fiction, written over the past eighty years.

A NOTE ON THE TYPE

The text of this book is set in Linotype Sabon, named after the type founder, Jacques Sabon. It was designed by Jan Tschichold and jointly developed by Linotype, Monotype and Stempel, in response to a need for a typeface to be available in identical form for mechanical hot metal composition and hand composition using foundry type.

Tschichold based his design for Sabon roman on a fount engraved by Garamond, and Sabon italic on a fount by Granjon. It was first used in 1966 and has proved an enduring modern classic.